Loss, Dying and Bereavement in the Criminal Justice System

Life is characterised by movement, change and development, including transitions, losses and grief. People experiencing loss must learn to accommodate it and, sometimes, relearn new roles. Whether the offender is accommodating general loss (such as transition), the loss of others or facing their own impending death, the bereavement process can become a particularly complicated experience for those involved in the criminal justice system.

Criminal offenders may be excluded from participating in grief rituals and may receive few explicit opportunities to talk about a loss they have experienced, sometimes resulting in disenfranchised grief. Informing thinking around assessment, care and support procedures, this volume seeks to bring together a range of perspectives from different disciplines on crucial issues surrounding the impact of loss, death, dying and bereavement for criminal offenders. The book will explore inherent challenges and responses to the criminal justice system by considering to what extent offenders' loss, death, dying and bereavement experiences have been – or should be – recognised in policy and practice. The first section considers theoretical approaches to loss; the next section translates these issues using professional perspectives to explore practical applications; and the final section introduces an offender perspective.

Through identifying challenges and consolidating evidence, this multidisciplinary book will interest researchers interested in loss and bereavement in vulnerable communities, concepts of disenfranchised grief, end-of-life care and mental healthcare in the criminal justice system.

Sue Read is Professor of learning disability nursing and Chair of the Palliative and End of Life Care Research Group at Keele University, UK.

Sotirios Santatzoglou is Teaching Fellow in law at Keele University, UK.

Anthony Wrigley is Senior Lecturer in ethics at Keele University's Centre for Professional Ethics, UK.

Routledge Key Themes in Health and Society

Available titles include:

The Story of Nursing in British Mental Hospitals
Echoes from the Corridors
Niall McCrae and Peter Nolan

Living with Mental Disorder
Insights from Qualitative Research
Jacqueline Corcoran

A New Ethic of 'Older'
Subjectivity, Surgery and Self-Stylization
Bridget Garnham

Social Theory and Nursing
Edited by Martin Lipscomb

Older Citizens and End-of-Life Care
Social Work Practice Strategies for Adults in Later Life
Malcolm Payne

Digital Technologies and Generational Identity
ICT Usage across the Life Course
Sakari Taipale, Terhi-Anna Wilksa and Chris Gilleard

Partiality and Justice in Nursing Care
Marita Nordhaug

Loss, Dying and Bereavement in the Criminal Justice System
Edited by Sue Read, Sotirios Santatzoglou and Anthony Wrigley

For more information about this series, please visit: www.routledge.com/Routledge-Key-Themes-in-Health-and-Society/book-series/RKTHS

Loss, Dying and Bereavement in the Criminal Justice System

Edited by Sue Read, Sotirios Santatzoglou and Anthony Wrigley

Routledge
Taylor & Francis Group

LONDON AND NEW YORK

First published 2018
by Routledge
2 Park Square, Milton Park, Abingdon, Oxon OX14 4RN

and by Routledge
711 Third Avenue, New York, NY 10017

Routledge is an imprint of the Taylor & Francis Group, an informa business

British Library Cataloguing-in-Publication Data
A catalogue record for this book is available from the British Library

Library of Congress Cataloging-in-Publication Data
A catalog record for this book has been requested

ISBN: 978-1-138-28357-2 (hbk)
ISBN: 978-1-315-27016-6 (ebk)

Typeset in Times New Roman
by Apex CoVantage, LLC

MIX
Paper from
responsible sources
FSC® C013056
www.fsc.org

Printed and bound in Great Britain by
TJ International Ltd, Padstow, Cornwall

Contents

Contributors

Dr Sue Ashby is a lecturer in nursing in the School of Nursing and Midwifery, Keele University, UK. Her teaching and research interests focus on primary care and the patient experience.

Kevin Benson is a counsellor at the Donna Louise Children's Hospice who also uses creative arts such as painting as a means of engagement and support.

Bree Carlton is Senior Lecturer in Criminology in the School of Social Sciences, Monash University, Australia.

Steve Cartwright is a community palliative care clinical nurse specialist based at the Walsall Palliative Care Centre in the West Midlands.

Gill Clifford is a paediatric nurse and education and development lead at the Donna Louise Children's Hospice. She is a passionate advocate for children and young people with palliative care needs.

Dr Mary Corcoran is a senior lecturer in criminology at Keele University, UK. She publishes widely on imprisonment, resettlement and the voluntary sector.

Andrew Henley is a lecturer in criminology in the School of Social Science and Public Policy, Keele University, UK.

Katie Hunt is a doctoral researcher at the Law School at the University of Southampton. Her PhD explores pastoral care provision for bereaved non-religious prisoners.

Jane Jervis is a lecturer in nursing at the School of Nursing and Midwifery, Keele University, UK. Her teaching and research interests focus on advanced practice, resuscitation, end-of-life care and participatory action research.

Dr Kate Lillie is a lecturer in nursing at the School of Nursing and Midwifery, Keele University, UK. Her practice, teaching and research interests focus on palliative and end-of-life care.

David Pitt is a senior practitioner/psychotherapist with Barnardo's Here and Now Service at HMP & YOI Polmont. He works with clients experiencing trauma, bereavement and loss.

Dr Sue Read is a professor of learning disability nursing at the School of Nursing and Midwifery, Keele University, UK, whose research interests are around marginalised groups, loss, dying and bereavement.

Joe Sim is a professor of criminology at Liverpool John Moores University. He has written a number of books on prisons and is a trustee of the charity INQUEST.

Dr Sotirios Santatzoglou is a teaching fellow at the Law School, Keele University, UK.

Alison Soulsby is a bereavement counsellor with Stafford Bereavement Service who practises in prisons and palliative care settings.

Lisa Thomson provides psycho-educational and therapeutic support to young men affected by experiences of trauma and bereavement held within HMP & YOI Polmont. Additionally, she is involved in further research within this field for female offenders.

Nina Vaswani is Research Fellow at the Centre for Youth and Criminal Justice, University of Strathclyde. Nina's research explores the bereavement experiences of young people.

Alexis Warrilow is a teaching fellow at the School of Nursing and Midwifery, Keele University, UK, whose teaching and research interests focus on primary mental health and mental healthcare in the criminal justice system.

Martin Wasik is an emeritus professor of law at Keele University and author of much published work. He is also a Crown Court judge.

Dr Anthony Wrigley is a senior lecturer in ethics at the Centre for Professional Ethics, School of Law, Keele University, UK. His research interests surround ethical and philosophical questions on the margins of life, with a particular focus on vulnerability, dying and end-of-life care.

Foreword

By bringing together two powerful themes, this book is bound to be the source of some extremely strong messages, especially to those who are actively involved in criminal justice policy and practice. Although there has been some interest in the subjects of loss and death in penal settings, this substantial collection offers a uniquely comprehensive overview of the topic, incorporating a wide range of perspectives and analyses. Despite this, there are undoubtedly common strands and imperatives arising from these contributions when seen as a whole. There is clearly, a consistent sense of 'double jeopardy', with the losses incurred via the justice system being compounded and intensified by the additional losses associated with death and harm to oneself or others. There is a further sense of rupture in that what might be seen as 'normal' processes of understanding, coming to terms with and moving on from 'loss' are distorted by the institutional regime, and of course, harms are further exacerbated. Both the legitimacy of one's own feelings and the need to follow the highly personal rhythms of emotion, insight and adaptation are compromised by the requirements of highly structured and essentially brutalising regimes. These dynamics obviously apply to those on both sides of the wall, where the opportunity to share, to address and to resolve hurt, confusion and the need to understand together are denied by fixed routines and implacable institutional regulatory systems.

As Carlton and Sim remind us here, though, the 'symbolic violence' of the system is mirrored by the 'routine' physical violence which remains a persistent and persistently unacceptable feature of the institutions of the justice system. Of course, this is no accident; in both senses, the consistent message is that the feelings, experiences and in some cases the very lives of those subject to the impositions of (legitimised) criminal processes and systems do not matter, and they are not entitled to normal human respect and dignity. By bringing this to our attention so powerfully and in so many different ways, this book acts as a major wake-up call. Whatever rights the justice system may claim to make decisions over people's lives, for whatever reason and however justified, this does not include the entitlement to devalue and demean those for whom it takes responsibility when their 'cases' are adjudicated and when they are subjected to confinement and constraint in the name of lawful punishment. The state's 'duty of care' should in fact remain its paramount obligation when it takes the decision to remove someone's liberty. This collection brings this home in so many powerful and important ways.

Roger Smith
Professor of Social Work
Durham University
November 2017

Introduction

Sue Read, Sotirios Santatzoglou and Anthony Wrigley

Life is inevitably characterised by movement, change and development and, by its very nature, by transitions, losses and grief (Thompson, 2002). Death is often perceived as the ultimate loss and is the only certainty within life itself. Whether anticipated, unexpected, welcomed or disguised, death can create a huge chasm in the lives of surviving individuals (Read, 2006) as individuals learn to accommodate their loss and have to relearn new roles (Attig, 1996). The context in which loss occurs can have a huge impact on that loss and how people deal with the loss, both at the time and much later. Many people learn from loss experiences, recognising coping strategies that might help them to deal with other losses in the future, identifying particular losses that may affect them more than others, and appreciating where support might best be found (or not) when needed.

Whilst loss and death are universal experiences, responses to them can be unique, individual and personal. People grieve in their own ways; everyone sheds different tears for the same loss; death means different things to different people; and reactions to death can be different for each person. However, research indicates that there are common responses to loss. Some of these may be firmly embedded in a cultural context but, fundamentally, certain responses such as sadness, anger, guilt, disbelief and denial may be seen to greater or lesser degrees across all groups of bereaved people.

Loss in itself can often be difficult to navigate, even for autonomous individuals who fully appreciate its complexities and its potential impact. However, for certain individuals, as well as groups of individuals, whether it be due to cognitive impairments, disability, age or social circumstances, dealing with loss can be fraught with difficulties and challenges. Disenfranchised grief (Doka, 1989, 2002) is a traditionally recognised concept which highlights the needs of marginalised, disadvantage groups of individuals who often find it difficult to have their losses recognised and who may easily have their responses to loss ignored and, therefore, their sadness (and other associated feelings) go unnoticed. Disenfranchised grievers may not be told about the death of their loved ones for many weeks, months or even years; some may not be allowed to attend any funeral rites or rituals; and many will not be encouraged to grieve or express sadness for the loss. Obviously, this can cause an immediate and long-term impact upon the disenfranchised individual, which can manifest in many forms for many years after the death. Those recognised as having the potential for disenfranchised grief include older people, children, people with mental health issues, people with learning disabilities, people with HIV and AIDS, those diagnosed with dementia and prisoners (Doka, 1989). One broad group where the possibility of disenfranchised grief is particularly prevalent includes those who experience loss or bereavement or are dying within the criminal justice system.

Whilst there may be found, albeit in a somewhat limited sense, research, published academic papers or chapters within textbooks around this topic area, never has a book been totally focused around this important, sensitive area of support. Therefore, although many of the themes will be familiar to anyone who has an interest in issues of loss, end-of-life care and bereavement, the unique nature of this book lies in the way that it integrates and considers these issues. The approach deliberately integrates a range of perspectives from different disciplines on crucial issues surrounding the impact of loss, death, dying and bereavement for criminal offenders across the criminal justice system. By addressing a range of contemporary practice issues, it identifies the inherent challenges these issues pose for criminal offenders and consolidates existing evidence to generate a foundation that will support best-practice approaches and provide potential opportunities for future loss support in a dynamic, ever-changing, restrictive care context.

In bringing together a range of perspectives from different disciplines on crucial issues surrounding the impact of loss, death, dying and bereavement for offenders, this book explores the inherent challenges and responses to the criminal justice system by considering to what extent the loss, death, dying and bereavement experiences of offenders have been – or should be – recognised in policy and practice. Ultimately, our aim is to challenge existing beliefs around criminal justice and punishment by informing thinking around assessment, care and support procedures. Although there is no intention of solving the issue as to exactly how policy makers and practice providers should address the issues of loss across the varying contexts of the criminal justice system, the book should be seen as encouraging readers to identify their own questions, both regarding this subject area and in relation their own areas of practice.

The editors originate from three diverse but interconnected professional disciplines (health, law and ethics), and all share a common understanding and passion for this translational topic which firmly unites them in their thinking. Consequently, the contributing authors of this book have been carefully selected to bring together vitally important skill sets and expertise when addressing these issues. This includes expertise on issues of loss and grief, as well as notable and varied expertise in the field of criminal justice. Many are well-established researchers and authors who bring unique, extensive expertise on the issues of loss, death and bereavement, whilst others are earlier-stage researchers and authors with fresh and developing expertise. Such a combination of contributions adds variety and provides a rich tapestry from which to explore issues of loss for criminal offenders within restrictive environments, something which is echoed in the contents.

Contents

This book is divided into three sections.

Section 1: appreciating dimensions of loss, death, dying and bereavement

The first section encourages the reader to appreciate the complexity of loss, death, dying and bereavement in relation to the particular population and context of the criminal justice system. These chapters are considered the foundation from which contemporary practice and ongoing support should be developed, establishing theoretical threads that underpin the topic area and weave throughout the text. They provide a broad platform by incorporating a critical analysis of the key issues that arise in this context.

Chapter 1: death, social losses and the continuum of disenfranchised grief for prisoners

This chapter considers the experience of loss and bereavement within the marginalised prisoner community, based on a number of pivotal papers related to bereavement care and support in prisons. The stories illustrate well the experiences of prisoners, and their powerful meanings behind the continuum of losses, not solely those related to death. The theory strongly highlights the potential for disenfranchised grief for this specific population, particularly in relation to the restrictive prison environment. However, this chapter also recognises the importance of the continuum of losses (from general transitional issues, to ill health, to death). As such, this first chapter provides a firm foundation for the following chapters around this sensitive and often controversial area of support across the criminal justice system.

Chapter 2: death, dying and maintaining hope: ethical tensions and responsibilities for end-of-life care in the prison setting

Restrictive environments already present numerous ethical challenges due to a combination of factors used to justify imprisonment (deterrence, retribution and rehabilitation). When it comes to issues of loss, dying and bereavement, these justifications can impact in areas central to our ethical concerns about provision of care, including privacy and confidentiality, autonomy, minimising harms, access to resources, environment and maintaining dignity through the dying process. Institutional settings can therefore strongly influence the ways in which both prisoners and healthcare practitioners can manage issues of loss, dying and bereavement. As such, it may be doubtful whether prisoners can receive the same standard and quality of care in this area that is received by those who are not detained or imprisoned, contrary to the United Nation's (1982) Principles of Medical Ethics. The aim of this chapter is to discuss the tension between the ethics of imprisonment and the ethics of what we can reasonably expect governments to provide in terms of treatment and support for prisoners, focusing on just one area of facilitating a good death – the maintenance of hope for the dying.

Chapter 3: 'sympathy to the offender': the Hobbesian account and the sympathy to the offender as an issue in end-of-life care (part A)

Compassion is a central tenet in palliative and end-of-life care practice. This chapter considers the question of the sympathy and compassion towards the offender. In part A, the focus is on the public sentiments towards the offender and the question about whether prisoners, and all those who otherwise are dealt with by the criminal justice system, can be seen as persons with needs beyond the criminal stigma. Towards this aim, the authors base their analysis on the Hobbesian account about compassion and pity. The authors argue that Hobbes' old account still feels contemporary and examine whether there are any alternative accounts in the public sphere with respect to the question of sympathy to the offender.

Chapter 4: loss at the end of life: palliative care in prisons

With an increasingly older prison population, the potential for palliative (non-curable) conditions is increased. This chapter explores the challenges of providing holistic palliative care within restrictive environments for the healthcare worker, the prison staff and the patients and their families. The chapter focuses on issues that affect losses, including anticipatory losses, during the dying process. It considers bodily (physical) losses, exploring how the dying person's autonomy is promoted or restrained by the disease process itself. This is then expanded to discuss how these different dying trajectories present a range of losses for families and numerous opportunities and barriers to psychosocial care for professionals working within healthcare and the criminal justice system.

Chapter 5: deaths in sites of state confinement: a continuum of routine violence and terror

This chapter considers the deaths that occur within and across sites of state confinement that are produced through systemic, routine and mundane forms of state and corporate violence. It aims to critically analyse deaths through the lens of terror and violence, which the authors argue are inculcated into the very structures and routines of daily life within various sites of confinement. The chapter is based on a new research project on deaths across sites of confinement in England and Wales. The authors provide a preliminary snapshot detailing the nature and extent of deaths in state confinement, particularly with respect to self-inflicted deaths, and the establishment of a framework for conceptualising the routine conditions and experiences that produce deaths as violence and terror.

Chapter 6: civil and social death: criminalisation and the loss of the self

This chapter seeks to broaden the conception of 'loss' and 'bereavement' in criminal justice by drawing attention to those social processes through which people subjected to state punishment are then rendered marginal in their *post-sentence* lives. To some extent this marginality is explained by formal *de jure* requirements to disqualify people with offending histories from certain opportunities. However, it is more often the case that those who have passed through the criminal justice system are subjected to *de facto* forms of discrimination grounded in negative stereotypes and a generalised public animus towards 'wrongdoers'. The author argues that the *exclusionary tendency* against former lawbreakers is generated within ritualised judicial processes of 'othering' and denunciation which coalesce with broader public and criminal justice discourses that construct convicted people as irredeemable 'criminals' or 'offenders'. Following this negative labelling, former lawbreakers may often go on to experience a *sense of loss* grounded in the ongoing denial of opportunities to (re)develop a positive sense of self.

Section 2: professional development of bereavement, loss and end-of-life practice

This section of the book shifts the focus from the theoretical to issues of professional practice, in particular practice needs and practice lessons (both often illustrated by case studies) in relation to the support of loss and bereavement of offenders in a variety of contexts and stages within the criminal justice system. This section includes important perspectives on how to support sentencing decision making in relation to loss and bereavement. Furthermore, it addresses successful paradigms, comparative ideas and policy practice questions involving the voluntary sector, which compassionately supports the offender within the prison context. Finally, reflective experiences from nursing professionals around end-of-life care are translated to the criminal justice setting, providing rich examples to inform future practice both in prison and in the community environment.

Chapter 7: bereavement and loss at the sentencing stage

This chapter examines the relevance of loss and bereavement as an issue in the criminal justice process up to and including the sentencing decision. The main focus is on bereavement and loss in relation to the accused, whilst also recognising the needs of bereaved victims of crime (e.g. their right to address the court at sentencing). Issues personal to the offender might in principle be taken into account at a number of points of discretion within the process, especially whether to prosecute and on mitigation prior to sentencing. The less serious the offence, the greater the scope there will be for exercising discretion in favour of the offender. Whilst there is no sentencing guideline or single appellate case that deals in detail with the issue of loss or bereavement, there are cases where the matter has received indirect consideration in the Court of Appeal. This limited guidance is assessed.

Chapter 8: bereavement work in the criminal justice system

The voluntary sector has historically viewed itself as a compassionate witness which supports prisoners, their families and others affected by the harms, losses and grief arising from custody. Conducting this work generates a shared understanding by those involved that 'custody' encompasses not only the detained but also their families, communities and social networks. This chapter examines the many ways in which the voluntary sector supports detained individuals and those connected with them at times of loss and bereavement. The chapter maps the different types of organisations and various supports that they offer, both within and outside custodial establishments. The author also identifies the discursive construction of the voluntary sector as interlocutor in grief and managing emotional struggles.

Chapter 9: 'sympathy to the offender': the Hobbesian account and the sympathy to the offender as an issue in end-of-life care (part B)

Building on chapter 3, this chapter addresses the issue of sympathy to the offender within the context of professionals. In this part B, the authors indicate the differentiating issue of distance as a key factor for the development of compassionate attitudes within the practice sphere of criminal justice. Whilst they provide a brief account about the overall state of compassion within the contemporary criminal justice system, the authors place the emphasis on the sentiments and the practice of palliative care practitioners. The discussion of holistic, palliative care practice and its compassionate attitude (or lack thereof) towards the offender is approached through Lipsky's seminal account of the dilemmas of street-level bureaucrats.

Chapter 10: working in the shadows: reflections on counselling in prison and hospice settings

This chapter provides a personal reflection of a person-centred counsellor. It introduces the main approach and key requirements of the person-centred approach to counselling, in particular the need to be empathetic, non-judgemental and congruent with the client, before exploring the wider nature of loss in the context of both the palliative care and prison settings. The chapter then explores the author's personal experience of counselling those suffering many forms of loss within the hospice community and within the prison community. This exploration seeks to highlight the similarities and differences between the two populations of clients and draw out how these impact on the experiences of counselling in these populations.

Chapter 11: the evolution of change: factors involved in the design and delivery of a therapeutic service within the confines of a custodial setting

This chapter presents unique and contemporary insights into the development of bereavement and loss support in a prison context.

Chapter 12: offenders and the challenges of palliative care in the community setting

Community palliative care is provided in a range of differing contexts to a range of different people. This chapter introduces a different dimension to the issue of loss: exploring nursing involvement with and within the criminal justice system, including the psychiatric and general nursing contributions to this subject. It identifies the potential for nursing involvement – before sentencing, in institutions or on release – from a palliative care perspective. This chapter also explores current practices in relation to risk assessment, and whether nurses are adequately prepared to support patients in the criminal justice system. The chapter concludes by advocating the need for nursing-evidence-based, compassionate guidelines for professionals who work within the criminal justice system to help identify these clients and prevent imprisonment where appropriate.

Section 3: insights to inform reflections for ongoing support

In this final and often very moving section, the contributors give voice to the voiceless by capturing the lived experiences of death and dying of offenders and their families. These topics are vitally important for a complete understanding of the issues of loss and bereavement in a criminal justice setting because the impact of loss arising from a range of scenarios and situations, such as sudden death, dealing with the death of a child, the impact of enduring mental health issues and ageing, can be multifaceted and the support needs varied. Therefore, by adopting a holistic approach regarding reactions to loss (psychosocial, emotional, spiritual and physical dimensions) across the life continuum, across the ages and across the conditions, the contributions in this section demonstrate how loss never happens in a vacuum but always in a social context, and that context will shape how the individual deals with that loss in the future. Accordingly, this means that the nature of the criminal justice setting will invariably influence how the person accommodates his or her loss.

Chapter 13: sorrow, loss and the transition of chronic disease to end-of-life care in prisons

The challenges of identifying the progression of chronic disease to end-of-life care in non-malignant conditions is well recognised in the literature and presents problems for healthcare professionals across inpatient and home environments. In this chapter, case studies are used to explore professional perspectives within the criminal justice context. Theses case studies include aspects of transition of DNAR status between primary and secondary care (the differing opinions of professionals, as well as the impact on the patient, family and healthcare team providing frontline care); managing end-of-life patients in the community (challenges for contemporary healthcare, i.e. acute care in community settings); and decision making in relation to the timing of advanced-care planning, recognition of presenting trends to determine deterioration of a chronic condition and commencement of end-of-life care. This generates an interesting exploration around the individual's continuing journey with a chronic health condition.

Chapter 14: the impact of loss on mental health: implications for practice in criminal justice settings

Many people within the criminal justice system have experienced loss in many forms and bereavement at some point in their lives. An individual's ability to cope with such life experiences relies on his or her ability to be resilient. This chapter initially explores the literature concerning the impact of loss and bereavement on an individual's mental health. It recognises that whilst mental health services in prisons may see individuals suffering from loss and bereavement and attempt to treat the symptoms, they are often not equipped to provide the interventions for addressing the root cause. The government has acknowledged the importance of the principle of 'equivalence' in healthcare provision and they advocate that 'prisoners should have access to the same range and quality of services appropriate to their needs as are available to the general population through the NHS'. Through exploring the available resources in the community and implications for practice within the criminal justice setting, recommendations for effective treatments of loss and bereavement are considered.

Chapter 15: mourning in custody: dealing with sudden death

This chapter considers sudden death and the criminal justice system. Sudden death is defined and contextualised, support needs described, issues associated when dealing with sudden death in criminal justice settings are identified and finally the training and development needs of staff in custodial settings related to this complex topic are considered. The chapter concludes by exploring the implications of culturally specific policy and support structures which could support the grief process in the criminal justice context. The chapter draws on different examples of sudden death, including sudden death of a relative whilst in prison, the experience of bereavement associated with gang-related deaths during fights and the traumatic experience of causing the death of a friend or relative due to drunk driving.

Chapter 16: freedom to grieve: a child and parent perspective

Families come in many shapes and sizes and a rigid definition is impossible to apply. The roles and relationships within families are as varied and diverse as the societies and cultures which they reflect. Each member, however, has a unique role to play, an individual identity still dependant on the whole and the stability of the dynamics within. The loss of an individual family member at a time of crisis can place an unbearable burden on the remaining members. For the absent family member, the inability to act autonomously and assume an active role in supporting the family unit can result in feelings of isolation and disconnection. The inability to share the emotional journey and the highs and lows inherent in the process of navigating the path through the shock, confusion and practical issues of caring for a child facing death will inevitably impact on an already impossibly difficult situation. This chapter sensitively explores and reflects on the impact on the physical and emotional well-being of the family, and its individual members, when a member is incarcerated within the criminal justice system before, during and after the death of a child.

Chapter 17: beyond loss of liberty: how loss, bereavement and grief can affect young men's prison journeys

Drawing on the research literature, this chapter adopts a broad conceptualisation of loss, encompassing bereavement as well as the full range of more ambiguous losses. The role that loss, bereavement and, in turn, grief can play in the journey to, through and from custody is discussed. The chapter begins by outlining how the nature and experience of loss, bereavement and grief in childhood can affect young men's behaviour and ultimately lead to involvement in offending. The chapter then goes on to explore how institutional responses to offending, such as the use of residential care, secure care or custody, often amplify or create additional losses, and also how the institutional context itself can significantly affect young men's ability to cope with loss and grief. The impact that these losses have on young men's self-concept and the practical and perceptual barriers that exist for personal change, social reintegration and desistance are critically discussed. The chapter concludes with an exploration around the implications for practice, both inside and outside the institutional environment.

Chapter 18: grief, chaplaincy and the non-religious prisoner

Indicative to the holistic nature of support, spirituality and faith remain important facets, regardless of context. This chapter indicates that in prison, it may prove difficult to identify and ensure access to appropriate religious and faith leaders. The experience in criminal justice practice is that many inmates feel uncomfortable accessing religious services and do not receive the help they need. The authors argue that multi-faith spaces, which seek to cater to inmates of all faiths and none, may be unable to support all offenders equally, and that the importance of effective pastoral care in the criminal justice system puts pressure on the Prison Service to do more to support those whom the chaplaincy cannot reach.

References

Attig, T. (1996). *How we grieve: Relearning the world*. New York: Oxford University Press.

Doka, K.J. (1989). *Disenfranchised grief: Recognising hidden sorrow*. Toronto, Canada: Lexington Books.

Doka, K.J. (Edit.). (2002). *Disenfranchised grief: New directions, challenges and strategies for practice*. Illinois: Research Press.

Read, S. (Edit.). (2006). *Palliative care for people with learning disability*. London: Quay Books.

Thompson, N. (2002). *Loss and grief: A guide for human services practitioners*. London: Palgrave Macmillan.

United Nations (1982). *Resolution 37/194: Principles of medical ethics annex Principles of medical ethics relevant to the role of health personnel, particularly physicians, in the protection of prisoners and detainees against torture, and other cruel, inhuman or degrading treatment or punishment*. Available at: http://www.un.org/documents/ga/res/37/a37r194.htm Accessed 03/10/17.

Section 1

Appreciating dimensions of loss, death, dying and bereavement

1 Death, social losses and the continuum of disenfranchised grief for prisoners

Sue Read and Sotirios Santatzoglou

Introduction

Death never occurs in a vacuum but within a social context, the nature of which can influence greatly how the person deals with that loss, or how individuals cope when confronted with the inevitability of the end of their lives, and how others accommodate the death of their friend or family member (Read, 2006). Particular social contexts can have a huge impact on how the experience is lived, where individuals receive their support, when they can expect care and support and indeed who they receive this care and support from.

Whilst death is a tangible loss, and for the most part the most difficult of losses to accommodate, people experience many other losses throughout their lives that can feel equally painful, but may be less tangible or visible, and subsequently not be as easily acknowledged or openly, constructively and consistently supported (Read, 2014). Life is characterised by movement and change and therefore by its very nature, by transitions, losses and grief (Thompson, 2002). Oswin poignantly reminds us of the importance of loss when she described how 'it sometimes seems as if all our lives we are trying to cope with loss – either the fear of it, or the memory of it or its raw immediate presence' (Oswin, 1991: 15). Subsequently loss remains omnipresent (Read, 2011).

There are many different types of loss. Schultz and Harris (2011) describe these losses as either being common (such as losses experienced through growing up and growing old), uncommon (such as abandonment, abuse, migration and violent death) or non-finite. The latter is described as a continuing presence of the loss, which, because it may not necessarily involve death, may go unrecognised and thus be difficult to articulate and explain. Machin (2009) identifies three distinct types of loss: *developmental*, which occur across the life course; *circumstantial*, unpredictable loss, incorporating changes in relationships, ill health and disability and death; and *invisible* grief and undervalued people, where marginalised communities rarely receive the support they need following a loss (Machin, 2009). Arguably, this *invisible* loss is particularly evident in the marginalised community of prisoners and offenders in general, and remains an under-researched issue (Vaswani, 2014). As Olson and McEwen indicate, 'Very little information can be found in the literature on bereaved prisoners, and it appears that their grief may not be of great concern to others' (2004: 226).

This chapter will consider the experience of loss and bereavement within the community of prisoners, which is based on papers related to bereavement care in prison. The chapter is also informed by the stories and views of professionals, which were collected during a small-scale qualitative research study.[1] The overarching aim of this research study was to explore existing bereavement support mechanisms with respect to offenders. The study involved focus groups and interviews with professionals, such as prison bereavement counsellors, community palliative care professionals, prison nurses, hospice workers and a prison chaplain.

The bereaved prisoner and the types of losses

Schetky's paper (1998), titled 'Mourning in Prison: Mission Impossible?' provided an early account about types of losses within a prison setting. Her account considered five groups of losses reflecting her learning experiences from the implementation of a support group scheme. Schetky's account did not distinguish between death and other losses, but primarily between incarceration-associated and non-incarceration-associated losses. The former were distinguished into two groups: (a) the loss of contact with 'children and loved ones', which was discussed first, and (b) the loss of self-esteem, professional identity, choice of medical care and material possessions, which were addressed second. With respect to the loss of contact, Schetky explained that

> men lost contact with children and, in some cases, had their parental rights terminated . . . [whilst] [s]ome lost all contact with siblings with whom they had once been close and had no knowledge of family of their whereabouts.
>
> (Schetky, 1998: 386)

Loss of contact could also include the difficulty in receiving news about 'terminally ill relatives'. As Schetky indicated, some of the inmates 'described the frustration of trying to get through to them on the prison phone system' whilst others 'described their anguish at being informed of the deaths of loved ones only after their funerals' (Schetky, 1998: 386). Schetky also considered losses which had 'occurred in the course of the group and included transfers of inmates, absences of the co-facilitators due to vacations or professional meetings, deaths or terminal illness in family members, moves by family members, and the deaths of several inmates' (1998: 386). Some of these losses, such as 'the transfers or the deaths of several inmates', should be seen as incarceration-associated losses. The consideration of similar incarceration-associated losses were addressed in further papers, such as Bolger's (2005), on dying in prison and the palliative care challenges therein, or Hendry's (2009) review of bereavement and prison nursing papers from 1998 to 2007. Bolger (2005) and Hendry (2009), both pointed to the 'obvious' forms of loss arising from incarceration, such as 'loss of liberty, loss of family contacts and loss of life years' (Hendry, 2009: 271; Bolger, 2005: 619). Hendry also listed the loss of 'material possessions, heterosexual contact, privacy, personal autonomy and personal security' as 'identified losses of prison life' (Hendry, 2009: 272).[2]

With respect to losses which did not arise due to incarceration as they were concerned with other life phases, Schetky considered '[c]hildhood losses and abuse'. Schetky indicated that these losses 'were common' amongst the group of inmates and she addressed them after the first group of incarceration-associated losses, the loss of contact with 'children and loved ones'. Schetky mentioned the experience of one inmate who 'was dealing with his adoption and reconciliation with his birth mother' (Schetky, 1998: 386). A further group of losses was the loss of 'a child through death, adoption, or alienation'. Schetky did not clarify whether these were experiences before or during incarceration but said that this loss 'was shared by several members' of the group, who had 'noted that the hurt never leaves and how much harder it is to deal with the loss of a child' (Schetky, 1998: 386). Therefore, Schetky's account did not distinguish between death and other losses, but primarily between incarceration-associated and non-incarceration-associated losses.

Further ways of listing types of losses can be found in other papers concerning children and young people in custody, such as the report of the Childhood Bereavement Network (CBN), which considered only the experience of death (and no other losses) by children and young people before they came into custody, as well as 'while they are there' (CBN, 2008). In relation to the period before custody, the report referred to 'deaths of parents, siblings, grandparents, extended family members, partners, friends and children' (CBN, 2008: 1). Regarding the deaths of grandparents, the report indicated that 'their death is likely to be very significant,' when they had 'been involved in caring for a young person or providing rare stability' (CBN, 2008: 1). Furthermore, the report indicated the 'small number of cases' where the deaths, which were 'very significant in the young person's life such as a partner or friend', had resulted from young people's 'own offences' (CBN, 2008: 1). With respect to the period in custody, the report stated that the deaths concerned 'both staff members and peers' (CBN, 2008: 1). In a further account also concerning young male inmates in England and Wales and their death bereavement experiences, Vaswani distinguished between multiple 'substantial' and 'recent' bereavements (rather than before or during custody) (2014: 345). Vaswani further categorised these bereavements into two types: 'traumatic' bereavements, which were 'caused by overdose, accident, murder or suicide, regardless of the participant's experience of that bereavement'; and 'parental', which were caused by the death of a 'biological parent, step-parent or main carer' (2014: 345). Therefore, these accounts pointed out the significance of death and bereavement experiences in the lives of young inmates in England and Wales.

Importantly, in a subsequent article, titled 'A Catalogue of Losses', Vaswani (2015) considered an overarching typology of losses beyond the experience of death bereavements for young men in custody. The typology included loss of future; loss of relationships; loss of status, in particular the loss of power and agency that can arise from the need to assimilate into prison culture; and loss of stability – often due to a disrupted and troubled childhood. The overarching typology of losses reflected Vaswani's interest in the significance of life 'uncertainties' experienced amongst young people involved in offending, such as 'family breakdown, abuse and neglect, and periods in placements away from home' (2015). Vaswani indicated that 'each of these can be experienced as a devastating loss' which 'many young people in prison . . . carry with them' (2015). Notably, Vaswani's latter account made a bold distinction between death and other losses in order to signify their importance. This raises the issue as to whether there is actually a hierarchy of losses and whether some losses are more important than others in the lives of prisoners.

Hierarchy of losses and disenfranchised grief

In her paper, 'A Catalogue of Losses', Vaswani criticised that 'most studies of loss tend to focus predominantly on loss *through* death' (2015: 28). Indeed, grief experiences of prisoners arising from death are central in a wide number of papers which address specific death-related losses only. For example, Harner *et al.* stated that '[o]ur study aim was to describe the experience of losing a loved one through death while incarcerated' (2011: 454). Ferszt examined 'the experience of three women who suffered the death of a significant person' whilst in prison (Ferszt, 2002). Wilson's study focused on a variety of death experiences, such as

> deaths from war and political unrest; death of children . . .; suicide . . .; . . . limited/restricted attendance at funeral rituals due to imprisonment, and unprompted discussions about sensing a presence of the deceased.
>
> (2011: 13)

Finally, Taylor studied the chaplains' efforts to manage the bereavement experiences of prisoners arising from 'four uniquely difficult deaths: murder, suicide, death of the parental figure, death of a child' (2012: 40). Arguably, these papers have implicitly defined the meaning of loss or, in other words, have implicitly set death, and more specifically death of relatives, as the primary focus.

The focus on death experiences does not necessarily reflect a lack of recognition of the existence of other social losses involved in the life stories of inmates. A number of papers refer to those losses. However, they still divert the focus to the death experiences singularly. For example, Olson and McEwen indicated that '[m]any prison inmates have experienced significant losses prior to as well as during their incarceration' and referred to the 'loss of possessions, jobs, control, freedom, relationships, childhood, spirituality, and dreams and goals' (2004: 226). However, their paper did not address them any further, as the focus was on the experience of 'four grief counselling groups' and how their members dealt with the 'reality of the deaths' (Olson & McEwen, 2004: 226). Similarly, Wilson also recognised that emotions of loss 'are not only associated with death but can be triggered [by] many other significant, non-death related losses . . . such as loss of stability through a dysfunctional family situation or being placed in care' and so on (2010: 10). However, the grieving project in prison, which was the paper's subject, was about death only (Wilson, 2010). The overwhelming majority of the studies place their focus on death, regardless of the recognition or not about the existence of social losses in the lives of prisoners.

The same pattern was also seen in the accounts of the interviewees of this qualitative small-scale research on bereavement care and criminal justice (see endnote 1), where bereavement experiences of prisoners arising from death-related losses of persons close to them were also central in the accounts of the practitioners-interviewees. For example, the stories of the bereavement counsellors (BC) were concerned with a prisoner whose 'mum had died . . . and came to terms with his mother's death'; 'a prisoner who was responsible for the death of his partner' (BC 1); 'somebody who lost an eight-year-old brother, but he to all intents and purposes was the carer for this little brother as well' (BC 2); and 'a grandparent's death' (BC 2). BC 2 further indicated that death of a child is 'one of the most difficult areas . . . it is indeed extremely difficult when you're dealing with somebody who's lost a child and they themselves are in prison,' indicating (through a story) that 'the younger they are, the more helpless they feel.' Death was also central in the interview with the chaplain, who indicated that 'as a chaplain, you can get as a reputation being the Angel of Death,' as the chaplain deals with 'receiving information of the death of a relative' and processing this to the prisoner. The BCs indicated the 'chaotic lives' of the bereaved prisoners, and agreed that their condition of being 'left abandoned when they're in prison', or simply 'being incarcerated', 'in essence, it sort of mirrors bereavement.' Nevertheless, the 'chaotic' life histories of the prisoners were not seen as embodying losses, namely social losses. It was only in one instance, of a bereaved prisoner who was a former vicar, that BC 1 stressed that '[h]e was abandoned by the Church . . . and that was a huge loss,' therefore linking the concepts of loss and bereavement to social losses. Remarkably, the chaplain-interviewee indicated that

> loss for me is not just about loss of . . . you know, bereavement through death, it's loss through abuse, loss through a whole variety of issues . . . and people have really struggled because things have happened, especially if there have been breakdowns in the relationships and they've lost the contact with the father or the mother or whatever it is, you know. So I don't narrow it down to death.

Nevertheless, the chaplain still observed that

> sometimes with loss the thing can be recouped, it can be in some way brought back, whereas with death, that's not gonna be a possibility . . . So, with loss I think you can actually retrieve some of those things often, or there is a possibility, not necessarily you can, but there's always the hope that you might actually make amends for it, or you might make it different, but you're never gonna make it different with a death.

In this way, the chaplain supported the existence of a hierarchy of losses which subsequently defined the scope of their practice.

Both the literature and the aforementioned empirical evidence demonstrate that perceptions of losses within the criminal justice system are aligned with the wider perception that death is usually the hardest, greatest loss to accommodate, perhaps because of its finality, permanence and irreversibility. This predominance demonstrates the existence of a perception, within research and of practitioners, of a hierarchy of significance about the types of losses. Against this perception, Vaswani argues that 'it is important [to] understand that loss does not have to be outwardly huge, nor devastatingly permanent' (2015: 34). Moreover, people experience many other losses throughout their lives that can feel equally painful, but may be less tangible or visible, and subsequently not as easily acknowledged or constructively and consistently supported (Read, 2014). However, it is also true that death is often perceived as the ultimate loss and the only certainty within life itself. Indeed, in the eyes of the chaplain interviewed, this was the perception, which signified the comparative importance of death against the social losses of prisoners. No doubt, whether anticipated, unexpected, welcomed or disguised, death can create a huge chasm in the lives of surviving individuals (Read, 2011), as individuals learn to accommodate their losses and have to relearn new roles (Attig, 1996).

Nevertheless, as the proponents of disenfranchised grief indicate, 'each loss must be recognised and validated' (Grollman, 2002: xi). This principle of disenfranchised grief points to the need to move beyond hierarchical perceptions of loss and understand the underpinning structures of loss, especially in relation to marginalised groups such as prisoners. Disenfranchised grief is defined as a loss which 'may be not recognised or validated by others' and 'the grief subsequently experienced is disenfranchised: The loss cannot be openly acknowledged, socially validated, or publicly mourned' (Doka, 2002: xiii). A number of papers regard 'disenfranchised grief' as the concept which can capture the mental and social state of inmates with unsupported grief (Harner et al., 2011; Hendry, 2009; Young, 2003; Ferszt, 2002). Most literature on prisoners' grief has focused on the impact of the prison environment and conditions, demonstrating the point that 'prisons are environments of enduring loss' (see Hendry, 2009: 271; Bolger, 2005: 619). In this way, the literature indicates the relevance of prisoners' grief to the premises of disenfranchised grief. For example, Ferszt indicates how women 'suspend their grief' in prison (2002: 251). Similarly, Hendry argues that '[t]he obstacles to dealing with loss and grieving for men in prison are formidable,' and 'men often grieve in silence, both in and out of custody' (2009: 275). However, Schetky's categorisation of prisoners' losses, which was earlier discussed, further demonstrated the endurance of 'cumulative losses' amongst prisoners who had 'little experience with grief' (Schetky, 1998: 385–386). Vaswani's overarching typology of losses not only demonstrates the occurrence of a multiplicity of losses in the lives of young inmates, but also that small-scale and temporary losses, especially as they accumulate, can be equally 'traumatic and manifest as externalising and challenging behaviours or complicated attachment relationships' (Vaswani, 2015: 34). It is the understanding and recognition of both the existence and impact of all losses (and not only death) on prisoners that matters in relation to disenfranchised grief.

Depth and multiplicity of prisoners' losses

The reported experience of death and bereavement for prisoners is not necessarily limited to non-incarcerated periods of their lives. Indeed, as Taylor purports, prisoners may 'have experienced multiple deaths' whilst incarcerated (2012: 40). Taylor's point illustrates well the multifaceted nature of death, which actually becomes particularly significant within the context of social losses. Some of the prisoners' narratives in these papers provide insight into the existence of additional losses and even their relevance (or not) to the prisoners' bereavement experience, though these issues may be overlooked by the researchers who focus on death. For example, Wolfenden's paper (1997), 'Open Space', which described the experience of a bereavement group run by the author in a closed women's prison, provided the inmates' stories regarding the deaths of their parents. Their narratives revealed experiences of traumatic lives amounting to a loss of childhood. Disappointingly, Wolfenden did not explore more deeply these multiple losses. The chaplain-interviewee indicated the significance of the buried memory of a loss of a childhood due to abuse:

> In one young offender institution I ran a programme called Being Dad, which was about parenting skills, and . . . we asked them all sorts of things about 'What comes into your mind when you think about the word "Dad"?' . . . And then I'm writing the words up on the board, 'abusive', 'violent', 'drunk' . . . In a service in a church . . . some of us actually pray through some of the prayers that have been left by people visiting the church, and one of them says 'Please pray for my daddy, he beats me up every time he comes back, but I think he still likes me'. And you suddenly realise, you know, and they listen to other people and realise that they've lost so much, because the other experience is 'Oh, I like my dad, he takes me to the football' or 'He's my friend.'

Similarly, Crawley's paper, which dealt with the issue of general care provisions for older inmates who will die in prison, also provides insight into the losses of this group of inmates, though there is no clear reference to the concept of loss generally (Crawley, 2005). The paper indicates the concerns of the old inmates with respect to their lives before prison and their wives 'who had been married for a very long time'. These men, as Crawley indicated, 'seemed to fare worse than those with no spouse and little family' (Crawley, 2005: 6). Therefore the paper clearly provides a picture of the social losses (and the subsequent needs) of a particular group of male inmates, those imprisoned whilst old due to historic prosecutions.

Furthermore, Stevenson and McCutchen refer to inmates who have used drugs (including alcohol) as a method of coping with emotion, pain and stress, and their loss of 'fellow users'. As each indicates these are important, notable people who were 'there' for the individual when others had left or been pushed away, at 'least they did not pass judgment on the addict because their own behavior mirrored theirs in many cases' (Stevenson & McCutchen, 2006: 105–106). Such accounts demonstrate strongly the social faces of death, and not solely the death itself. The death or transition to another prison of a fellow user can be an acknowledged loss as it perpetuates the stigma of substance misuse.

In all the cases previously mentioned, the principle of disenfranchised grief that 'each loss must be recognised and validated' (Grollman, 2002: xi) is of significant relevance. Vaswani's analysis (2014) was underpinned by an interest in understanding the voices of the individuals within a particular group (i.e. young people) about their feelings and their perceptions of their experiences of losses. Indeed, Vaswani indicated that '[t]he huge sense of loss experienced by these young men was often evident in their choice of language, using the symbolism of a hole, or the empty chair' (Vaswani, 2014: 352). This view is in the centre of a number of studies dealing with offenders' experiences from loss and bereavement. Consequently, the studies through their inherent narratives bring to the surface the importance of disenfranchised grief in relation to prisoners' social losses, including death. Indeed, as Bosworth observes, 'the reason such stories are told so readily in the prison context is precisely because of the deeply isolated and emotionally vulnerable position that prisoners find themselves in. The opportunity to offload, to engage with these feelings (buoyed by some intrusive and piercing questions from the researcher) can hardly stop this venting process' (cited in Phillips & Earle, 2010).

Conclusion

This chapter has considered the experience of loss and bereavement within the marginalised prisoner community, based on a number of pivotal papers related to bereavement care and support in prisons. The stories illustrate well the experiences of prisoners, and their powerful meanings behind the continuum of losses, not solely those related to death. The theory strongly highlights the potential for disenfranchised grief for this specific population, particularly in relation to the restrictive prison environment. However, this chapter also recognises the importance of the continuum of losses (from general transitional issues, to ill health, to death). As such, this first chapter provides a firm foundation for the following chapters around this sensitive and often controversial area of support across the criminal justice system.

Notes

1 Read, S., Santatzoglou, S., Corcoran, M., Lillie, K.S., Wrigley, A. (March–July 2015, unpublished). 'Exploring bereavement support mechanisms within the criminal justice system: A small scale qualitative study', In *Inter-Disciplinary Study, Funded by the Seedcorn Funding*. Keele University Research Strategy Fund.
2 In relation to these losses, Hendry cited the works of Sykes, G.M. (1958). *The Society of Captives: A Study of a Maximum Security Prison*. Princeton, NJ: Princeton University Press; and Johnson, R. & Toch, H. (1982). *The Pains of Imprisonment*. London: Sage Publications.

References

Attig, T. (1996). *How we grieve: Relearning the world*. Oxford: Oxford University Press.
Bolger, M. (2005). Dying in prison: Providing palliative care in challenging environments. *International Journal of Palliative Nursing*. 12: 619–620.

Childhood Bereavement Network (2008). *Bereavement in the secure setting delivering every child matters for bereaved young people in custody*. London: National Children's Bureau.

Crawley, E. (2005). Surviving the prison experience? Imprisonment and elderly men. *Prison Service Journal*. 160: 3–8.

Doka, K.J. (ed.) (2002). Preface. IN: K.J. Doka (ed.) *Disenfranchised grief: New directions, challenges and strategies for practice*. Illinois: Research Press Publishers. (pp: xiii–xv).

Ferszt, G.G. (2002). Grief experiences of women in prison following the death of a loved one. *Illness, Crisis & Loss*. 10(3): 242–254.

Grollman, E.A. (2002). Forward. IN: K.J. Doka (ed.) *Disenfranchised grief: New directions, challenges and strategies for practice*. Illinois: Research Press Publishers.

Harner, H.M., Hentz, P.M. & Evangelista, M.C. (2011). Grief interrupted: The experience of loss among incarcerated women. *Qualitative Health Research*. 21(4): 454–464.

Hendry, C. (2009). Incarceration and the tasks of grief: A narrative review. *Journal of Advanced Nursing*. 65(2): 270–278.

Machin, L. (2009). *Working with loss and grief: A new model for practitioners*. London: Sage Publication.

Olson, M.J. & McEwen, M.A. (2004). Grief counseling groups in a medium-security prison. *The Journal for Specialists in Group Work*. 29(2): 225–236.

Oswin, M. (1991). *Am I allowed to cry?* London: Souvenir Press.

Phillips, C. & Earle, R. (2010). Reading difference differently? Identity, epistemology and prison ethnography. *British Journal of Criminology*. 50: 360–378.

Read, S. (ed.) (2006). *Palliative care for people with learning disability*. London: Quay Books.

Read, S. (2011). End of life. IN: H. Atherton, & D. Crickmore (eds.) *Learning disabilities: Towards inclusion*. London: Churchill Livingston Elsevier. (pp. 537–549).

Read, S. (ed.) (2014). *Supporting people with intellectual disabilities experiencing loss and bereavement*. London: Quay Books.

Schetky, D.H. (1998). Mourning in prison: Mission impossible? *Journal of American Academy of Psychiatry and the Law*. 26(30): 383–391.

Schultz, C.L. & Harris, D.L. (2011). Giving voice to non-finite loss and grief in bereavement. IN: R.A. Neimeyer, D.L. Harris, H.R. Winokuer, & G.F. Thornton (eds.) *Grief and bereavement in contemporary society: Bridging research and practice*. London: Routledge.

Stevenson, R.G. & McCutchen, R. (2006). When meaning has lost its way: Life and loss "Behind bars". *Illness, Crisis & Loss*. 14(2): 103–119.

Taylor, P.B. (2012). Grief counselling in the jail setting. *American Jails*. July/August: 39–42.

Thompson, N. (2002). *Loss and grief: A guide for human services practitioners*. London: Palgrave Macmillan.

Vaswani, N. (2014). The ripples of death: Exploring the bereavement experiences and mental health of young men in custody. *The Howard Journal of Criminal Justice*. 53: 4.

Vaswani, N. (2015). A catalogue of losses: Implications for the care and reintegration of young men in custody. *Prison Service Journal*. 220: 26–35.

Wilson, M. (2010). "This is not just about death: It's about how we deal with the rest of our lives": Coping with bereavement in prison. *Prison Service Journal*. 190: 10–16.

Wilson, M. (2011). Exploring the efficacy of a bereavement support group for male category C prisoners. *Bereavement Care*. 30(3): 10–16.

Wolfenden, J. (1997). Open space: A bereavement and loss group in a closed women's prison. *Psychodynamic Counselling*. 77–82.

Young, V. (2003). Helping female inmates cope with grief and loss. *Corrections Today*. June: 76–94.

2 Death, dying and maintaining hope

Ethical tensions and responsibilities for end-of-life care in the prison setting

Anthony Wrigley

Introduction

The underlying ethical justifications for utilising imprisonment as a form of punishment for offenders (Hart, 1968; Duff, 1986) quickly run into conflict with ethical concerns about provision of care (Pont et al., 2012). These concerns are particularly pronounced when it comes to issues of death and dying because many of the goals, aims and means of providing good end-of-life care are precisely those that are difficult or impossible to secure in a prison environment. The ethical concerns this care raises include issues such as privacy and confidentiality, respecting autonomy, minimising harms, access to resources, suitability of environment, safeguarding dignity and the duty to prevent despair by fostering hope through the dying process (Trestman, 2014; Garrard & Wrigley, 2009). Institutional settings can therefore strongly influence the ways in which both prisoners and those charged with their care are able to manage issues of the dying process. This situation is more pressing than ever because of increases in the numbers of elderly offenders and in-prison deaths (Stensland & Sanders, 2016; Turner et al., 2011), and the significant problems prison populations have when facing issues of loss, bereavement or their own impending deaths when compared to other groups (Doka, 1989; Hester & Taylor, 2011; Vaswani, 2014). This leaves us with two significant ethical concerns. First, it may be doubtful whether prisoners can receive the same standards of care that are received by those who are not detained or imprisoned. Second, how can we establish that this matters when there is a notable tension between provision of such care and the justifications for imprisonment?

This situation therefore presents us with a difficult ethical challenge in which we have to balance various competing demands. One is maintaining the coherency of our established ethical justifications for using imprisonment as a punishment in light of our knowledge that care and treatment of prisoners is likely to be compromised in certain aspects. Another is our regulatory and legal duties set out by international and national bodies stipulating minimum standards of treatment and care which require us to take a stance on implementing or following them (e.g. UN Resolution 37/194, 1982; UN Resolution 43/173, 1988; Council of Europe, 1989). Finally, there are competing demands between what is achievable and what we need to do to ensure a good death. We therefore have to consider the demands for care against other ethical tensions arising from the justifications we use for imprisonment and already-existing limitations on the kind of end-of-life care we can provide for people, regardless of whether they are in prison or not (Rick & Ashby, 2014). In essence, it comes down to a question of what we should do when the prison environment appears to impinge on our ethical duty to provide high-quality end-of-life care.

Although the list of ethical concerns that might arise in end-of-life care is substantial, I am here focusing on the need for one vital yet oft-ignored aspect of end-of-life care: that of hope. Hope is an interesting and telling case to focus upon. First, hope is a fundamental aspect of human existence. Therefore, to contribute to its loss and to deepen despair would be to deprive extremely vulnerable people of the very last vestiges of what makes them part of human society (Godfrey, 1987). Second, the maintenance of hope is also a fundamental aspect of end-of-life care in itself, and failure to ensure it is to allow an individual to descend into despair, thereby destroying any possibility of the person securing a good death (Garrard & Wrigley, 2009). As our ethical justifications for punishment by imprisonment, at least in the United Kingdom and many developed countries, do not extend to depriving an individual of either humanity or a good death, it would seem we have an ethical duty to foster hope in the face of death or else leave ourselves open to the charge of consigning someone to a terrible end as an unjustified aspect of his or her punishment. Given this, the question then becomes a more practical one of whether the prison environment genuinely impinges on our ability to foster hope at end of life and whether there is a way through the restrictions this imposes.

Medical ethics and criminal justice

When combined, the two rather distinct areas of 'medical care' and 'criminal justice' create a much more complex picture of ethical challenges than they do by themselves. Our broader ethical concerns, such as justice, fairness, autonomous decision making and access to healthcare, are often at odds with the justifications for and purpose of prisons, where the focus is on maintaining control and security which, in turn, inevitably result in restricting movement and choice of both prisoners and practitioners working in that environment. End-of-life care for prisoners is therefore delivered in a highly strict and rigid environment offering far from ideal end-of-life care conditions. The combination of security, views about justice and fairness, the specific patient population and inadequate resources all combine to inhibit the delivery of this care. Yet it is unclear whether the limitations on the provision of good end-of-life care in these circumstances amount to an ethical failure, as opposed to something akin to a political decision or something that is justified by appeal to other competing ethical demands from society.

Within criminal justice, the ethical justifications for imprisonment as a punishment for offenders are primarily divided into consequentialist, retributivist and expressivist arguments, albeit with a range of variations, hybrids and nuances (Walker, 1991). The consequentialist position can take a number of forms. For example, there may be a focus on the positive consequences of a reduction in the incidence of crime by appeal to the deterrence effect of imprisonment on future crime; by appeal to public safety by the containment of a perceived dangerous individual; or by appeal to some notion of rehabilitation of criminals. Alternatively, there may be a focus on the positive benefits for society in terms of reducing the fear of crime or promoting a sense of justice and protection by the state.

Retributivist theories, by contrast, are primarily based on a notion of desert: that punishment by incarceration is what those who engage in criminal activity deserve to receive, and it is thereby a central requirement of justice that offenders receive appropriate punishment (Bedau, 1978; Cohn, 1999). What is particular about retributivist theories is that they seek to justify punishment of an offender regardless of whether there were any genuine consequences resulting from the offence (hence allowing for criminal intention, etc.), although a point about just sentencing is still that it must in some way take into account not only the culpability of the offender but also the harms the offence has caused for victims and society. Whether every offender does, indeed, deserve to be punished and whether there is an acceptable non-arbitrary way of determining what the sentence should be for any given crime are questions that still trouble our theories of punishment. For example, the Roman law principle of *lex talionis* or 'an eye for an eye' is often appealed to by retributivists but has been widely criticised as being little more than retaliation or revenge rather than proportional punishment, particularly when the suffering caused through a poor dying experience is vastly disproportionate to the severity of the offence committed (Walker, 1991; Zaibert, 2006).

Expressivist theories of punishment revolve around punishment as an expression of social attitudes (Feinberg, 1965; Duff, 2001). Accordingly, punishment is meant to signify the very strong disapproval that society has towards criminal actions. What it takes to capture an expression of social attitude and whether that is justifiable, such as public views on capital punishment, are significant challenges to utilising such a theory in practice. Therefore, such expressivist functions are unlikely to be able to stand alone without also drawing on either consequentialist-type rationale, such as deterrence, or a form of the retributivist aim of punishment, such as the shaming of individuals in the eyes of society.

These basic theories form the underpinnings within criminal justice to justifying punishment by imprisonment. Although, potentially, such principles could be used as a justification for limiting access to healthcare for prisoners or for denying them a good death, such as by appealing to extreme notions of the deterrence effect or to enhance some conception of desert, such radical applications of theory have not been successful or widely countenanced. Nowhere in the United Kingdom or most other developed nations would deprivation of access to healthcare, especially end-of-life care, be an expected aspect of the punishment process itself. The problem arises not because the theories of criminal justice advocate limiting care for prisoners but because these theories advocate other restrictions that are well supported as an aspect of criminal justice, and it is these restrictions that indirectly inhibit the provision of such care. The question remains, therefore, as to what should take priority. Should the appeal to theories of punishment that justify imprisonment and restrictions of freedom be the primary concern, so that we must accept any other limitation on what can be achieved within that framework? Alternatively, should the appeal to provide important aspects of care that are not justified as being part of punishment be allowed to prevail, so that these are provided regardless of the restrictions imposed as part of the punishment? Our understanding of these theories of punishment does not give us a clear answer to this dilemma. However, there are some areas of the provision of care that are sufficiently important or fundamental to us as human beings that we should seek to provide them even under the most difficult of circumstances. I take certain aspects of end-of-life care to fall into this category because of the fundamental importance of achieving a good death.

Medical ethics, equivalence of care and limited resources

Another ethical tension arises between these ethical justifications for imprisonment and the duties outlined in international codes and guidelines. There appears a general position, following the United Nations' (1982) Principles of Medical Ethics and further endorsed by the BMA (2016), that prisoners are entitled to the same standards of healthcare as the rest of society. Looking at the underlying reasoning for this, it is based on the principle of justice concerning access to resources, generally referred to as the 'principle of equivalence'. That is, prisoners are entitled to the equivalent range and standard of treatment as any other patient (Handtke et al., 2012).

This, however, only tells us what the basis of this principle is. It doesn't explain why justice demands such equivalence and what might constitute sufficient equivalence. To understand this, we need to consider another aspect of the justice issue concerning deprivation of healthcare and how countenancing this for prisoners, either deliberately or as a corollary of imprisonment, would be an additional punishment. Such an addition would be something the state would not be entitled to inflict and, therefore, beyond the boundaries of what custodial sentences can impose on an individual. This implies that equality of care should continue to apply to prisoners as it does between other members of society because to fail to provide it would be to impose additional unfair punishment on individuals. However, this is a very simplified account of what is at play when considering such issues of justice, and there are some well-recognised limits, many of which are usually also resource based, where limited resources are combined with the added difficulty of administering and monitoring a range of treatments in the prison setting.

Nevertheless, the mere fact that someone is imprisoned is not *prima facie* a reason to fail to offer them the same standards of care as everyone else. Accordingly, if it is not possible to offer this in a prison setting due to constrictions of environment and facilities (Collins & Bird, 2007), this would be a reason to ensure appropriate care is provided elsewhere. Yet this too can have a significant resource impact and lead to pressure not to refer prisoners for treatment outside prison. However, lack of comparable provision would imply that a form of additional healthcare rationing of resources is taking place in prisons on top of the general rationing that is already taking place in a healthcare system facing increasing demand upon resources.

This leads to a question as to whether some justification for additional rationing is warranted by appeal to the competing ethical demands of imprisonment itself. However, given that the ethical reasons for imprisonment generally appeal to the three main elements described previously – deterrence, punishment and rehabilitation – the lack of provision of equivalence of healthcare looks as though it would gain little traction from appeal to any of these. For example, there is no basis for low-quality healthcare to be used as a punishment on the grounds of desert or proportionality; advocating deterrence based on low quality-of-life standards in prison would be to already endorse that deprivation of healthcare is an acceptable form of punishment; and deprivation of healthcare serves no purpose in rehabilitation.

The other major rationale for imprisonment tends to be the safety of society. This would mean that only in those situations where prisoners appear to pose a notable risk could exception be made to providing them access to healthcare. However, two obvious concerns arise here. First, it is significantly less likely that someone is a security risk at end of life, and, second, such a risk also exists in the context of other treatment issues, but there is still a requirement for treatment to be provided to prisoners, albeit with appropriate safeguards. Hence the only identifiable problem would be if demand outstrips the ability to provide such safeguards.

This, more than anything, leads us to the heart of the matter. It is not a credible answer to simply say there should be more resources or funding to facilitate provision of care within the demands of these safeguards, however much we might wish such a solution were available in cases of scarce resources. Instead, the more pertinent question is whether provision of end-of-life resources in the prison setting can be carried out within the constraints it imposes. It would then be a case of arguing whether or not end-of-life care should take priority over other issues of welfare where distribution of limited resources is an issue.

Fostering hope and preventing despair as key aspects of a good death

Rather than pursue the question of prioritising scarce resources between different types of health and welfare services to prisoners, the focus here is on why and how the maintenance of hope for dying prisoners is such an important aspect of their end-of-life care. From there, we can ask whether the prison environment significantly impinges on the maintenance of hope. If it does, this would be a clear manifestation of the tension arising between the justification for punishment through incarceration and an equity of provision of healthcare. However, if this is so, we can still ask whether it is possible to foster hope in such restricted environments. Should this be impossible, it would be to acknowledge a significant ethical failing in our end-of-life care and motivate a substantial reassessment of why we allow a continued imposition of an additional and unjustified punishment on prisoners because of it. Given the restrictions of environment and resources, I will argue in this section that we have a strong ethical duty to foster hope in dying prisoners. To let them descend into despair in the absence of hope would be to deny them a fundamental aspect of trying to achieve a good death, something that is absolutely central to the human experience and something that is not in conflict with any of the ethical arguments justifying their punishment by imprisonment. Finally, I outline in the limited space remaining that, despite limitations on what can be achieved in the prison setting, this does not mean that the maintenance of hope is impossible.

There are situations that we all may face by virtue of being human that are potentially so terrible that they may lead us to lose all hope and descend into despair. This not only means that appeal to hope is essential in such circumstances to prevent despair but also raises the question as to whether hope is possible in situations that might seem to be entirely hopeless. Two situations are seen to present the greatest likelihood of this: imprisonment and facing one's own inevitable death (Marcel, 1952; Godfrey, 1987). Coping with the prospect of one's own death can be extremely challenging under any circumstances, but the situation for those dying in prison is to compound this significantly. These situations can seemingly undermine any reason we may have to continue to maintain hope, as much of what might be considered a desirable outcome or object of hope is stripped away so that there seems to be nothing left to hope for. In order to meaningfully account for hope in these cases, a revision of what we understand by hope is vitally important.

There have been numerous studies amongst dying patients that have gathered information about the most pressing and commonplace fears that surround dying which can ultimately lead to a state of despair. These include pain in the process of dying; a loss of control that requires dependency upon others; isolation so that one dies alone; indignity in the dying process; the fear of what will happen to loved ones without you; and existential questions about the meaningfulness of life, entering the unknown and contemplating life after death (Authers, 2008; Billings, 1989; Cassem, 1988; Faull et al., 2012; Nyatanga, 2005; Saunders, 2006; Steinhauser et al., 2000). At the same time, the value of fostering and maintaining hope in the face of such substantial fears and difficult circumstances has also been widely acknowledged (Barilan, 2012; Ferrell & Coyle, 2005; Garrard & Wrigley, 2009; McGeer, 2008; Snyder, 1995).

Loneliness, hopelessness and despair are features of prison life that many might argue are inevitably a feature of existence in a restricted environment. Yet these are seen as substantial issues that need addressing in the dying process; there is no account of good palliative and end-of-life care that doesn't incorporate how and why loneliness, hopelessness and despair should be avoided. The prison environment, however, offers limited opportunity for this, making them extremely difficult to attain. Usual social relations that allow some of these aspects of end-of-life care planning are unavailable due to restricted means of communication and contact with those closest to the dying individual. Indeed, some prisoners, especially those serving long sentences, may have lost touch with their families altogether. The DoH (2008) End of Life Care Strategy also outlines choice of environment for dying prisoners, with the possibility of compassionate release to facilitate this, but recognises some dying prisoners may even choose prison as a place to die and even consider it their 'home', thereby forcing provision of care in the facility. This means that all the factors and needs surrounding the provision of a good death are still present but complicated by the restricted setting.

Although the language of hope is usually employed in terms of hoping for a cure or at least an improvement in one's condition in normal clinical settings, in the palliative setting the possibility of a cure is either non-existent or vanishingly small and, ultimately, even such tiny possibilities will run out. Moreover, there is no means of relieving someone of the conditions of a terminal illness, with all its concomitant existential fears, although there may be means of relieving symptoms they experience as part of that terminal illness. Under these circumstances, the ability to not give way to depression and despair might seem to be paramount in order to maintain a certain quality of life and a certain attitude towards death that will allow the possibility of attaining a good death. The question is, where does hope lie in circumstances where one is both terminally ill and imprisoned?

One way of answering that question might be to focus on things that are not about a cure but about the achievement of a certain quality of life or the readying of oneself for a good death. Even cases of abject misery may leave room for trying to foster certain aspects of hope, even within extremely limited boundaries (McGeer, 2008). Attempting to foster hope by exploring even the most restricted range of goals within the limits of a life is something that is deeply congruent with the palliative goal that patients "should live until they die" (Saunders, 2006). For example, a person can know they are dying and can find hope in the achievements of those around them, such as hope in the continued success of one's family after one's death, or hope in some identifiable goal in dying, such as hope in a personal formulation of what would count as a good death. All of these can be accommodated within our common understanding of hope because there is an object of hope to rationally hope for or hope in. Hope for amelioration of their conditions, for pain relief, or for all sorts of tangible occurrences is exactly what many would expect to have as the object of their hopes. Even these small objects of hope, however, might not be available to those in restricted environments. Given the fragile nature of fostering hope when dying, we need to reflect upon whether the prison environment prevents this in such a way as to preclude a good death in some circumstances.

If the prison environment creates a situation where various perceived goals that might be seen as potential objects of hope are unavailable, how are we to respond? One response is to admit there is no recourse to instil hope in certain cases, which would be to consign them to a state of total despair. Alternatively, one might countenance a certain amount of false hope to be generated, appealing to some form of paternalistic beneficence in order to justify leading the dying prisoner to falsely believe he or she may attain some tangible object of hope, such as seeing loved ones again, improvements in conditions and so on. As neither of these seems to form part of an appropriately ethical approach to end-of-life care, this leaves us with one option – to consider what we mean by hope and how this might be achievable even in the most limited of environments.

Some cases might just require us to help the dying person look for objects of hope in different directions from the usual, for example, to orientate the object of hope towards very modest goals, such as the hope that pain relief will be better tomorrow, or to turn the object of hope outwards so that it is a hope that one's family will continue to live a happy life after one's death. Such attempts at identifying possible objects of hope may prove useful, but they will not always be applicable, particularly in more challenging cases. Also, they will not always provide a means of addressing the sort of despair that people can experience when dying. Searching for an identifiable object of hope fails to manage what really matters in such circumstances that gives rise to despair: fear of the prospect of one's own death as a result of 'dying salience': a state of growing awareness of one's own inevitable death (Little & Sayers, 2004). Cases where such limited objects of hope run out involve experiences where dying holds only the prospect of protracted suffering and no scope for engagement with the wider world. How we understand hope becomes a much greater challenge through the absence of those things that we might normally find hope in.

Conclusion

Instilling and fostering hope in the face of inevitable death is therefore vitally important for those whose circumstances have stripped away all usual attainable goals in this process. Although imprisonment may generate such circumstances, there will also be situations outside the prison setting where the usual objects of hope are absent in the dying process. All such cases need a new approach to understanding hope, one that is not focused on objects of hope but on engagement with one's world as seen within limited boundaries. In principle, if it can be managed in one such extreme setting, it can be managed in all other similarly extreme settings. Approaches to hope in these types of circumstances have been offered and provide a potential route away from despair at end of life for those dying in prison, but it is still a desperately difficult thing to achieve (Marcel, 1952; Garrard & Wrigley, 2009). Nevertheless, hope in the face of death in restricted environments may still be achievable, allowing those imprisoned the possibility of avoiding despair at end of life and opening some chance at achieving as good a death as possible in otherwise deeply challenging circumstances.

References

Authers, D. (2008). *A sacred walk: Dispelling the fear of death and caring for the dying*. Virginia: A&A Publishing.

Barilan, Y.M. (2012). From hope in palliative care to hope as a virtue and a life skill. *Philosophy, Psychiatry, & Psychology* 19 (3): 165–181.

Bedau, H.A. (1978). Retribution and the theory of punishment. *Journal of Philosophy* 75: 101–120.

Billings, J. (1989). The doctor and the dying patient. IN: J. Billings, & J. Stoeckle (eds.) *The clinical encounter*. Chicago: Year Book Medical Publisher: 193–199.

BMA (2016). BMA response to the Justice Select Committee inquiry into prison reform. www.bma.org.uk/-/media/files/pdfs/collective%20voice/influence/uk%20governments/bma-briefing-justice-committee-inquiry-on-prison-reform.docx?la=en Accessed 03/10/17.

Cassem, E. (1988). The person confronting death. IN: A. Nikoli (ed.) *The new Harvard guide to modern psychiatry*. Cambridge: Harvard University Press: 728–758.

Cohn, F. (1999). The ethics of end of life care for prison inmates. *Journal of Law and Medical Ethics* 27 (3): 252–259.

Collins, D.R. & Bird, R. (2007). The penitentiary visit- a new role for geriatricians? *Age and Ageing* 36 (1): 11–13.

Council of Europe (1989). Recommendation R (98) 7 of the Committee of Ministers to member states concerning the ethical and organisational aspects of health care in prison, Council of Europe Committee of Ministers, Strasbourg. http://hrlibrary.umn.edu/instree/coerecr98-7.html Accessed 03/10/17.

Department of Health (2008). End of life care strategy: Promoting high quality care for adults at the end of their life. www.gov.uk/government/publications/end-of-life-care-strategy-promoting-high-quality-care-for-adults-at-the-end-of-their-life Accessed 03/10/17.

Doka, K.J. (ed.) (1989). *Disenfranchised grief: Recognizing hidden sorrow*. Lexington, MA: Lexington Books.

Duff, R.A. (1986). *Trials and punishments*. Cambridge: Cambridge University Press.

Duff, R.A. (2001). *Punishment, communication, and community*. Oxford: Oxford University Press.

Faull, C., de Caestecker, S., Nicholson, A., & Black, F. (2012). *Handbook of palliative care*. London: Wiley-Blackwell, ch. 7.

Feinberg, J. (1965). The expressive function of punishment. *The Monist* 49 (3): 397–423.

Ferrell, B.R. & Coyle N. (eds.) (2005). *Textbook of palliative nursing* (2nd ed.). Oxford: Oxford University Press.

Garrard, E. & Wrigley, A. (2009). Hope and terminal illness: False hope versus absolute hope. *Clinical Ethics* 4 (1): 38–43.

Godfrey, J.J. (1987). *A philosophy of human hope*. Dordrecht: Martinus Nijhoff Publishers.

Handtke, V., Bretschneider, W., Wangmo, T., & Elger, B. (2012). Facing the challenges of an increasingly ageing prison population in Switzerland: In search of ethically acceptable solutions. *Bioethical Forum* 5 (4): 134–141.

Hart, H.L.A. (1968). *Punishment and responsibility: Essays in the philosophy of law*. Oxford: Oxford University Press.

Hester, R. & Taylor, W. (2011). Responding to bereavement, grief and loss: Charting the troubled relationship between research and practice in youth offending services. *Mortality* 16 (3): 191–203.

Little, M. & Sayers, E.J. (2004). While there's life . . . hope and the experience of cancer. *Social Science & Medicine* 59: 1329–1337.

Marcel, G. (1952). *Homo viator: Introduction to the metaphysics of hope*. (Repr. 2010). Trans. E. Craufurd & P. Seaton, South Bend, IN: St. Augustine's Press.

McGeer, V. (2008). Trust, hope and empowerment. *Australian Journal of Philosophy* 86 (2): 237–254.

Nyatanga, B. (2005). Adapting to death, dying and bereavement. IN: C. Faull, Y.H. Carter, & L. Daniels (eds.) *Handbook of palliative care*. London: Blackwell: 98–115.

Pont, J., Stover, H., & Wolff, H. (2012). Dual loyalty in prison healthcare. *American Journal of Public Health* 102 (3): 475–480.

Rick, L.E. & Ashby, M.A. (2014). Crime and punishment, rehabilitation or revenge: Bioethics for prisoners? *Journal of Bioethical Inquiry* 11: 269–274.

Saunders, C. (2006). *Cicely Saunders: Selected writings 1958–2004*. Oxford: Oxford University Press (from articles originally published in the *Nursing Times*, 1959).

Snyder, C.R. (1995). Conceptualizing, measuring and nurturing hope. *Journal of Counselling and Development* 73: 355–360.

Steinhauser, K., Christakis, N.A., Clipp, E.C., McNeilly, M., McIntyre, L., & Tulsky, J.A. (2000). Factors considered important at the end of life by patients, family, physicians, and other care providers. *JAMA* 284: 2476–2482.

Stensland, M. & Sanders, S. (2016). Detained and dying: Ethical issues surrounding end-of-life care in prison. *Journal of Social Work in End-of-Life & Palliative Care* 12 (3): 259–276.

Trestman, R.L. (2014). Ethics, the law, and prisoners: Protecting society, changing human behaviour, and protecting human rights. *Bioethical Inquiry* 11: 311–318.

Turner, M., Payne, S., & Barbarachild, Z. (2011). Care or custody? An evaluation of palliative care in prisons in North West England. *Palliative Medicine* 25 (4): 370–377.

United Nations (1982). Resolution 37/194: Principles of medical ethics annex Principles of medical ethics relevant to the role of health personnel, particularly physicians, in the protection of prisoners and detainees against torture, and other cruel, inhuman or degrading treatment or punishment. www.un.org/documents/ga/res/37/a37r194.htm Accessed 03/10/17.

United Nations (1988). Resolution 43/173: Body of principles for the protection of all persons under any form of detention or imprisonment. www.un.org/documents/ga/res/43/a43r173.htm Accessed 03/10/17.

Vaswani, N. (2014). The ripples of death: Exploring the bereavement experiences and mental health of young men in custody. *The Howard Journal of Criminal Justice* 53 (4): 341–359.

Walker, N. (1991). *Why punish? Theories of punishment reassessed.* Oxford: Oxford University Press.

Zaibert, L. (2006). Punishment and revenge. *Law and Philosophy* 25: 81–118.

3 'Sympathy to the offender'

The Hobbesian account and the sympathy to the offender as an issue in end-of-life care (part A)

Sue Read and Sotirios Santatzoglou

Introduction

The question of the public legitimacy of sympathy to the offender is the subject of the first part of this essay. In the second part, the question of legitimacy is considered within the criminal context and more specifically with regards to the emotions of the end-of-life-care professionals. It should be noted that in this essay, the terms 'sympathy', 'compassion' and 'pity' are used interchangeably. Certainly, there is a difference between these terms, for example, 'the distinction between the ability to recognise someone else's pain and the impulse to do something about it' (de Waal, 1996: 41). However, the purpose of this essay is to consider the legitimacy of such emotions within the criminal context, public or professional, rather than addressing their conceptual structure.

End of life, compassion and the criminal context

In *R* (*Tracey*) (2014), a legal case which considers healthcare practice with respect the imposition of a 'Do-Not-Attempt-Cardio-Pulmonary-Resuscitation', the Court of Appeal recognised the significant and also critical nature of the management of the end-of-life phase, the 'closing days and moments of one's life', wherein difficult and sensitive care decisions, which affect 'personal autonomy, integrity, dignity and quality of life', have to be made and communicated (*R* (*Tracey*) [2014] at paras 32, 85 and 95). Hence, Larkin reasonably stressed that it 'would be almost sacrilegious to suggest' that the management of end-of-life care *is even possible without compassion* (2016a). Larkin's observation, which can be 'contentious' (Larkin, 2016b: 5), reflects the strong ever-existing link between compassion and the ability of professionals to address the plethora of challenges surrounding end-of-life care. In a rather ambitious account, Renzenbrink, a social worker involved in palliative care and bereavement support services, identified end-of-life compassionate care within the experience of *holistic* care: a 'patient-centred . . . whole-person approach' comprising 'caring for the staff [and] the bereaved' (2016: 176). Renzenbrink's account both enlarged and deepened the link between compassion to successful end-of-life care. However, at the same time, Renzenbrink, far from idealising this link, also indicated not only the problematic experiences of *burnout* or *compassion fatigue* but also the 'overwhelming and difficult' *politics* which, in a particular instance, led to 'a major crisis' and derailed the development of a new compassionate hospice programme in Melbourne (2016: 176). Importantly, Renzenbrink's account points to the significance of the context wherein the development of compassionate end-of-life practice takes place, in particular the organisational or policy context, which moulds compassion both in its function and scope.

The influence of context to the emergence or development of compassion is not a novel theme, but rather an old one in the history of thinking of compassion as a driving emotion or as a moral virtue. In *Nicomachean Ethics*, Aristotle indicated the relevance and significance of the *social*, such as 'human needs and purposes', in the search for defining excellence in decisions driven by emotions, such as compassion (NE 1106a28, 1006a35; Brown, 1997; Brown, 2014: 67; Ross, 2009: 215). In a contemporary account about the practice of compassion, Dutton *et al.* introduced the concept of *social architecture* which along with human agency 'transform individual compassion into a social reality' (2006: 74). 'Social architecture' was defined as 'the amalgam of social networks, values, and routines that structure an organization and that constrain and enable individual action' (2006: 74). Although the word 'context' has not notably been employed, in essence, from the Aristotelian times of virtue ethics to the contemporary organisational theory of Dutton *et al.*, context is nevertheless seen as a critical component in the emergence of compassionate action. This is a significant point about the value and scope of compassion when end-of-life care takes place beyond the healthcare context, in the criminal context, which is different in both values and routines.

The criminal justice context, which administers the imputation of criminal liability and punishment, is not foreign to ideas and values relevant to compassion. As Radzinowicz indicated, penal reform innovations were not necessarily 'devised on the strength of fresh and precise criminological knowledge' but rather they 'evolved . . . under the influence of . . . religious movements and philanthropic stimulus' (1961: 178, 179). Tomczak (2017) also points out the long history of involvement of the 'philanthropic tradition' in English criminal justice, further indicating the current 'increasing role for charities in the delivery of penal services under contract in England and Wales'. However, Faulkner argues that 'qualities such as compassion' do not seem to have any place 'in political, professional or academic debate' on contemporary criminal justice (2014). Faulkner's critical observation reflects the concern that the engagement of the philanthropic voluntary sector with modern neo-liberal penal policies raises 'troubling issues' for the sector's 'ethics of compassion' (Tomczak, 2017). The gradual and actual 'dominance' of punitive policies and conditions of 'overcriminalization' since the 1970s (Lacey, 2008; Husak, 2008; Loader & Sparks, 2011) sets the question about the impact of the overwhelming growth of punitive passion against compassion. This is a critical issue about the scope of compassion in relation to the offender.

This issue is directly relevant to the nature of compassion which, according to Gilman, comprises 'the other', 'the self' and importantly '*the relationship of self and other*' (1994: 754). The interplay of these main elements of compassion raise a number of critical questions when we consider them in the context of criminal justice, especially within a context of 'overcriminalization'. Therefore, what are the values or the ideas which influence our collective (namely social) *relationship* with the offender? How do we collectively *relate* to the offender? *Is there sympathy to the offender?* What is the impact of this *relationship* on the compassionate scope and its function within the criminal process? In his treatise on *Rhetoric*, Aristotle briefly considered the problem of expressing compassion within the context of difficult social relationships and observed by quoting Socrates: 'For it is true . . . that "the difficulty is not to praise the Athenians at Athens but at Sparta"' (Roberts, 2004: 1416a), namely within the land of their eternal enemies. In this way, Aristotle indicated the existence of an intrinsic difficulty in the nature of compassion, which arises when its scope has to be extended to those seen as undeserved, the moral enemy. To put it simply, can we be compassionate to everyone, even to offenders; or should they be seen as undeserving of such sentiments and acts of altruism? Indeed, we can ask what is compassion for within the criminal justice context? More specifically, is *sympathy to the offender* a legitimate feeling, and to what extent? It is exactly the question of the public legitimacy of sympathy to the offender which is the subject of this chapter.

'Sympathy to the offender': the Hobbesian account and the outsider

In seventeenth-century England, Hobbes offered an account about the public perceptions of 'pity', which he used in his writings as a synonym for 'compassion'. Hobbes' account was an account of *public morality*, namely an account which claimed to express a *recognised* and *established* morality embodying the community of moral ideas about 'what is good and what is evil' (Devlin, 1965: 9–15). In *The Elements of Law*, Hobbes argued that 'pity' 'is the greater [for] another man's . . . calamity [when] we think [they] have not deserved the calamity', indicating at the same time that 'we think' that those who 'have not deserved' the calamity are the 'innocent' (1889: 40). Accordingly, he argues that we feel less compassionate to offenders, claiming, 'when we see a man suffer for great crimes . . . the pity is the less' (1889: 40). This was a point also argued in his *Leviathan*: 'for Calamity arriving from great wickedness, the best men have the least Pity' (Hobbes, 1651: 28). Hence, Hobbes' account defined the scope of compassion to the offender through the distinction between those who deserve our compassion, because they don't deserve their suffering, and those who do not deserve our compassion or deserve only a little, because they are not 'innocent'. Therefore, the distance that people *feel* about those of 'great wickedness' lies at the heart of the Hobbesian moral distinction. Hobbes argued that 'we' find it difficult to feel compassion for those who 'suffer for great crimes', because we regard 'us' as different from 'them': 'we cannot easily think [the suffering for great crimes] will fall upon ourselves' (1889: 40). At the same time, there is no such distance in our feelings when the suffering concerns an 'innocent man', as he is the 'every' man', namely a member of our society, one of us; or in the words of the Hobbesian account, 'the evil that happeneth to an innocent man, may happen to every man' (1889: 40). It is that we regard the offender as a distant and different entity to us which defines the degree of our compassion. The feeling of this distance, which is a moral distance, constitutes a significant parameter in Hobbes' seventeenth-century public morality account of compassion to the offender.

The existence of such public feeling was addressed in the *Outsiders*, the seminal contemporary *critical* study about the social meaning of the deviant:

> [W]e think of the person who commits a traffic violation or gets a little too drunk at a party as being, after all, not very different from the rest of us and treat his infraction tolerantly. We regard the thief as less like us and punish him severely. Crimes such as murder, rape or treason lead us to view the violator as true outsider.
>
> (Becker, 1963: 3)

Therefore, following Becker's account, the bigger the criminal stigma, the bigger the public moral distance, which leads to the construction of the 'true outsider'. From this point of view, Becker's critical account indicates the nature of the moral distance: both the moral distance and the undeserved outsider are constructed through our feelings towards crime, which expectedly are negative for most (but not all) forms of criminal conduct. Therefore, the construction of the 'true' undeserved outsider is concurrent with the justified deconstruction of the acknowledgement of the human needs of the outsider, and therefore the limitation of compassion. This deconstruction constitutes what Smith et al. (2015) call, as a 'process of exclusion', a process of '*adiaphorisation*'. Adiaphorisation embodies the negation of our 'moral responsibility' to the stigmatised groups, by which 'they are dehumanised and, crucially, beyond reach of empathy and compassion' (Smith et al., 2015). The influence of criminal stigma, the construction of the underserved outsider and the deconstruction of our moral responsibility to the human dimension of the offender are all major and interrelated elements of the Hobbesian account.

Therefore, the Hobbesian account of public morality on the compassion to the offender seems to suffer from a sort of moral deficit, as social attitudes fostering ideas of dehumanisation and exclusion lack sufficient ethical justification. However, it could be claimed that the Hobbesian account represents a *pragmatic* perspective regarding embedded public emotions towards crime and offenders. Indeed, this pragmatism is reflected in statements such as in the one of Dutton et al. who, as they put it, claim a *stigmatised* pain is 'less likely to evoke emotions such as empathetic concern' (2006: 89), or in Martin Porter's QC observation that

> [m]otoring offences are far more likely than other serious crimes to invoke empathy and compassion from a jury . . . 'there but for the grace of God go I' is not a thought likely to cross many jurors' minds in cases of murder, rape, terrorism or knife crime.
>
> (2016: 446)

Notably, Wrong argued that Hobbes was not only an 'accurate observer of his own time', but his account is rather 'of universal applicability to all men in all societies' (1994). However, arguably, public morality could be open to the construction of different moral perceptions, and therefore open to different feelings and emotions, such as compassion. The occurrence of such differentiations in the public morality is mostly a historical question. The question at hand is whether an interest in the human needs of offenders was ever seen as a legitimate public issue and to what extent.

Compassionate elites and the problem of public legitimacy

Cultural developments within western societies have been seen as the driving force behind the emergence of penal reform which is associated with ideas of justice, decency, humanism and compassion (Garland, 1990; Manson, 2011). In particular, in *Punishment and Modern Society*, Garland discussed his argument about the emergence of a sympathy to the offender as part of a cultural development in Western Europe in a chapter with the telling title 'Punishment and Sensibilities'. His analysis relied on Elias' work on 'civilizing process', a notion which referred to the transformation in Western emotional life and social conduct from the 'Middle Ages to present' (Garland, 1990: 216–225). Within this 'civilizing process', which was characterised by the social development of noble sentiments, Garland stressed the concurrent emergence of the 'extension of sympathy to the offender' (1990: 236). There are two significant points in Garland's account. First, he indicates that the 'enhancement of sympathy to offender . . . and the amelioration of penal conditions' was the 'least well developed' change which occurred during the 'civilizing process' (1990: 236). Second, Garland argued that the sentiments associated with penal reform, such as justice, decency, humanity and compassion, were only part of 'the aspirational values of political elites rather than the sensibilities of the general public' (2001: 10). The link between penal reform and political elites has also been raised in Loader and Sparks' (2011) account about 'the penal philosophy . . . of the middle decades of the twentieth century in the United Kingdom', which set the preservation of 'civilized values' in the centre of the development of penal policy. Loader and Sparks regarded this philosophy as one of 'liberal elitism', comprising 'the sensibilities and dispositions shared amongst opinion-formers, including strategically placed academics, and policy-makers' (2011: 66–67). A rather different perspective can be found in MacCormick's account about the penal developments of this era. MacCormick regarded penal reform as part of wider sociocultural trends which brought about a 'new morality': 'To those who lived through those years, it seems obvious that there was across them a great change in the moral climate' (2008). Moreover, MacCormick further argued about the existence of a harmony between parliamentary ideas and public opinion (2008). However, one of the important penal reforms of this era, the parliamentary abolition of death penalty (which MacCormick included in the new morality of the 'swinging sixties'), had been enacted in clear disharmony with public sentiment. Arguably, MacCormick's account of the wideness of the reform emotions within the public sphere is not as accurate as the account which narrowly links compassionate ideas to penal elitism.

Following the latter account, the problem arising is that the development of compassionate penal reform appears to be a trend which does not concern the wider public moral context and, therefore, lacks public legitimacy. The lack of wider public legitimacy poses a serious risk for the viability of compassionate penal reform. To paraphrase Nils Christie, 'a penal system based on [compassion] from above is a vulnerable one' (1993: 45). In other words, it needs wider public legitimacy for its long-term development. However, contemporary history has shown that, unlike with compassionate penal reform, the intolerant and authoritarian penal policy models can be 'clearly at home' with social thinking (Rutherford, 1996: 131). As Garland put it, with respect to late modernity, within the public sphere, 'crime [has] acted as a lens through which to view the poor – as undeserving, deviant, dangerous, different – and as a barrier to lingering sentiments of fellow feeling and compassion' (2001: 102). As a result, within the limits of this public thinking, the question of social order has been 'viewed not as a Durkheimian problem of solidarity but as a Hobbesian problem of order' (Garland, 2001: 102), namely as a problem of discipline and punishment. In other words, the fight for public legitimacy between ideas of compassionate penal reform and ideas of punishment takes place in the cultural grounds, which are critically located within the Hobbesian moral territory. A late-1970s public correspondence with respect to an alternative to the prison programme provides a characteristic example of this war of ideas and the limits that it poses on penal reform.

Public legitimacy and the 'soft option' problem

In 1977, the editorial of *Justice of the Peace*, under the telling heading 'Soft Option', pointed to a photograph of a young man playing ping-pong, which had been first published in the *Social Services* newspaper under the heading 'Community Service, an Outstanding Success', and over the caption 'An offender performs community service at a Nottingham youth club'. The editorial commented caustically, 'If this is how we wage the relentless war against crime little wonder that the annual statistics keep on rising so' (Brougham, 1977: 509). In a letter which tried to respond to this sarcastic comment, the information officer of the National Association for the Resettlement of Offenders referred to the long criminal record of the young person and also on the impact of the community service order (CSO) on him, who according to the letter, when he was interviewed, said, 'I have found in me something that I did not know existed – the ability to do something constructive' (Cavadino, 1977). However, the critical account of the responding letter was not so much the reference to the impact of the CSO, but rather the detailed description of letter with respect to what this order practically entailed:

> The club [where the young offender served] caters for, to put it bluntly, truants, vandals and shop-lifters . . . on the first night, on walking through the door he was ambushed by several teenagers, his hair was pulled, his girlfriend

was nearly dragged on to the floor and his rough reception continued for the rest of that evening and the next evening.

(Cavadino, 1977)

In short, the descriptive account of the letter aimed at persuading the readers that the young offender did not enjoy any sort of compassion. Indeed, the letter writer explicitly argued that community service was *not* a soft option – this was the main point of the letter. Apparently, in this war of words aiming at gaining public legitimacy, the responding letter clearly conceded to the idea of being *tough on crime*, as, probably, the letter author regarded it as dominant within the public sphere. In this way, the compassionate drive of the CSO was actually diminished, as its value as a constructive alternative to imprisonment was not utilised against the deceptive rhetoric of the 'soft option'. This was despite the fact that the emergence of CSO had been inspired, envisioned and implemented as an alternative to the punitiveness of imprisonment (Harding, 2015). For the historical record, Richard (the name of the young offender), later became an assistant warden in a probation hostel in Bristol, studied politics and social work and, in the late 1980s, joined the Hampshire probation service (Harding, 2015).

This public correspondence shows that within a public context which leans towards authoritarian perceptions, compassion can be easily ill defined as a moral virtue irrelevant to the penal reform system rather than as a vital one. Aristotle himself had indicated the semantic problems arising within a context of 'extremes' by pointing to the ability of 'the people at the extremes' to ill define the meaning of a moral virtue: 'the brave man is called rash by the coward, cowardly by the rash man' (Ross, 2009: 35). This can be, more or less, the fate of compassionate penal reform as 'punishments which lack moral reprobation are not [regarded as] really punishments' (Sadurski, 1985: 49) but rather shamed as a 'soft option', or even rejected as a vision of 'reductionism and sentimentality' (Acorn, 2004: 161). Therefore, on the road to public legitimacy, the rhetoric of penal reform will probably tend to hide its compassionate dimension so as to become established within a public context inclined or even friendly towards Hobbesian non-sympathy against crime and criminals. The question is whether within this context of a war of ideas, a mostly symbolic war, there is another avenue for ideas of compassion to gain public legitimacy.

The avenue of rationalisation for public legitimacy

Ideas of compassionate penal reform may seek legitimacy through the logic of the rationalisation of crime control. This logic corresponds to a crime prevention theme and its ideas of the scientific analysis of crime reduction. The idea is that crime is something which can be managed in a scientific way through the contribution of a wide spectrum of sciences, such as statistics, psychology, psychiatry and so on. Unlike, the Hobbesian approach, crime prevention appears free from emotions with only one purpose, to reduce crime, and therefore is something of a utilitarian approach. Arguably, the ideologies of rehabilitation or treatment, which are both part of a logic of crime prevention or reduction, can also become partly compatible with ideas of compassionate reform. Indeed, Christie (1981) clearly referred to 'compassion, relief, care and goodness' as all composing the 'hidden message' of the treatment/rehabilitation ideology. In this way, the rationalisation of the sympathy to the offender as a crime prevention/reduction policy can become the avenue for the wider public legitimacy of visions of empathy and compassion. A book review published in *The Sunday Telegraph* in 1993 shows the symbolic significance of the preventative logic within the public sphere as an alternative to Hobbesian morality. The review was written by Roger Hood, then director of the Centre for Criminological Research at Oxford University, and it was concerned with Rutherford's book titled *Criminal Justice and the Pursuit of Decency*, a book which clearly addressed the issue of care and compassion within criminal justice practice. The review-article was titled 'Caring Can Go with Justice' and was accompanied by an editorial indication: 'Roger Hood puts the case for more crime prevention, and less pointless punishment' (Hood, 1993). Actually, the word 'preventive' was mentioned only once in the two-column review and undoubtedly did not constitute the main point of Hood, who instead had placed his emphasis on the core issue of Rutherford's book, namely the 'humanitarian approach, the "caring credo"' and the need to prevent abuse in criminal justice (Hood, 1993). Arguably, an explanation behind the inconsistency of this editorial indication was the concern with the readers' reaction: the public legitimacy issue. The humanitarian and clearly anti-punitive content of the book (which was extensively addressed by the reviewer) was presented in the subtitle as a rational vision of crime prevention against the 'pointless' (namely irrational) use of punishment. The humanitarian and anti-punitive ideas were wrapped within the scientific message, 'more acceptable to the readers', of crime prevention. Historically, a number of compassion-inspired penal reform projects subordinated their public aims to the rationalisation of compassion, namely to the prevention of crime.

However, this model of public legitimacy still may fail to establish sympathy to the offender within the public sphere. The case of the 'rehabilitative ideal' (Bottoms, 1980) is rather characteristic. During the 1960s, the treatment-oriented 'rehabilitative ideal' had 'provided a focal point for liberal and humanitarian values' (Rutherford, 1994). However, at the same time, in public, the vision of treatment was disassociated from the humane values. Indeed, Bottoms indicated the transition in the kind of semantics and ideology which marked the rationalisation of compassionate reform: 'in the post-war period, "reform" became "rehabilitation" – that is religious and moral impulses in reformation became secularised, psychologised, scientised' (Bottoms, 1980). The treatment vision operated within the 'bloodless language of social science' and the 'rationality of value-neutral science', where the 'moral evaluation' was 'displaced by scientific understanding' (Garland, 1990: 185–187). As Garland further indicated, during the life of the 'rehabilitative ideal', the moral values of compassion and welfarism 'had not become, after all, solidly entrenched in public attitudes or in penal policy' (Garland, 1990: 186). In the opinion of Rutherford, to 'tie' the 'fate' of the caring values to that of preventative ideals was the wrong way forward for the public legitimacy of those values (Rutherford, 1994: 26). True, when the interest in the needs of the offender is justified through the rationale of crime reduction, the arising problem is that both the interest and the needs of the offender become conditional on the aims of the 'war against crime'; namely, their scope is shaped by the language and the ideology of the crime reduction programmes, and simply the notion of crime. Therefore, the same as with Hobbesian morality, the concept of crime remains the single dominant public lens to view the needs of the offender. As a result, both *otherness* and *undeservedness* remain mostly unquestioned issues whilst compassionate attitudes are withdrawn to the outskirts of the public sphere and policy. This is very much reflected in Faulkner's contemporary statement about criminal policy and 'qualities such as compassion and forgiveness':

> There is none in the Government's policy as it is formulated at present . . . Their only interest to Government is in whether they can be shown to 'work' in reducing re-offending or increasing public confidence. All those affected by crime or involved in criminal justice, in whatever capacity, need some sense of hope and belief in the possibility of progress.
>
> (Faulkner, 2014)

The identification of crime reduction with 'progress' demonstrates the limited visual range of the public lenses with respect to the offender. Their range is more part of the Hobbesian order which devalues the sympathy to the offender, rather than part of the Durkheimian solidarity, as Garland argues (2001).

Conclusion

Within the wider public sphere '*the relationship of self and other*' has not been conditioned by ideas of compassion; both adiaphorisation and the punitive emotion rather than *sympathy to the offender* constitute the dominant public emotions. Therefore, the Hobbesian account both represents and summarises rather successfully the wider public attitudes. The public moral view to the offender is shaped by the lenses of crime (and criminality) which deprive the offender of a human dimension, as a person with needs. The offender is greatly dehumanised and seen as a *distant* and *undeserving* being. The concepts of crime and the criminal *are* the dominant contextual values which influence the scope of the public sympathy to the offender. Therefore, the Aristotelian observation is correct, namely 'it is true . . . that "the difficulty is not to praise the Athenians at Athens but at Sparta" '.

In the second part of this essay, chapter 9, the question of legitimacy of 'sympathy to the offender' is considered within the smaller but socially busier criminal context with regard to the emotions of criminal justice professionals and even more so the emotions of those regarded as compassionate by definition, namely the end-of-life professionals.

References

Acorn, A., (2004), *Compulsory Compassion: A Critique of Restorative Justice* (UBC Press, Vancouver – Toronto).

Becker, H.S., (1963), *Outsiders: Studies in the Sociology of Deviance* (The Free Press – Collier Macmillan Canada Ltd, New York).

Bottoms, A.E., (1980), 'An Introduction to "The Coming Crisis"' in A.E. Bottoms & R.H. Preston (Eds.) *The Coming Penal Crisis: A Criminological and Theological Exploration* (Scottish Academic Press, Edinburgh).

Brougham, (1977), 'Soft Option' *Justice of the Peace*, 141: 509.

Brown, L., (1997), 'What Is "The Mean Relative to Us" in Aristotle's Ethics?' *Phronesis*, 42/1.

Brown, L., (2014), 'Why Is Aristotle's Virtue of Character a Mean? Taking Aristotle at His Word' in R. Polansky (Ed.) *The Cambridge Companion to Aristotle's Nicomachean Ethics* (Cambridge Companions to Philosophy – Cambridge University Press, Cambridge).

Cavadino, P., (1977), 'Soft Option' *Justice of the Peace, Correspondence*, 141: 569, 70.

Christie, N., (1981), *Limits to Pain: The Role of Punishment in Penal Policy* (Martin Robertson, Oxford).

Christie, N., (1993), *Crime Control as Industry* (Routledge, London and New York).

Devlin, P., (1965), *The Enforcement of Morals* (Oxford University Press, Oxford).

de Waal, F. (1996), *Good Natured: The Origins of Right and Wrong in Humans and Other Animals* (Harvard University Press, Cambridge, MA).

Dutton, J., Worline, M.C., Frost, P. J., & Lilius, J., (2006), 'Explaining Compassion Organizing' *Administrative Science Quarterly*, 51: 59–96.

Faulkner, D., (2014), *Servant of the Crown: A Civil Servant's Story of Criminal Justice and Public Service Reform* (Waterside Press, Hampshire).

Garland, D., (1990), *Punishment and Modern Society: A Critical Study in Social Control* (Oxford University Press, Oxford).

Garland, D., (2001), *The Culture of Control: Crime and Social Order in Contemporary Society* (Oxford University Press, Oxford).

Gilman, J.E., (1994), 'Compassion and Public Covenant: Christian Faith in Public Life' *Journal of Church and State*, 36: 747–771.

Harding, J., (2015), 'From Planning to Practice: Pioneering Community Service Order in England and Wales', 1972–1974 in M. Wasik & S. Santatzoglou (Eds.) *The Management of Change in Criminal Justice* (Palgrave Macmillan, Hampshire).

Hobbes, T., (1651), *Leviathan* (Printed for Andrew Crooke, at the Green Dragon in St. Paul's Churchyard) (Anodos Books, Dumfries and Galloway).

Hobbes, T., (1889), *The Elements of Law: Natural and Politic*. Edited by F. Tonnies (Simpkin, Marshall, & Co., London).

Hood, R., (1993), 'Caring Can Go with Justice' *The Sunday Telegraph*, 31st January.

Husak, D., (2008), *Overcriminalization: The Limits of the Criminal Law* (Oxford University Press, Oxford).

Lacey, N., (2008), *The Prisoners' Dilemma: Political Economy and Punishment in Contemporary Democracies* (The Hamlyn Lectures) (Cambridge University Press, Cambridge).

Larkin, P., (2016a), 'Preface' in P. Larkin (ed.) *Compassion* (Oxford University Press, Oxford).

Larkin, P., (2016b), 'Compassion: A Conceptual Reading for Palliative and End-of-Life Reading' in P. Larkin (ed.) *Compassion* (Oxford University Press, Oxford).

Loader, I. & Sparks, R., (2011), *Public Criminology?* (Routledge, Abingdon, UK).

MacCormick, N., (2008), *H L A Hart* (Edward Arnold, London).

Manson, A., (2011), 'The Search for Principles of Mitigation: Integrating Cultural Demands' in J. Roberts (ed.) *Mitigation and Aggravation at Sentencing* (Cambridge University Press, Cambridge).

Porter, M., (2016), 'Road Traffic Offences: A Right to a Jury' *Criminal Law & Justice Weekly*, 25 June, 180: 446–447.

Radzinowicz, L., (1961), *In Search of Criminology* (Heinemann, London).

Renzenbrink, I., (2016), 'Compassionate Organisations' in P. Larkin (ed.) *Compassion* (Oxford University Press, Oxford).

Roberts, W.R., (2004), Aristotle, *Rhetoric*. Translated by R.W. Roberts (Dover Publications Mineola, New York).

Ross, D., (2009), Aristotle, *Nicomachean Ethics*. Translated by D. Ross, Revised with an Introduction and Notes by L. Brown (Oxford World's Classics – Oxford University Press, Oxford).

Rutherford, A., (1994), *Criminal Justice and the Pursuit of Decency* (Waterside Press, Hampshire).

Rutherford, A., (1996), *Transforming Criminal Policy* (Waterside Press, Hampshire).

Sadurski, W., (1985), 'Distributive Justice and the Theory of Punishment' *Oxford Journal of Legal Studies*, 5: 47–59.

Smith, M., Clapton, G., & Cree, V.E., (2015), 'Conclusion: Moral Panics and Beyond' in V.E. Cree, G. Clapton, & M. Smith (Eds.) *Revisiting Moral Panics* (Policy Press, Bristol).

Tomczak, P., (2017), *The Penal Voluntary Sector* (Routledge, Abingdon, UK).

Wrong, D.H., (1994), *The Problem of Order: What Divides and Unites Society* (The Free Press, New York).

Cases

R.(Tracey) v Cambridge University Hospitals NHS Foundation Trust and another (Equality and Human Rights Commission and another intervening) [2014] EWCA Civ 822.

4 Loss at the end of life

Palliative care in prisons

Kate Lillie

Introduction

The journey to the end of life can be conceived as a series of losses. Indeed, it has been claimed that the primary task of the dying patient is to deal with multiple losses (Hottensen, 2010). This is summed up in the Tibetan book of living and dying:

> Often we forget that the dying are losing their whole world: their house, their job, their relationships, their body and their mind – they're losing everything. All the losses we could possibly experience in life are joined together when we die.
>
> (Rinpoche, 2002: 176)

This chapter will consider how dying in a custodial setting affects the losses experienced, focusing on deaths from natural causes. It will critically consider the challenges involved in promoting a good death through palliative care within the criminal justice system.

The World Health Organisation (WHO, 2002) defines palliative care as

> an approach that improves the quality of life of patients and their families facing the problem associated with life-threatening illness, through the prevention and relief of suffering by means of early identification and impeccable assessment and treatment of pain and other problems, physical, psychosocial and spiritual.

There has been rapid development in palliative care since Dame Cecily Saunders founded St Christopher's hospice in 1967 (Clark, 2007). From the start, research and teaching were integrated with clinical practice and an interdisciplinary approach to providing holistic assessment of the needs of the dying and their families and carers. The philosophy was pithily summed up in one of Cecily's most renowned quotes:

> You matter because you are you, and you matter to the end of your life. We will do all we can not only to help you die peacefully, but also to live until you die.
>
> (Saunders, 1976)

Although palliative services initially concentrated on the needs of people with cancer, there is an increasing focus on supporting anybody with an advancing progressive incurable disease, including people with dementia and those living with end-stage heart, renal and respiratory disease (Moens *et al.*, 2014). There is also an active desire to ensure that marginalised and disenfranchised groups are able to access services (Department of Health (DoH), 2008).

One important objective within palliative care is the enablement of a 'good death' (DoH, 2008). This is difficult to define, and the concept remains controversial as every individual may have his or her own ideas about what constitutes an acceptable way to die. However, the UK Department of Health (2008: 9) advocates that it involves being:

- treated as an individual, with dignity and respect;
- without pain and other symptoms;
- in familiar surroundings; and
- in the company of close family and/or friends.

This can be difficult to achieve in any setting. The Parliamentary and Health Service Ombudsman (2015) stated that poor end-of-life care is a recurring and consistent theme. It documents substandard care in hospitals, homes and even hospices, emphasising that the construction of a good death is not a straightforward or easily achieved outcome in any setting. There are, however, unique challenges to providing palliative care in prisons (Richter and Hostettler, 2017), which can affect both the physical and psychosocial dimensions of palliative care provision. Despite these challenges, prisoners have a right to an equivalent standard of healthcare as the rest of society (Till *et al.*, 2014). This is explicit in the UK End of Life Care Strategy which states,

> People who are detained in prison, or under the Mental Health Act in secure hospitals, should be treated with dignity and respect and given as much choice as is possible about the care they receive as they approach the end of their lives.
> (DoH, 2008: 103)

Hence, the issue is not whether palliative care should be offered in secure environments, but how appropriate systems of care can be utilised and modified to meet the individual needs of people with advancing incurable disease (Fowler-Kerry, 2003) to ensure they receive equitable access to care. This is an increasingly important issue due to the growing number of elderly prisoners and a tendency towards longer custodial sentences resulting in more people reaching old age in prison (Richter and Hostettler, 2017).

Physical care: enabling equitable access to symptom control

The prevention of suffering through the alleviation of physical symptoms is integral to palliative care (WHO, 2002). Advancing incurable disease is commonly associated with a range of debilitating symptoms including pain, breathlessness, nausea, vomiting, constipation and fatigue (NICE, 2015). The aim of care is to minimise symptoms to promote optimal quality of life. This requires accurate assessment of the cause to enable effective treatment with minimal side effects. Although discussion of the control of individual symptoms is beyond the scope of this chapter, it is important to be aware that each person requires an individualised and holistic approach to care (NICE, 2015). There can be significant barriers to the assessment and treatment of physical symptoms within a prison environment, even when terminal disease has been appropriately diagnosed. This will be illustrated using pain as an exemplar symptom.

Pain is an unpleasant sensory and emotional experience associated with actual or potential tissue damage (IASP, 1994). In palliative care the concept of total pain, which acknowledges that an individual's pain perception is influenced by one's physical, psychosocial and spiritual state, is central (Portenoy, 2011). Hence it is recognised that the way pain is perceived can be moderated by the mood, moral and meaning that the individual associates with that experience (Twycross, 2003). No research was located that specifically considered how (or whether) being imprisoned affected prisoners' perceptions of pain.

The accurate comprehensive assessment of pain is vital to ensure appropriate, targeted and effective treatment (Rayment and Bennett, 2015). There is some evidence that being in prison may affect pain reporting. A 'macho' prison culture has been described, resulting in prisoners perceiving pain as weakness, leading to reluctance to report pain and complicating assessment (Burles *et al.*, 2016). Reluctance to acknowledge pain can hinder effective and timely treatment. It is also important to note that pain assessment in advancing disease is an iterative process that requires ongoing communication between patient, carer and clinician (Rayment and Bennett, 2015).

Optimal pain treatment is dependent on the cause of pain. There is evidence that the provision of analgesic medication and other treatments for pain may be constrained in prisons. For mild pain, non-pharmacological measures are frequently effective. Gentle exercise, distraction and pacing are frequently recommended (NHS Choices, 2017), but security measures can restrict individual autonomy to utilise these freely within a secure environment. Similarly a risk assessment is required to determine if an individual can hold medications for mild analgesics (such as paracetamol) that can be purchased over the counter in the community (NICE, 2016). If this is not deemed appropriate it can be difficult to obtain analgesia in a timely fashion, especially at night as cells may be locked and only opened in emergencies (Lum, 2005). Similarly opioids, which are an integral component of palliative pain control (NICE, 2015), are primarily seen through a security lens as narcotics, with the primary aim of preventing drug misuse and illegal trading within a prison environment (Burles *et al.*, 2016). Delay in accessing medication may cause symptoms to deteriorate, making it more difficult to achieve sustained periods of pain control (Twycross, 2003). The difficulty in achieving a balance between the security and palliative care requirements of prisons can therefore result in people receiving inadequate or untimely access to treatment for pain and other symptoms (Turner and Peacock, 2017).

In addition, there is a need for systems to support prisoners who are experiencing loss of mobility, continence and cognitive functioning (Moll, 2013; Prison Reform Trust, 2008). These fundamental bodily losses can make prisoners intrinsically vulnerable, causing them to struggle physically and psychologically with systems that are primarily designed for physically fit men (NACRO, 2009). Moll (2013) summarised the existing research on the experiences of older people with dementia in prison as replete with examples of detainees oblivious to their surroundings and mentally incapable of participating in activities required for release.

Psychosocial and spiritual care: being treated as an individual, with dignity and respect

Ensuring that individuals dying within the criminal justice system are treated equally, with both dignity and respect, requires a sympathetic awareness of the complexities of the experience of dying in prison (Turner *et al.*, 2011). Being told an illness is both advancing and incurable can present a major psychological challenge and frequently leads to emotional distress, including anger, grief, fear and depression (Hottensen, 2010; Deaton *et al.*, 2009). Prisoners have a fundamental right to the social, psychological, emotional and spiritual aspects of palliative care, as well as symptom control (Wood, 2007). The aim is to support people to cope in the face of loss and suffering and even enable the potential for growth and personal development that can result from overcoming adversity (Cherny, 2015).

Dying in prison may be perceived as stigmatising (Deaton *et al.*, 2009) and indeed the ultimate failure (Bolger, 2005). Raised death anxiety is associated with concern about separation from family, loss of a final chance at restoration and perceived lack of timely access to healthcare (Deaton *et al*, 2009). Although there is a dearth of research about how people with terminal illness cope in restricted environments, the research on bereavement documents that prison can be an intolerant environment in which the opportunity to express and process emotions is restricted (Vaswani, 2014). The lack of privacy and personal space and the pervasiveness of prison rules have been identified as barriers to inmates' ability to grieve the death of others (Ferszt, 2002) and are likely to present significant barriers to coping with the emotions that arise when living with terminal disease.

The principle of equivalence of care for prisoners (Till *et al.*, 2014) means not only access to diagnostic, therapeutic and nursing care but also the right to self-determination, information and confidentiality (Handtke *et al.*, 2012). Towards the end of life, people with terminal illnesses have very limited control over their lives; in prison, there is even less personal control (Wood, 2007). Healthcare professionals have a vital role in helping people to understand their situations and deal with the emotions that may follow. However, developing the trusting relationship required between the care provider and the patient at the end of life can be more challenging in prison than other healthcare environments, as prisoners are less likely than the population in general to assume the system is working in their best interests (Laird, 2015). This may be compounded by the limited access to sources of information about disease and dying within restricted environments.

Access to the Internet is normally severely limited. Moreover, many people in prison have poor educational attainment and reduced reading abilities which can limit access to independent health information about their conditions (Laird, 2015). Mistrust of professionals can reduce the opportunities to discuss the dying process and make autonomous decisions. This is further compounded as opportunities to involve family members and loved ones are limited (Bolger, 2005).

The experience of loneliness and isolation is common in the dying, even amongst those who have committed caregivers (Ettema *et al.*, 2010). The experience is composed of at least three interrelated components: social loneliness, emotional loneliness and existential loneliness. Existential loneliness is commonly associated with dying in the literature, and the increasing weakness that is associated with physical deterioration normally leads to a gradual loss of social networks and social roles (Ettema *et al.*, 2010). Moreover, friends and family may struggle to connect with the dying as their condition deteriorates for a whole host of reasons. The social loneliness associated with the dying is likely to be magnified in people who have experienced the disruption to their social networks through imprisonment and live in an environment where social interaction is highly regulated (Bond *et al.*, 2005). The stigma associated with criminal conduct alongside imprisonment can lead to people being conspicuously alone at the time of death even if they have been released on compassionate grounds (MacWilliams *et al.*, 2014).

The support of family and friends is consistently emphasised as a mainstay of psychosocial support in palliative care and a family-centred approach is frequently promoted to support a good death (Lethborg and Kissane, 2015). Although access to family and other trusted friends is restricted in secure settings, this does not negate the importance of family. In fact, a study exploring general concepts of health with prisoners found that the maintenance of family connections and the preservation of the family unit were critical facets of individuals' definitions of health (Woodhall, 2010). It has long been suggested that prisons should become more flexible for terminally ill prisoners, with increased visiting hours and more regular opportunities for communication between staff, prisoners and the prisoner's family (Craig and Craig, 1999).

However, it is important to acknowledge that some prisoners may have experienced lifelong alienation from family as well society. This can lead prisoners to experience feelings of hopelessness with fear of dying alone, shame at dying as a prisoner and regret at dying without atonement or forgiveness (Deaton *et al.*, 2009; Craig and Craig, 1999). Wood (2007) urges that dying prisoners need respect, companionship and compassion to avoid feelings of loneliness and hopelessness and adds that treating dying prisoners with respect can also have a positive effect on other inmates by demonstrating that even prisoners have the right to die with dignity.

One model of care that has been well evaluated is the development of an in-house peer-support system of inmate volunteers (Cloyes *et al.*, 2017; Wood, 2007; Craig and Craig, 1999). Prisoners may be the most appropriate people to support their peers at the end of life, as they have the personal experience of the pains of imprisonment. It is suggested that dying prisoners more readily trust and confide in other inmates or outside volunteers than in the prison staff (Wood, 2007). They also have more access to fellow prisoners than family or healthcare professionals and can provide reliable companionship, as well as assistance with physical needs. However, caring for the dying is skilled work, and volunteers need to be carefully selected and appropriately trained and supported in their role (Cloyes *et al.*, 2017; Craig and Craig, 1999). There are concerns that peer support does not enable a real equivalence in care and the potential for psychological abuse or exploitation by other inmates needs to be carefully thought through (Handtke *et al.*, 2012). Despite these concerns, peer volunteers may be a valuable component of the palliative care package that ensures prisoners are treated with dignity and respect (Cloyes *et al.*, 2017; Wood, 2007; Craig and Craig, 1999).

The experience of advancing incurable disease can lead people to question their religious and spiritual beliefs (Cheatham, 2015). Religious care may include, but is not restricted to, ensuring that people have support to develop a relationship with a divine being and timely access to rituals and practices in accordance with an organised system of belief (McClement, 2015). Spiritual care is frequently defined more broadly, for instance as

> that care which recognises and responds to the needs of the human spirit when faced with trauma, ill health or sadness and can include the need for meaning, for self-worth, to express oneself, for faith support, perhaps for rites or prayer or sacrament, or simply for a sensitive listener.
>
> (Royal College of Nursing, 2011: 3)

The need for religious and pastoral care for those facing death within the prison system is explicitly acknowledged by the Ministry of Justice (2013), and the prison multi-faith chaplaincy team is explicitly tasked with the provision of pastoral and religious support (Ministry of Justice, 2013). However, there has been very limited research into the effectiveness of care within the criminal justice system (Todd and Tipton, 2011). Case studies suggest that concerns about judgement in the afterlife can be a significant issue for certain individuals in the general population (Griffith, 2007), but there has been no systematic study to see whether there are concomitant concerns in those who have been judged and found guilty in life.

Enabling a good death in prison

Death in prison need not be viewed as shameful or frightening if it can be afforded dignity, sensitivity, care and understanding (Bolger, 2005). In the United Kingdom, the Prison and Probation Ombudsman independently reviews all deaths, including those from natural causes. It is not uncommon for the report to conclude that care was equivalent to that which the prisoner could have expected to receive in the community. An evaluation of palliative care in six prisons in England (Turner *et al.*, 2011) uncovered examples of good practice where hospice and prison staff worked together to combine knowledge and skills. The *Journal of*

Correctional Care issued a special section looking at end-of-life care in France, Switzerland, the United Kingdom and the United States showing how different systems were adapting their structures and processes to enable end-of-life care (Cloyes *et al.*, 2017; Turner and Peacock, 2017; Chassagne *et al.*, 2017). Nevertheless, there is no evidence that there is systematic equivalence in care provision, and there remain significant structural barriers to ensuring high-quality palliative care in prisons. These include identifying people who are approaching the end of life, managing the tensions between security and care provision and staff training.

Identifying the dying

To implement palliative strategies and services successfully, it is important to be able to identify individuals who are dying and to anticipate, and plan for, the challenges that lie ahead. Failure to identify need in a timely manner prevents adequate planning and leads to inappropriate aims of care and leads to people dying without dignity irrespective of the setting (Parliamentary and Health Service Ombudsman, 2015). As treatments for individual diseases have improved many people die with multiple co-morbidities alongside progressive incurable disease. This change is associated with both an increase in life expectancy and an attenuated dying process, where individuals, families and health and custodial professionals have the time to plan and prepare for death (Murray *et al.*, 2005). However, diagnosing dying remains a difficult and uncertain process even in the last days of life (NICE, 2015).

There are a wide range of prognostic indicator tools to support accurate indication of prognosis, but these are predominantly statistically based tools and it remains very difficult to predict when an individual will deteriorate and die (Glare *et al.*, 2015). The challenges that this can provide for healthcare professionals working in the criminal justice system are clearly illustrated in the case of Abdelbaset al-Megrahi, 'the Lockerbie Bomber'. He was released, on compassionate grounds in August 2009, with terminal cancer and an anticipated life expectancy of less than three months but lived for two years nine months following his release (The Independent, 2012). This prompted questions, and indeed criticism, of the Scottish criminal justice system from political leaders in both United Kingdom and the United States (The Independent, 2012). More commonly the fact that people are dying is not recognised in a timely manner, leading to patients and their families not receiving the support they require, which is frequently associated with inappropriate care provision including unnecessary hospital admissions, investigations and preventable suffering before death (NICE, 2015).

Knowing when to stop treating disease and change the aims of care to palliative is particularly difficult for people with illnesses interspersed with episodes of acute deterioration and partial recovery, a pattern that is observed in many common non-malignant diseases such as chronic obstructive airways disease and end-stage heart failure. This can lead to complex decisions about how to balance the Prison Service's duty to protect the public and the humanity of care. The propensity to focus on security can lead to unnecessary diminishment of dignity in the dying. For instance, the inappropriate use of restraints on elderly, infirm and dying prisoners remains an ongoing public concern (Allison and Hattenson, 2013).

Tensions between security and care provision

Prison staff perceive the primary purpose of the prison estate to be the provision a safe, secure and restraining environment rather than the provision of health-care, even when sympathetic to the health needs of individual patients (Chassagne *et al.*, 2017; Penrod *et al.*, 2014). There are tensions between the rehabilitative and correctional roles of prisons that can lead to healthcare provision for the dying being perceived negatively (Burles *et al.*, 2016). Correctional personnel may fear deaths in prison, which they know will trigger an investigation regardless of the cause (Turner *et al.*, 2011). The suggestion that prisons should become more flexible for terminally ill prisoners (Craig and Craig, 1999) may also lead to concerns about putting additional pressure on overstretched staff and resources (Turner *et al.*, 2011).

Need for training and expertise

Experience is essential to gain clinical expertise (Benner, 2001). As the proportion of prisoners requiring palliative care is low, maintaining the skills and knowledge required to competently care for this group of prisoners is challenging (Scott, 2016). It can require a change in organisational culture and challenge personal beliefs, with staff encouraged to manage anticipated deaths with kindness and empathy towards offenders in their facilities (Wood, 2007). The emotional labour involved in caring for the terminally ill is influenced by the professional attitudes towards death and dying (Sorensen and Iedema, 2009). Even trained healthcare professionals find caring for the dying stressful and may need support coping with the emotional demands of their work, and there is little organised support for cus-todial persons in this area. For instance, the most recent NICE (2016) guidance on the physical health of people in prison does not mention death. In response there have been calls for prison staff to have not only initial training in end-of-life care (particularly in relation to pain and symptom management) but also ongoing edu-cation and personal contact with experienced hospice professionals (Turner *et al.*, 2011; Bolger, 2005; Craig and Craig, 1999).

Conclusion

The experience of loss at the end of life depends on a complex interplay of mul-tiple personal, physical, psychosocial, spiritual and environmental factors. Ensur-ing high-quality palliative care requires an individualised holistic approach that assesses and tends to each factor as death approaches. Palliative care developed as a reaction to the attitude that nothing more can be done when curative treatment fails (Twycross, 2003). Although there are structural barriers to the implementa-tion of palliative care within prisons, there are exemplars of good practice which suggest that it is possible to achieve a good death in prisons. More work is needed to ensure this occurs in a more consistent manner. However, the fundamental principle is that prisoners should receive equitable care (Till *et al.*, 2014; DoH, 2008) and that restricting access to a good death should not, and need not, be part of the penal consequences of crime.

References

Allison, E., Hattenson, S. (09/11/2013). Dying in chains: Why do we treat sick prisoners like this. *The Guardian*. www.theguardian.com/society/2013/nov/09/sick-prisoners-handcuffing-terminally-ill (accessed 02/11/16).

Benner, P. (2001). *From novice to expert: Excellence and power in clinical nursing practice*. New Jersey: Prentice Hall Health.

Bolger, M. (2005). Dying in prison: Providing palliative care in challenging environments. *International Journal of Palliative Nursing*, 11(12), 619–621.

Bond, G.D., Thompson, L.A., Malloy, D.M. (2005). Lifespan differences in the social networks of prison inmates. *International Journal of Aging and Human Development*, 61(3), 161–178.

Burles, M.C., Peternelj-Taylor, C.A., Holtslander, L. (2016). A good death for all? Examining issues for palliative care in correctional settings. *Mortality*, 21(2), 93–111.

Chassagne, A., Godard, A., Cretin, E., Pazart, L., Aubry, R. (2017). The collision of inmate and patient end-of-life issues in French prisons. *Journal of Correctional Health Care*, 23(1), 66–75.

Cheatham, C. (2015). *Hospice whispers: Stories for life*. Austin: SCIE Publishing.

Cherny, N.I. (2015). The problem of suffering and the principles of palliative care. IN: N.I. Cherney, M.T. Fallon, S. Kaasa, R.K. Portenoy, D.C., Currow (eds). *Oxford textbook of palliative medicine*. Oxford: Oxford University Press. (pp. 35–49).

Clark, D. (2007). From margins to centre: A review of the history of palliative care in cancer. *The Lancet Oncology*, 8(5), 430–438.

Cloyes, C.G., Rosenkranz, S.J., Supiano, K.P., Berry, P.H., Routt, M., Llanque, S.M., Shannon-Darcy, K., (2017). Caring to learn and learning to care: Inmate hospice volunteers and the delivery of prison end-of-life care. *Journal of Correctional Health Care*, 23(1), 43–55.

Craig, E., Craig, R. (1999). Prison hospice: An unlikely success. *American Journal of Hospice and Palliative Care*, 16(6), 692–693.

Deaton, D., Aday, R.H., Wahidin. A. (2009). The effect of health and penal harm on aging female prisoners' views of dying in prison. *Omega*, 60(1), 51–70.

Department of Health. (2008). *End of life care strategy: Promoting high quality care for adults at the end of their life*. London: DoH.

Ettema, E.J., Derksen, L.D., van Leeuwen, E. (2010). Existential loneliness and end-of-life care: A systematic review. *Theoretical Medicine and Bioethics*, 31(2), 141–169.

Ferszt, G. (2002). Grief experiences of women in prison following the death of a loved one. *Illness, Crisis & Loss*, 10(3), 42–53.

Fowler-Kerry, S. (2003). Palliative care within secure forensic environments. *Journal of Psychiatric and Mental Health Nursing*, 10, 53–59.

Glare, P., Sinclair, C.T., Stone, P., Clayton, J.M. (2015). IN N.I. Cherney, M.T. Fallon, S. Kaasa, R.K. Portenoy, D.C. Currow (eds). *Oxford textbook of palliative medicine*. Oxford: Oxford University Press. (pp. 65–77).

Griffith, L.,J. (2007). Good palliative care for a patient with schizophrenia dying of emphysema and heart failure. *Psychiatry*, 4(8), 61–65.

Handtke, V., Bretschneider, W., Wangmo, T., Elger, B. (2012). Facing the challenges of an increasingly ageing prison population in Switzerland: In search of ethically acceptable solutions. *Bioethica Forum*, 5(4), 134–141.

Hottensen, D. (2010). Anticipatory grief in patients with cancer. *Clinical Journal of Oncology Nursing*, 14(1), 106–107.

IASP Task Force on Taxonomy. (1994). Part III: Pain terms, a current list with definitions and notes on usage. IN: H. Mersky, N. Bogduk (eds). *Classification of pain* (Second Edition). Seattle: IASP Press. (pp. 209–214).

The Independent. (21/05/2012). Convicted Lockerbie bomber dies of cancer years after release. www.independent.co.uk/news/world/africa/convicted-lockerbie-bomber-dies-of-cancer-years-after-release-7769685.html# (accessed 06/15).

Laird, B.J.A. (2015). Barriers to the delivery of palliative care. IN: N.I. Cherney, M.T. Fallon, S. Kaasa, R.K. Portenoy, D.C. Currow (eds). *Oxford textbook of palliative medicine*. Oxford: Oxford University Press. (pp. 105–112).

Lethborg, C., Kissane, D.W. (2015). The family perspective. IN: N.I. Cherney, M.T. Fallon, S. Kaasa, R.K. Portenoy, D.C. Currow (eds). *Oxford textbook of palliative medicine*. Oxford: Oxford University Press. (pp. 1101–1110).

Lum, K. (2005). Palliative care in a New Zealand prison. *International Journal of Palliative Nursing*, 11(12), 621.

MacWilliams, J., Bramwell, M., Brown. S., O'Connor, M. (2014). Reaching out to Ray: Delivering palliative care services to a homeless person in Melbourne, Australia. *International Journal of Palliative Nursing*, 20(2), 83–88.

McClement, S.E. (2015). Spiritual issues in palliative care. IN: N.I. Cherney, M.T. Fallon, S. Kaasa, R.K. Portenoy, D.C. Currow (eds). *Oxford textbook of palliative medicine*. Oxford: Oxford University Press. (pp. 1057–1059).

Ministry of Justice, National Offender Management Service. (2013). *Faith and pastoral care for prisoners*. PSI 51/2011 Ministry of Justice. London: Crown Copyright.

Moens, K., Higginson, I.J., Harding, R. (2014). Are there differences in the prevalence of palliative care-related problems in people living with advanced cancer and eight non-cancer conditions? A systematic review. *Journal of Pain and Symptom Management*, 48(4), 660–667.

Moll, A. (2013). *Losing track of time: Dementia and the ageing prison population: Treatment challenges and examples of good practice*. London: Mental Health Foundation.

Murray, S.A., Kendall, M., Boyd, K., Sheikh, A. (2005). Illness trajectories and palliative care. *British Medical Journal*, 330(7498), 1007–1011.

NACRO. (2009). *A resource pack for working with older prisoners*. GR 12279. London: DoH.

National Institute for Health and Care Excellence. (2015). *Care of dying adults in the last days of life NICE guideline*. NG31. London: NIHCE.

National Institute for Health and Care Excellence. (2016). *Physical health of people in prison*. NICE Guideline NG57. London: NICE.

NHS Choices. (2017). *Living with pain*. ww.nhs.uk/Livewell/Pain/Pages/Painhome.aspx (accessed 11/08/17).

Parliamentary and Health Service Ombudsman Report. (2015). *Dying without dignity: Investigations by the parliamentary and health service ombudsman into complaints about end of life care*. London: Parliamentary and Health Service Ombudsman.

Penrod, J., Loeb, S.J., Smith, C.A. (2014). Administrators' perspectives on changing practice in end-of-life care in a state prison system. *Public Health Nursing*, 31(2), 99–108.

Portenoy, R.L. (2011). Treatment of cancer pain. *The Lancet*, 377(9784), 2236–2247.

Prison Reform Trust. (2008). *Doing time: The experiences and needs of older people in prison*. London: Prison Reform Trust.

Rayment, C., Bennett, M.I. (2015). Definition and assessment of chronic pain in advanced disease. IN: N.I. Cherney, M.T. Fallon, S. Kaasa, R.K. Portenoy, D.C. Currow (eds). *Oxford textbook of palliative medicine*. Oxford: Oxford University Press. (pp. 519–525).

Richter, M., Hostettler, U. (2017). End of life in prison: Talking across disciplines and across countries. *Journal of Correctional Health Care*, 23(1), 11–19.

Rinpoche, S. (2002). *The Tibetan book of living and dying: Revised and updated*. London: PerfectBound™ HarperCollins Publishers, Inc.

Royal College of Nursing. (2011). *Spirituality in nursing: A pocket guide*. London: RCN.

Saunders, C. (1976). Care of the dying 1. *Nursing Times*, 72(26), 1003–1005.

Scott, G. (2016). *Prisoner healthcare*. Macmillan Cancer Care. www.macmillan.org.uk/aboutus/healthandsocialcareprofessionals/newsandupdates/macvoice/prisonerhealthcare.aspx (accessed 02/11/16).

Sorensen, R. Iedema, R. (2009). Emotional labour: Clinicians' attitudes to death and dying. *Journal of Health Organization and Management*, 23(1), 5–22.

Till, A., Forrester, A., Exworthy, T. (2014). The development of equivalence as a mechanism to improve prison healthcare. *Journal of the Royal Society of Medicine*, 107(5), 179–182.

Todd, A., Tipton, L. (2011). *The role and contribution of a multi-faith prison: Chaplaincy to the contemporary prison service*. Cardiff: Cardiff Centre for Chaplaincy Studies.

Turner, M., Payne, S., Barbarachild, Z. (2011). Care or custody? An evaluation of palliative care in prisons in North West England. *Palliative Medicine*, 25(4), 370–377.

Turner, M., Peacock, M. (2017). Palliative care in UK prisons: Practical and emotional challenges for staff and fellow prisoners. *Journal of Correctional Health Care*, 23(1), 56–65.

Twycross, R. (2003). *Introducing palliative care* (4th Edition). Abingdon: Radcliffe Medical Press.

Vaswani, N. (2014). The ripples of death: Exploring the bereavement experiences and mental health of young men in custody. *The Howard Journal*, 53(4), 341–359.

Wood, F. (2007). The challenge of providing palliative care to terminally ill prison inmates in the UK. *International Journal of Palliative Nursing*, 13(3), 131–135.

Woodhall, J. (2010). Exploring concepts of health with male prisoners in three category-C English prisons. *International Journal of Health Promotion and Education*, 48(4), 115–122.

World Health Organization. (2002). *World Health Organization definition of palliative care*, Geneva, www.who.int/cancer/palliative/definition/en/ (accessed 10/11/2016).

5 Deaths in sites of state confinement

A continuum of routine violence and terror

Bree Carlton and Joe Sim

Introduction

With the exception of a few studies and collections (Moore & Scraton, 2014; Scraton and McCulloch, 2006; Scraton and McCulloch, 2009), there is a marked absence of critical, academic research which examines and provides a theoretical and political framework for analysing deaths in sites of state confinement. This critical work has directly challenged the positivist discourses which have dominated state policies, expert definitions and liberal scholarship in this area, whose primary and enduring focus around deaths in police custody, prisons and in other sites of state confinement has been largely on the pathological deficiencies of the deceased, the poor practices and attitudes of individual state servants and the failure to adhere to broader, preventative policies such as risk assessment and management. However, its reliance on generalised concepts related to the violence of incarceration (see Scraton and McCulloch, 2006, 2009) and the violence of neglect (Cunneen, 2006) needs development in order to capture the nuanced mechanics of how institutional environments produce harm, death and trauma.

The state's discourse, augmented by liberal academic research (Liebling, 1999, 1992), with its endlessly recurrent emphasis on crisis, inquiry and policy reform, is insufficient because it obscures and mystifies systemic issues of institutional and corporate violence, wounding processes of neglect and domination as well as sheer incompetence which provide the context for deaths in state confinement. Additionally, experiences of fatal harm and injustice are differentiated and structured by vectors and axes of structural inequality and oppression built on social class, gender, race, age, sexuality and ability/disability. The key issue of democratic control and accountability is also insufficiently addressed, if at all, within liberal scholarship, whilst it is given passing reference in state inquiries into deaths in its institutions.

Building on the aforementioned critical work, this chapter has four areas of focus. First, it provides a preliminary snapshot of the nature and extent of deaths in sites of state confinement, whilst advocating an expansion of the definition of state confinement to include a range of satellite institutions, both public and private. Second, it critically considers the issue of deaths in these sites as a form of violence. Third, it outlines a theoretical framework for conceptualising the routine, dehumanising and punitive conditions and experiences which produce individual and collective harm and death; herein, we argue that deaths in sites of incarceration are better understood as being located along *a continuum of violence and terror*. Fourth, it concludes by advocating an abolitionist position regarding sites of state confinement. Ultimately, this is about generating analyses that enable the long-term project of transforming and dismantling the structures, contexts and institutions at the foundations of state-generated violence, harm and death.

A critical reading of the meaning of sites of state confinement

What is meant by 'sites of state confinement'? This chapter adopts an approach that stretches beyond the traditional confines of the criminal justice system to include deaths in other forms of institutions. In this sense, a central task is to consider *where* confinement takes place. In doing so, it becomes possible to map the proliferation of sites and processes of state confinement and to explore connections and continuums of violence across different social and criminal justice institutions. These include, but are not restricted to, prisons and police custody centres, court custody facilities, immigration and border detention centres, sites of juvenile detention, secure facilities which house the elderly, secure rehabilitation centres and hospitals, secure psychiatric units, probation hostels and military detention as well as transportation to and from these various sites.

The deprivation of liberty is defined within the UN Optional Protocol for the Prevention of Torture (OPCAT) as any place 'where persons are or may be deprived of their liberty, either by virtue of an order given by a public authority or at its instigation or with its consent or acquiescence' and more broadly as 'any form of detention or imprisonment or the placement of a person in a public or private custodial setting which that person is not permitted to leave at will by order of any judicial, administrative or other authority' (Office of the United Nations High Commissioner for Human Rights, 2002, Article 4).

The National Preventive Mechanism (NPM) has been established in the United Kingdom to meet the requirements of OPCAT. It serves as an independent oversight body monitoring the treatment of incarcerated 'detainees' (NPM, nd).

The NPM also includes the broad category of 'deprivation and other safeguards in health and social care' and identifies the practice referred to as '*de facto* detention' in a range of social and health institutions where individuals have been deprived of liberty in contexts not necessarily deemed legal or covered by existing protection standards and protocols (NPM, 2015, p. 47). These include care homes, hospitals, low-security units, supported-living service and supported living for children or adolescents. Whilst these sites are governed by different regimes, characteristics and sets of power relations and actors, there are characteristics related to deprivation of liberty that commonly cut across them.

Characteristics accepted by the NPM for determining deprivation of liberty within '*de facto* detention' include whether individuals are confined in restricted spaces for non-negligible periods of time, whether individuals have provided valid consent to their confinement, whether the state is responsible (in some cases where this is not the case, confinement could be illegal), whether the person has the freedom to leave, the duration of the confinement, the extent to which sedation is used, the extent of contact the individual has with the outside world and the extent to which an individual's movement is controlled or restricted.

Such criteria provide a rationale for collating data relating to deaths across a range of institutions which, despite their apparent differences, are ultimately linked not only through the deprivation of liberty but also through the harm, punishment and pain being delivered directly and indirectly as a result of the routine realities of regimented institutional environments. This is explored in greater detail in the following sections.

A snapshot of deaths

What knowledge is currently available about deaths in different sites of state confinement? A statistical snapshot from some of these sites – here, using data from England and Wales – demonstrates the need for further quantitative and qualitative inquiry to help map, then contextualise and understand, continuums of institutional violence which generate deaths (and, of course, a range of other physical, emotional, psychological, financial, economic and cultural harms). Thus, for example, we know that

- between 1990 and December 2016, 4,126 people died in prisons and 1,944 of these deaths were self-inflicted (inquest.org.uk);
- within this total, black and minority-group prisoners accounted for 423 of these deaths, 242 of which were self-inflicted (inquest.org.uk);
- of this total, there were also 193 deaths amongst women prisoners, 116 of which were self-inflicted (inquest.org.uk);
- in the same period, 305 children and young people died in custody, 275 of which were self-inflicted (inquest.org.uk);
- between April 2011 and March 2015, 10,306 patients died whilst in the care of the Southern Health NHS Foundation Trust; whilst the majority of these deaths were expected, 1,454 of them were unexpected, and whilst only 30 per cent of deaths of adults with mental health issues were investigated, this figure dropped precipitously to 1 per cent of those with learning difficulties and 0.3 per cent of those over 65 with mental health issues (*The Guardian*, 10 December 2015);
- between 2010 and 2015, 3,196 individuals died under probation supervision, of which 646 were on licence from prison; 66 deaths were classified as 'non-natural' and occurred within 28 days of the individual being released from prison (Phillips et al., 2016);
- the UK-based Institute for Race Relations has been documenting deaths in short-term immigration holding centres, during removal and shortly after release from detention centres since 1989, and has documented 22 deaths that occurred between 1989 and May 2014 (Institute for Race Relations, 2014);
- between 2000 and 2013, there were 4,573 deaths in psychiatric detention in England and Wales, which accounted for 60 per cent of all deaths in state custody during this time (Independent Advisory Panel on Deaths in Custody, 2013 cited in Speed, 2017a);

- furthermore, statistics from the Care Quality Commission stated that during April 2014 to March 2015, they were informed of the deaths of 227 patients, 29 more than the 198 deaths that were reported between 2013 and 2014 (Care Quality Commission, 2015, cited in Speed, 2017b);
- between 1970 and 1988, 48 children died in children's homes in Lambeth, London (*Private Eye* no. 1436, 27 January–9 February 2017); and
- finally, between 1990 and January 2017, there were 1,592 deaths in police custody in England and Wales (inquest.org.uk).

These data highlight three important issues.

First, the scale of deaths in sites of state confinement is significant and ongoing, with many of these deaths taking place beyond prison and police custody, which have been the principal focus for critical research and activist engagement.

Second, accessing data and then developing consistent data sets are key tasks in themselves if a realistic portrayal of the actual numbers of deaths in the various sites is to be quantified.

Finally, the fact that much work is needed to retrieve even these bald data indicates something about the lack of any political and social priority attached to such deaths and the state's abject failure, or indeed lack of desire, to learn lessons from them.

Deaths in sites of state confinement as violence

How, then, to conceptualise such deaths? One starting point is perhaps how *not* to understand them. For us, such deaths cannot be explained by the actions of rogue individuals working within the state or those contracted by the state, nor through classifications around degrees of risk and vulnerability, nor through individual-ised discourses of victim blaming. The experience of INQUEST, which has pro-vided case worker support for those bereaved by deaths in custody in England and Wales for over 30 years, is exemplary insofar as it suggests these deaths are sys-temic and often have very similar causes. This can be seen in relation to the use of certain kinds of restraint techniques in custody and the lack of care and protection afforded to the detained. A further and significant factor is the corrosive sense of impunity that is endemic within the occupational cultures of state servants. This impunity is rarely, if ever, challenged by government ministers who are, in theory, accountable for the everyday actions of criminal justice personnel. A critical anal-ysis, then, requires developing a position which does not absolve state servants of individual responsibility but which is *not* reducible to individual actions or omis-sions, whether as bad apples, rogue employees or non-responsibilised detainees incapable of accepting and recognising the benevolence of the state's intentions.

However, it is theoretically inadequate simply to cast deaths across a whole series of sites of state confinement as effects of structures or as 'structural' harms. This obscures the differences between the types of deaths produced in different institutions and, indeed, the complex lived realities of what incarceration across these different sites is, how incarceration is managed, by whom, to what ends and so on. Thus, it is important to be sensitive to 'sectoral' and organisational-level practices and cultures, since these are likely to differ between a prison, a residential care home and a bail hostel. Additionally, a critical analysis needs to be even more nuanced to take into account the similarities and differences between different categories of prison, or the micro-exercises in power in different prison wings, police custody suites or psychiatric units as examples, amongst many.

Furthermore, thinking critically about the varieties of harm across sites of state confinement means conceptualising these harms as violence. To refer to such deaths as violence jars with dominant common-sense, legal and indeed criminological understandings of the term 'violence'. A critical understanding requires overcoming two inherent assumptions in dominant legal, cultural and criminological definitions of violence: first, the primacy granted to intention, and second, the focus upon individual, interpersonal conflict as opposed to collective sources of violence. We consider both of these in turn.

Intent enjoys significant legal status. However, the notion of intent presupposes, and then concretises, a moral hierarchy which, once examined, is counter the commonsensical. Reiman (1998) makes this point in a simple but striking fashion. He contrasts the motives (and moral culpability) of most acts recognised as intentional murder with what he calls the indirect harms on the part of absentee killers, by which he means deaths which result where employers refuse to invest in safe plant or working methods, where manufacturers falsify safety data for new products or where illegal discharges are made of toxic substances into the environment. Additionally, he notes that intentional killings generally result from acts directed explicitly at one (or, rarely, more than one) specific individual. In such cases, the perpetrator – who in many respects fits our archetypal portrait of a criminal – 'does not show general disdain for the lives of her fellows' (Ibid, p. 67).

These intentional killings are contrasted with deaths that result from 'indirect' harms, so that the relative moral culpability of the intentional killer on the one hand and the mine executive who cuts safety corners on the other is quite distinct. Locating these different types of offenders on a moral hierarchy arguably inverts, or at least collapses, the hierarchy of culpability around which criminal law operates. Thus, the mine executive

> wanted to harm no-one in particular, but he knew his acts were likely to harm someone – and once someone is harmed, the victim is someone in particular. There is no moral basis for treating one-on-one harm as criminal and indirect harm as merely regulatory.

> (Ibid, pp. 67–70)

Reiman concludes that offenders of intentional, one-on-one harm are less likely to represent some generalised threat to others than the mine executive. The reasoning is plausible, and points to indifference or 'indirect' harm as at least as, if not more, culpable compared with intention and 'direct' harms.

The fact many deaths in prisons occur as a result of the failure to learn lessons from previous deaths or from the inept, incompetent and indifferent behaviour of state servants, either individually or collectively, has been well documented by INQUEST, the Chief Inspector of Prisons, the Prisons and Probation Ombudsman and different coroners. Given this, and given the arguments outlined previously, it is not necessary for intent to be present in the conventional, legalistic sense for deaths in prison to be conceptualised as a form of violence. Indifference and neglect can and do kill and, further, generate a sense of bereavement and deeply felt loss which can be as wounding for the families of the deceased as the intentional killing of their relatives.

If intent is central to dominant legal and academic understandings of violence, also significant is the primacy attached to individualised explanations. As Salmi has written, the 'usual treatment of violence' is infected with '[e]xcessive individualisation', 'attributing solely to individual factors actions that cannot in reality be accounted for in individual terms. By so doing, the possibility of a causal link between the violence observed and the surrounding social structure is systematically dismissed' (Salmi, 1993, p. 8). Rather, the focus remains upon 'the individual and the eradication of such deplorable behaviour' (Catley, 2003, p. 4).

However, if an epistemological commitment to individualism is abandoned, then more encompassing definitions and considerations of violence become possible. For example, Bowie has sought to develop the category of 'organisational violence', and although this is partially limited by some commitment to intention, it is far more useful than other definitions of violence. Thus, for Bowie, organisational violence, developed in the context of the workplace, is applicable across organisations. It 'involves organisations knowingly placing their workers or clients in dangerous or violent situations or allowing a climate of abuse, bullying or harassment to thrive in the workplace' (Bowie, 2002, p. 6).

If this position still retains some commitment to intention, it at least moves beyond simple understandings of individual action, not least because it acknowledges how a general organisational demeanour of generating or turning a blind eye towards violence can be fostered 'in a growing economic rationalist climate of decreasing job security, massive retrenchments and expanding unemployment that pitted workers and unions against employers' (Bowie, 2002, p. 9).

If the limitations of intent and individualism can be transgressed, then more accurate ways of describing, analysing and theorising about violence become available. For example, in one well-known effort to develop a more holistic understanding of violence, Jamil Salmi, following Galtung amongst others, has set out a systematic, analytical framework which aims to explore the different dimensions of this phenomenon; he then identifies the patterns and relationships linking the various manifestations of violence to the prevailing economic, social and political power structures. Such a frame might usefully be developed to conceptualise the causal dynamics which produce deaths in sites of incarceration, as well as the multifaceted consequences of these.

Deaths in sites of state confinement: a continuum of violence and terror

If we accept these claims both with regard to the limits of dominant discourses of violence and with regard to the need to develop wider definitions of this term

(Tombs, 2007), then how can this be applied to deaths in sites of state confinement, and what do they have in common as forms of violence and what differentiates them? These questions raise two issues.

First, violence takes a variety of forms within, and across, different sites and processes of incarceration. At the same time, those forms of violence which result in death are not necessarily logically distinct from the other forms of routinized, normalised forms of violence which characterise and circulate through such sites. Thus, following Kelly (1988), violence resulting in deaths can be understood as at one extreme of a 'continuum of violence'.

Second, then, a key issue here is understanding the forms of power that underpin or characterise confinement across different institutions and the socially and psychologically harmful processes that they generate on an everyday basis.

As a concept, the 'continuum of violence' draws connections between structural and institutional forms of power, violence and neglect. Scholars such as Harris have illustrated the ways in which criminal justice institutions, and the prison in particular, compose a continuum of structurally produced violence that is linked to the reproduction of gendered violence (Harris, 2011). This analysis can be extended to examine the different forms of violence which emerge from spaces, logics and processes of state/corporate incarceration. In various ways, spaces of incarceration are too structured by axes of domination and subordination. Understanding the continuum between structural and institutional power is critical if we are to grasp that, whatever form it may take, conditions within incarceration both emulate and reproduce structural power, social divisions, harm and violence.

Additionally, this raises the question about the relationship between violence and terror in the context of what Rodriguez calls 'punitive carcerality'. This involves thinking about state terror in relation to the 'fundamental inseparability between acute forms of state coercion and the subject, discourses and places that they conceive and reproduce. State terror is, in this sense, uncontained and *inescapable*' (Rodriguez, 2006, pp. 148 and 156, emphasis in the original).

This point, in turn, raises a further issue, namely the relationship between terror and trauma which underpins and gives meaning to self-harm and self-inflicted deaths in different institutions. For the confined, and, indeed, for those at the razor-sharp end of neo-liberal welfare practices, the exercise of state power is experienced as incapacitating and senselessly producing uncertainty and is therefore traumatic and traumatising (Sim, 2014). For those at the bottom of the ladder of social inequality, the imprisoned and the welfare claimant, for example, the exercise of institutional power is psychosocially experienced through destructive 'zones of contact' such as the prison, the benefit office, the welfare agency and private job-seeking agencies which are built on rules which are 'uncertain, changing and indecipherable'. These 'zones of contact' have become the 'incomprehensible other' which are grafted through the use of 'senseless injunction[s]' (Zizek, 1989, p. 44).

These psychological conditions are not pathological in the positivist sense but are the result of a series of deeply embedded social processes which operate in different sites of confinement leaving those incarcerated within them, or who come into contact with them, feeling bereft, a word that has the same etymological roots as 'bereaved'.

All prisoners can feel bereft and terrified through living in often-abject penal regimes that are built on the delivery of punishment and pain. Feeling bereft can generate a deep sense of loss and a lack of self-worth and self-esteem, underpinned by feelings of alienation, humiliation and uncertainty. If they feel humiliated, this 'strips [them] of their self-esteem and reduces them to vulnerable creatures rather than significant beings in a world of meaning' (Solomon et al., cited in Sim, 2016, p. 9). In short, they have a 'despairing belief in personal nothingness' (Epstein, 1996, p. 65). Within institutions, the discourse of rehabilitation and resettlement is so far removed from the everyday reality of prisoners that they 'become literally "dis-illusioned" because they lack a functional blueprint of reality. Without such a map, there is no basis for determining what behaviours are appropriate or desirable, leaving no way to plot a course to self-esteem' (Ibid).

Feeling bereft – of family, friends, possessions, safety and belonging – is reinforced by a sense of social abjection, defined by Imogen Tyler as

> [t]he action or an act of casting down, humbling, or degrading; an act of abasement; [t]hat which is cast off or away, esp. as being vile, unworthy, scum, dregs. The state of being cast down or brought low; humiliation, degradation, dispiritedness, despondency.
>
> (*Oxford English Dictionary*, cited in Tyler, 2013, p. 20)

For those in prisons and other institutions of state confinement, their experience is one of penal abjection built on a series of 'officially approved torments' (Maloney, 2013, p. 208) which underpin and give meaning to the actions of those who kill themselves or engage in self-harm. These places traumatise the already traumatised. Contrary to the state's official discourse, they make *all* prisoners vulnerable, not just those who are defined as at risk by the state's 'judges of normality' (Foucault, 1979, p. 304). Additionally, self-inflicted deaths are all treated as similar. This neglects the fact that each death 'represents a different set of reactions to individually experienced pain' (Medlicott, 2001, p. 17).

Ultimately, in spite of the differences between sites of state incarceration, they are linked not only through the process of depriving the individual of liberty but also in the conscious and unconscious delivery of harm, punishment and pain which is underpinned by a corrosive process of 'depersonalisation' and 'corruption of care'. Therefore 'if individuals are viewed as less than human and not "like us" then abuse of those individuals becomes more explicable, if not justifiable' (Wardhaugh and Wilding, cited in Penhale, 1999, p. 9). More broadly, what happens within them can be tied into to what Mick Taussig has called 'terror as usual' (Taussig, cited in Wall 2014, p. 6).

For example, many of the accounts of those who have self-harmed or killed themselves in confinement indicate that they are terrified. The idea of being terrified is important because it raises the central issue not about what places of state incarceration such as prisons *are* but what they *do*. Contrary to the state's often mendacious discourse, they are, despite the odd exception such as Grendon Underwood in England and Wales, sites for the infliction of pain, punishment and terror built on a network of horizontal and vertical power relationships that are targeted, cruel and unrelenting. It is these everyday cruelties – the banality of terror, to paraphrase Hannah Arendt, or in Katz's phrase the 'banal terrorism' which refers to ' "those everyday, routinized, barely-noticed" reminders of terror, or the threat of terrorism' (cited in Liebert, 2014, p. 221) – which provide the context for understanding not only why deaths in confinement occur but also the form, shape and magnitude that they take.

Conclusion

The fatal consequences of systemic and routine neglect within sites of state confinement must be understood as violence. By extension, and beyond the regimes and experiences associated with penal and other institutions, the failures of liberal penal reform agendas to redress structural causes underpinning death and particularly the lack of adherence to coronial recommendations that could prevent future deaths also constitute violence by state and private actors. In examples related to deaths in penal custody, as documented by Razack (2015) and Cunneen (2006), penal reform agendas have largely served to reinforce the legitimacy of state agents in maintaining a duty of care rather than doing anything which qualitatively prevents death.

Quite simply, the implementation of policy reform packages has coincided with penal expansion in the form of therapeutic and healthy prison environments and the abject failure to implement coronial inquest recommendations and findings. In this context, the continuum of violence is less exceptional or even preventable and more a matter of the system working routinely and exactly as it is intended. Ultimately, if the abolitionist imperative is to prevent state and structurally generated harm and death in relation to that occurring in and across sites of state confinement, then there is a need for developing theoretical and political frameworks for understanding the way they are a manifestation of the processes through which power operates within, and beyond, institutional environments to reproduce violence.

References

Bowie, V. (2002). *Workplace violence*. New South Wales: Workcover.

Catley, B. (2003). Philosophy: The luxurious supplement of violence. Paper presented at Critical Management Studies 2003, Lancaster, July.

Cunneen, C. (2006). Aboriginal deaths in custody: A continuing systemic abuse. *Social Justice*, 33 (4), 37–51.

Epstein, M. (1996). *Thoughts without a thinker*. Cambridge: Basic Books.

Foucault, M. (1979). *Discipline and punish*. Harmondsworth: Penguin.

Harris, A. (2011). Heteropatriarchy Kills: Challenging Gender Violence in a Prison Nation. *Journal of Law and Policy*, 37(1): 14–65.

Institute for Race Relations. (2014). *May 8, 2014: News*. www.irr.org.uk/news/deaths-in-immigration-detention-1989-2017/

Kelly, L. (1988). *Surviving sexual violence*. Cambridge: Polity.

Liebert, R.J. (2014). Psy policing: The borderlands of psychiatry and security. IN: D. Holms, J.D. Jacob, and A. Perron (eds). *Power and the psychiatric apparatus*. Farnham: Ashgate, 217–232.

Liebling, A. (1992). *Suicides in Prison*. London: Routledge.

Liebling, A. (1999). Doing Research in Prison: Breaking the Silence? *Theoretical Criminology*, 3(2): pp. 147–175.

Medlicott, D. (2001). *Surviving the prison place*. Aldershot: Ashgate.

Moloney, P. (2013). *The Therapy Industry: The Irresistible Rise of the Talking Cure and Why It Doesn't Work*. London: Pluto.

Moore, L. & Scraton, P. (2014). *The Incarceration of Women: Punishing Bodies, Breaking Spirits*. Basingstoke: Palgrave Studies in Prison and Penology Series.

National Preventive Mechanism. (2015). Monitoring places of detention. Sixth Annual Report of the United Kingdom's National Preventive Mechanism, London: HMSO, 1 April 2014–31 March 2015.

National Preventive Mechanism. (nd). *Introducing the UK's National Preventive Mechanism*. https://s3-eu-west-2.amazonaws.com/npm-prod-storage-19n0nag2nk8xk/uploads/2015/05/NPM-factsheet-1_Introducing-the-UK-NPM.pdf (accessed 30 June 2017).

Office of the United Nations High Commissioner for Human Rights. (2002). *Optional Protocol to the Convention against Torture and Other Cruel, Inhuman or Degrading Treatment or Punishment*. www.ohchr.org/EN/ProfessionalInterest/Pages/OPCAT.aspx (accessed 30 June 2017).

Penhale, B. (1999). Introduction. IN: N. Stanley, J. Manththorpe, and B. Penhale (eds). *Institutional abuse: Perspectives across the life course*. London: Routledge, 1–15.

Phillips, J., Gelsthorpe, L., Padfield, N., and Buckingham, S. (2016). *Non-natural deaths following prison and police custody*, Research Report 106. London: Equalities and Human Rights Commission.

Razack, S. (2015). *Dying from improvement: Inquests, inquiries into aboriginal deaths in custody*. Toronto: University of Toronto Press.

Reiman, J. (1998). *The rich get richer and the poor get prison* (fifth edition). Boston: Allyn & Bacon.

Rodriguez, D. (2006). *Forced Passages: Imprisoned Radical Intellectuals and The U.S. Prison Regime*. Minneapolis: University of Minnesota Press.

Salmi, J. (1993). *Violence and democratic society: New approaches to human rights*. London: Zed Books.

Scraton, P. & McCulloch, J. (2006). Deaths in Custody: Introduction. *Social Justice*, 33 (4), 1–14.

Scraton, P. & McCulloch, J. (eds.) (2009). *The Violence of Incarceration*, London: Routledge.

Sim, J. (2014). Prison, terror and trauma: From an ethos of punishment to an ethos of care. Paper presented at Keele University Conference, Loss, Bereavement and Compassionate Care: Challenges and Opportunities in the Criminal Justice System, December 2016.

Sim, J. (2016). *Changing prisons, saving lives: Report of the independent review into self-inflicted deaths in custody of 18–24 year olds (the Harris review): Unpublished briefing paper*. London: INQUEST.

Speed, C. (2017a). Deaths in psychiatric detention. IN: S. Morley, J. Turner, K. Corteen, and P. Taylor (eds). *Companion of state power, liberties and rights*. Bristol: Policy Press.

Speed, C. (2017b). As little regard in life as in death: A critical analysis of subjugation and accountability following deaths in psychiatric detention. *Illness, Crisis and Loss*, 25 (1), 27–42.

Tombs, S. (2007). Violence, safety crimes and criminology. *British Journal of Criminology*, 47 (4), 531–550.

Tyler, I. (2013). *Revolting subjects*. London: Zed Books.

Wall, T. (2014). Legal Terror and the police dog. *Radical Philosophy*, 188 (November/December), 1–7.

Zizek, S. (1989). *The sublime object of ideology*. London: Verso.

6 Civil and social death
Criminalisation and the loss of the self

Andrew Henley

Introduction

In this chapter I offer an alternative perspective to the themes of 'dying', 'loss' and bereavement' within criminal justice and explore the relationships which exist between social practices of punishment and the status or positioning of former lawbreakers who have *been punished*. First, I provide a brief history of punishments in England whose object was to bring about not only the literal death of the condemned person but also their 'civil death'. Second, I connect these historical practices of juridical 'othering' to the 'pains of criminalisation' which exist in the present. These, I argue, are manifestations of 'social death' which are experienced by people with convictions due to the stigma of having a criminal record. Drawing on Erving Goffman, I then suggest that this 'mortification of the self' disrupts pre- and post-conviction social identity in ways which require us to develop wider conceptions of 'loss' and 'bereavement' in criminal justice research.

Death as punishment and 'death' beyond punishment

The social practice of punishment has long been associated with the idea that the convicted party must suffer painful or 'unpleasant consequences' following a breach of the law (Lacey 1988: 7–8) and that, by doing so, lawbreakers expiate their guilt for offences. Indeed, many post-Enlightenment theories of punishment are predicated on the idea that lawbreakers have incurred a notional 'debt to society' by 'breaching the social contract' between state and citizens which must be 'paid back' by suffering a proportionate punishment (Beccaria 1764/1819). However, a cursory examination of the history of English punishment – and particularly the use of the death penalty – reveals a number of examples which undermine the idea that even the finality of death was sufficient for a convicted party to fully expiate his or her guilt and be emancipated from the juridical status as irretrievably 'other'.

The hanging, drawing and quartering of those convicted under the Treason Act of 1351 was a prime example of *posthumous* punishment. The destruction of the offender's body was intended not only to reflect the seriousness of attacks on the authority of the monarch in comparison to other 'lesser' capital offences (Bellamy 2004: 13) but also to continue punishment into the afterlife. In many Christian traditions, the burial of an intact corpse facing eastwards was a necessary precondition for resurrection of the body on the final day of judgement (Abbot 1996: 33). It could, therefore, be argued that this posthumous destruction of the corpse was designed to extend the effects of punishment *beyond* the point of death.

In 1814, the legal reformer and parliamentarian Sir Samuel Romilly proposed to reduce the penalty for high treason to death by hanging with the body being merely placed 'at the King's disposal' (Romilly 1820: xlvi). However, an amendment to Romilly's proposal argued that such a reform would leave the punishment for high treason in a state 'less than the punishment annexed to murder' (1820: xlvi). It was therefore resolved that posthumous decollation (beheading) would be retained ' "as fit punishment and appropriate stigma" in such cases' (Romilly 1820: xlvi).

The Murder Act of 1752 allowed for the corpses of convicted murderers to be either hung in irons (gibbeting) as a deterrent or used for public dissection so 'that some further terror and peculiar mark of infamy be added to the punishment' (Harrison 1983: 6). Posthumous dissection, often conducted in public, had the effect of rendering a death sentence for murder as more 'notorious' than that which was commonly available for theft during this period. The sentence of 'death with dissection' was retained until the Offences against the Person Act of 1828 and was only rendered obsolete four years later following the Anatomy Act of 1832, which permitted the donation of bodies for medical research purposes. However, the principle that those who were executed for their crimes could not, even in death, return to a state of equality to other 'innocent' people was also retained by the act, which included a direction that the bodies of executed convicts belonged to the Crown. Consequently, they were to be buried within the prison grounds in unmarked graves (often containing several bodies) rather than returned to family members for private burial. Section 5 of the Capital Punishment Amendment Act of 1868 added the provision that a formal inquest be held following execution, but section 6 retained the requirement that the body be buried within the grounds of the prison where the execution took place – a practice which continued until the abolition of the death penalty for murder in the 1960s.

Capital punishment in England had, therefore, a long tradition of adding further post-mortem indignities to the condemned. However, in addition to suffering execution, those convicted of treason or felonies could also be subjected to a wider range of legal consequences which effectively extended the effects of punishment *beyond death* (Damaska 1968). During the Middle Ages, bills of attainder were often passed 'as an adjunct to a death sentence or following a commuted capital sentence' (Edgely 2010: 405). The consequence of such bills was to pronounce the 'civil death' of the condemned and to inflict the additional punishment of 'corruption of blood' upon them. In effect, attainder meant that whilst individuals were still *physically* alive, they were *legally* dead, even if only for the short period prior to their executions. As a result, attainted persons' property was forfeited to the Crown and they were forbidden from entering into contracts and inheriting property. Also, their wives legally became widows and their children were orphaned. Moreover, any civil or political rights enjoyed by the attainted were stripped from them. Consequently, they could not give evidence in court or begin legal proceedings against another person. Neither could they sit on a jury or, in later centuries when the franchise had been extended, vote in any elections (Edgely 2010: 405).

Damaska (1968: 354) suggests that the motive behind the infliction of such measures was that of 'degrading the offender'. Significantly, this involved the reduction of noblemen and women to the status of commoners, thus rendering them liable to forms of torture and execution which would otherwise have been forbidden. The corruption of blood which accompanied a bill of attainder also had the effect of stripping individuals of the right to pass on property or any titles to their heirs. Once again, these were forfeited to the Crown and thus another practical effect of such a bill was the termination of the legal entitlements of the attainted person's family (Saunders 1970: 989).

Bills of attainder were typically passed by medieval kings and queens against political enemies or others who posed a threat to the security of the monarch's position. Whilst they were mostly made against men, notable women made subject to bills of attainder included Anne Boleyn and Catherine Howard, who were stripped of their titles and had their marriages to Henry VIII annulled prior to their executions. Henry VIII also famously attainted his chief minister Thomas Cromwell on charges of treason in 1540 (Schofield 2008). Later, in events which helped precipitate the English Civil War, a bill of attainder was passed by Parliament against Thomas Wentworth, the first earl of Strafford and one of the King Charles I's leading advisers (Lerner 2002). Whilst not strictly a bill of attainder, a 'bill of pains and penalties' was also tabled by Gladstone's government as recently as 1869. The bill was intended to deprive Daniel O'Sullivan, the elected mayor of Cork and a magistrate, of his offices in response to comments he had made which were supportive of an assassination attempt on the duke of Edinburgh made by Irish nationalists. In the event, O'Sullivan was persuaded to resign and the potentially inflammatory effects of his 'attainder' were avoided (MacDonagh 1974).

Sullivan's case perhaps contextualises certain provisions in the Forfeiture Act of 1870. Whilst the act abolished the automatic forfeiture of goods and property to the Crown following a conviction for felony or treason (thus ending many of the common law consequences of 'civil death'), section 2 of the act stated that those convicted of treason shall be disqualified from holding public office, shall lose their right to vote in elections, and shall also lose their pensions. For the most part, these disqualifications remain in force today – albeit they have subsequently been restated or amended by additional legislation. For example, the removal of state pension rights from serving prisoners was achieved through the National Insurance Act of 1911, whilst the ban on prisoners serving more than twelve months from standing in parliamentary elections was introduced by the Representation of the People Act of 1981. This legislation sought to prevent Irish republican prisoners from replicating the election success of Bobby Sands in the Fermanagh and South Tyrone by-election in April of that year. Section 3 of the Representation of the People Act of 1983 maintains a blanket ban on convicted prisoners from voting in local and national elections in the United Kingdom. Despite the European

Court of Human Rights (in *Hirst v. UK [No. 2] – 74025/01 [2005] ECHR 681*) ruling that this was incompatible with article 3 of protocol 1 of the European Convention (on the 'right to free elections'), this prohibition remains in place (see Behan 2014; Drake and Henley 2014).

That the origin of these contemporary civil disqualifications can be traced back to the archaic practice of attainder demonstrates a certain ambiguity about precisely what the limitations or boundaries are to the effects of legal punishments in the present. Just as historically execution and civil death *as punishment* did not bring about a definitive end to the torment of the condemned, cessation of the formal aspects of a convicted person's sentence offers limited safeguards against the social death which often *follows punishment* in the present.

The pains of criminalisation and their impact on the self

As I have explored elsewhere (see Henley 2014, 2016, 2017) the 10.5 million people with convictions in the United Kingdom (Unlock 2014) are potentially subjected to a wide range of *de jure* prohibitions on participation in full and meaningful citizenship. They are also particularly vulnerable to *de facto* discrimination – that is, whilst there may often be no specific law authorising discrimination against them, they are nonetheless regarded as potentially risky, dangerous or 'less eligible' than other citizens and excluded from equal consideration. Thus, if we extent Sykes' (1958) notion of the 'pains of imprisonment' – which suggests that penal confinement is experienced as painful due to the deprivation of liberty, security, autonomy, goods and services and heterosexual relationships – it is possible to also conceive of a number of 'pains of criminalisation' which apply to ex-prisoners and other people with convictions as a result of the stigma associated with criminal records (for further details, see Henley 2016, 2017 and also the work of the charity Unlock, who campaign on such issues). In the United Kingdom, these 'pains' include, but are by no means limited to the deprivation, restriction or outright denial of

- *employment* (since people with convictions are over-represented amongst the ranks of the unemployed and are subjected to both *de jure* and *de facto* exclusion from many occupations, exacerbated by widespread criminal background checking);
- *financial services* (because many major mortgage providers will not lend to people with unspent convictions, who may also find they are routinely charged far more for insurance products);
- *accommodation* (as private landlords may legitimately refuse a tenancy to anyone declaring an unspent criminal conviction and where several local authorities have introduced restrictions regarding access to social housing);
- *international mobility* (since criminal records can cause difficulties obtaining entry visas for travel outside of the European Union);
- *educational opportunities* (particularly when criminal records acquired in childhood cause difficulties with acceptance into university or vocational training courses requiring criminal background checks);

- *victimisation* (since unspent convictions have the effect of eliminating the possibility of receiving compensation from the government-funded Criminal Injuries Compensation Scheme for those physically or mentally injured as the victim of a violent crime); and
- *civic participation* (because previous convictions can place limitations on a person's right to stand for elected office, serve on a jury or, in some cases, sit as a charity trustee).

When regarded in their totality, these pains of criminalisation represent a form of premature *social death* (see Bauman 1992; Králová 2015) which exists as an adjunct to the formal 'unpleasant consequences' (Lacey 1988) or 'hard treatment' (Duff 2001) associated with legal punishment.

It has been common for scholars (particularly in the United States) to describe such effects as the 'collateral consequences' of punishment (see Demleitner 1999; Chin 2012; Uggen and Stewart 2015). There are, however, reasons to question whether this term does justice to the personal and social harm which arises when those who have served their sentences and paid their 'debt to society' are then subjected to further discriminatory conduct. First, the term 'collateral' suggests that this discrimination is merely ancillary to the formal judicially approved sanction. This is problematic because the wide-ranging nature of the discrimination possible and the potential frequency with which it is encountered suggests that it is likely to be experienced as inherently punitive in its own right and, potentially, as more severe than the main judicial sanction (see Aresti *et al.* 2010; Earle 2016: 77–94). Thus, it is necessary to think of these pains of criminalisation as *central* to the social process of punishment rather than merely as 'collateral' effects of it. Second, the word 'consequences' suggests a certain inevitability about post-sentence discrimination – as though it were merely a natural result of a conviction. This ignores the fact that such discrimination involves a whole range of social actors (e.g. employers, insurers, landlords and others) becoming involved in an *active social process* of exclusionary or hostile conduct towards those who they discover have previous convictions. Other forms of discrimination such as racism, homophobia or disablism are not, of course, the inevitable consequence of stigmatised characteristics which are either inherent or acquired, but the result of a negative bias or prejudice on the part of those who have decided to treat the stigmatised person less favourably.

Due to the moral condemnation or censure attached to criminally offending (see von Hirsch 1993; Duff 2001) it might, of course, be argued that the stigma attached to a criminal record is in some way 'deserved'. However, there are good reasons for arguing against such a position. This is because a distinction can be made between the censure of illegal behaviour which accompanies a punitive sanction and what happens to a person because of a decision to disclose the *record of that sanction*, often years later after the punishment has been served and most other people have forgotten about the original conduct (see Larrauri 2014a on the relationship between disclosure of criminal records and the right to privacy). A further problem arises because, for the most part, the pains of criminalisation outlined previously are completely unregulated by constraints of proportionality when compared to formal, legal sanctions.

The idea that post-sentence discrimination can be akin to social death is no exaggeration when one considers that there appear to be no strict limits to the hardships which people with convictions might face post-sentence, other than those offered by the limited protections of the Rehabilitation of Offenders Act of 1974. This legislation allows certain convictions to become 'spent' (and thus non-disclosable) for most purposes after a set period of time. However, it does not apply to anyone who has served a prison sentence of four years or more (see Ministry of Justice 2014; Henley 2016). Therefore, the pains of criminalisation outlined previously have the potential to severely damage life chances because, whilst the practice of civil death represented in bygone laws of attainder has lapsed, the social death of people with convictions arises from exclusionary rules, policies and conducts which are both widespread and, for the most part, unregulated.

Similarities can be drawn here with the status of '*homo sacer*' ('the accursed man') imposed upon lawbreakers in ancient Rome (see Agamben 1998). This status rendered individuals unprotected by law, meaning that they could be killed with impunity. They were also excluded from sacrificial rituals meaning that their death held no significance in religious ceremony. Thus, just as the ancient *homo sacer* was left in a state of what Agamben described as 'bare life' – permanently exposed to the possibility of death and unprotected by the law – the modern-day person with convictions remains continually vulnerable to the possibility of *social* death should his or her conviction be revealed.

The impact of this precarious status on the social identities of people with convictions is potentially profound. Goffman (1961) described a 'mortification of the self' affecting individuals confined to asylums, prisons and other 'total institutions'. This mortification, Goffman explained, involved a 'series of abasements, degradations, humiliations, and profanations of self' (p. 24). He suggested that the pre-existing identity which an 'inmate' carried with him into an institution was reliant upon 'stable social arrangements in his home world' (*ibid.*) but that these were disrupted by the experience of confinement. One potential effect of this was a reduction of the individual (and their self-concept) to the status of 'non-person' – a process exacerbated by the moral stigmatisation which can 'taint' former mental health patients and ex-prisoners (see Goffman 1963).

Goffman (1963: 13) defined stigma as 'an attribute that is deeply discrediting' and described stigmatisation as involving a conflict between actual social identity (incorporating the attributes which an individual *actually* possesses) and virtual social identity (composed of characteristics which an individual is *assumed* to possess by others). When a negative social reaction occurs to these assumed characteristics, this has the potential to 'spoil' normal identity. In the context of this chapter, the negative reaction will most likely arise as a result of the disclosure or discovery of an individual's criminal record. In some instances, of course, people with convictions are able to conceal this stigma, but in others it may be a legal requirement for them to disclose their records, for example in certain job applications. Stigmatisation can negatively impact those trying to desist from criminal offending since a core part of the desistance process involves leaving behind the 'criminal self' and instead cultivating a prosocial identity (see Maruna 2001; Aresti *et al*. 2010). This identity shift is likely to be frustrated when those at an early stage in the desistance process experience negative social reactions from others with knowledge of their criminal records. However, there are also implications for the longer-term maintenance of a defensible 'sense of self' amongst *all* people with convictions, even many years after their last offences were committed. This is because certain forms of 'standard' and 'enhanced' criminal record checks involve the disclosure of almost all previous convictions and cautions, and the use of such checks has expanded significantly in recent years (see Larrauri 2014b). There are therefore good reasons for being concerned about whether an *intensification* of certain pains of criminalisation might be occurring – particularly the 'denial of employment', since most criminal background checks are conducted on job applicants.

In summary then, criminalisation can give rise to a profound sense of loss amongst people with convictions. This loss is twofold, comprising both a potential loss of *preconviction identity* through the 'mortification of the self' which Goffman (1961) identified, and also a loss of *future identity* due to the broader stigmatisation of people with convictions in their post-sentence lives. Thus, a sense of bereavement and mourning for both the 'past self' which has been lost and the potential 'future self' which cannot be are likely to be experienced by many of those who have passed through the criminal justice system. Therefore, when considering issues of loss and bereavement in criminal justice, we must carefully evaluate our responses to not only those who literally die in the care of the state but also those who experience the 'social death' after already having been punished and the very real harms which can arise from the pains of criminalisation.

References

Abbot, M. (1996). *Life Cycles in England, 1560–1720: Cradle to Grave*. London: Routledge.

Agamben, G. (1998). *Homo Sacer: Sovereign Power and Bare Life*. Stanford, CA: Stanford University Press.

Aresti, A., Eatough, V. and Brooks-Gordon, B. (2010). Doing time after time: An Interpretative Phenomenological Analysis of reformed ex-prisoners' experiences of self-change, identity and career opportunities. *Psychology, Crime and Law*, 16 (3): 169–190.

Bauman, Z. (1992). *Mortality, Immortality, and Other Life Strategies*. Stanford, CA: Stanford University Press.

Beccaria, C. (1764/1819). *Essay on Crimes and Punishment* (2nd American edition). Philadelphia, PA: Phillip H. Nicklin Publishers.

Behan, C. (2014). Embracing and resisting prisoner enfranchisement: A comparative analysis of the Republic of Ireland and the United Kingdom. *Irish Probation Journal*, 11: 156–176.

Bellamy, J. (2004). *The Law of Treason in England in the Later Middle Ages*. Cambridge: Cambridge University Press.

Chin, G.J. (2012). The new civil death: Rethinking punishment in the era of mass conviction. *University of Pennsylvania Law Review*, 160: 1789–1833.

Damaska, M.R. (1968). Adverse legal consequences of conviction and their removal: A comparative study. *The Journal of Criminal Law, Criminology and Police Science*, 59 (3): 347–360.

Demleitner, N.V. (1999). Preventing internal exile: The need for restrictions on collateral sentencing consequences. *Stanford Law & Policy Review*, 11 (1): 153–171.

Drake, D.H. and Henley, A.J. (2014). 'Victims' versus 'offenders' in British political discourse: The construction of a false dichotomy. *The Howard Journal of Criminal Justice*, 53 (2): 141–157.

Duff, R.A. (2001). *Punishment, Communication and Community*. Oxford: Oxford University Press.

Earle, R. (2016). *Convict Criminology: Inside and Out*. Bristol: Policy Press.

Edgely, M. (2010). Criminals and (second-class) citizenship: Twenty-first century attainder? *Griffith Law Review*, 19 (3): 403–437.

Goffman, E. (1961). *Asylums: Essays on the Social Situation of Mental Patients and Other Inmates*. London: Penguin.

Goffman, E. (1963). *Stigma: Notes on the Management of Spoiled Identity*. London: Penguin.

Harrison, R. (1983). *Bentham*. London: Routledge and Kegan Paul.

Henley, A.J. (2014). Abolishing the stigma of punishments served. *Criminal Justice Matters*, 97 (1): 22–23.

Henley, A.J. (2016). *Criminal records and the regulation of redemption: A critical history of legal rehabilitation in England and Wales*. Unpublished PhD Thesis. Keele: Keele University.

Henley, A.J. (2017). Criminal records and conditional citizenship: Towards a critical sociology of post-sentence discrimination, in S. Fletcher and H. White (eds.). *Emerging Voices: Critical Social Research by European Group Postgraduate and Early Career Researchers*. Bristol: European Group Press.

Králová, J. (2015). What is social death? *Contemporary Social Sciences*, 10 (3): 235–248.

Lacey, N. (1988). State punishment: Political principles and community values. London: Routledge.

Larrauri, E. (2014a). Criminal record disclosure and the right to privacy. *Criminal Law Review*, 10: 723–737.

Larrauri, E. (2014b). Legal protections against criminal background checks in Europe. *Punishment and Society*, 16 (1): 50–73.

Lerner, C.S. (2002). Impeachment, attainder and a true constitutional crisis: Lessons from the Strafford trial. *University of Chicago Law Review*, 69 (4): 2057–2101.

MacDonagh, O. (1974). The last bill of pains and penalties: The case of Daniel O'Sullivan, 1869. *Irish Historical Studies*, 19: 136–155.

Maruna, S. (2001). *Making Good: How Ex-Convicts Reform and Rebuild Their Lives*. Washington: American Psychological Association.

Ministry of Justice. (2014). *New guidance on the rehabilitation of Offenders Act of 1974*. Available on www.gov.uk/government/publications/new-guidance-on-the-rehabilitation-of-offenders-act-1974 (Accessed 17th May 2017).

Romilly, S. (1820). *The Speeches of Sir Samuel Romilly in the House of Commons: In Two Volumes* (Volume 1). London: James Ridgway and Sons.

Saunders, H.D. (1970). Civil death: A new look at an ancient doctrine. *William and Mary Law Review*, 11 (4): 988–1003.

Schofield, J. (2008). *The Rise & Fall of Thomas Cromwell: Henry VIII's Most Faithful Servant*. Stroud: The History Press Ltd.

Sykes, G.M. (1958). *The Society of Captives: A Study of Maximum Security Prison*. Princeton, NJ: Princeton University Press.

Uggen, C. and Stewart, R. (2015). Piling On: Collateral consequences and community supervision. *Minnesota Law Review*, 99 (5): 1871–7912.

Unlock. (2014). *Number of People with Convictions: Home Office Freedom of Information Release CR33517*. Maidstone: Unlock.

Von Hirsch, A. (1993). *Censure and Sanctions*. Oxford: Clarendon Press.

Section 2

Professional development of bereavement, loss and end-of-life practice

Section 2

Professional development
of bereavement, loss and
end-of-life practice

7 Bereavement and loss at the sentencing stage

Martin Wasik

Introduction

This chapter examines issues of bereavement and loss as they are likely to arise in the course of a criminal trial, with particular focus on the sentencing of a defendant after conviction. The chapter falls naturally into two parts. In the first part I consider criminal cases pursuant to a fatality (e.g. murder, manslaughter, causing death by dangerous driving, or a workplace death infringing on health and safety laws) and examine the ways in which bereavement and loss occasioned to the victim's family is addressed and managed during the court process. Cases of such seriousness will always be heard in the Crown Court.

In the second part of the chapter I turn to consider the different question of the relevance of a defendant's experience of bereavement or loss as a factor in the sentencing by a court of that defendant for a criminal offence. This issue might arise in the Crown Court or in a magistrates' court. If the defendant is aged under 18, the magistrates' court is constituted as a youth court.

The chapter is necessarily of limited scope and is confined to coverage of criminal cases. Bereavement as it arises in the course of civil disputes, such as fatal accident litigation, is referred to here only briefly. Nor is the jurisdiction and specialised role of the Coroners Court dealt with.

Part 1

A highly influential report by Casey, which was published in 2011, contains the largest survey yet undertaken of families who have been bereaved by homicide (Casey, 2011). The survey is instructive. All respondents in the survey said that their physical or mental health had been affected by what had happened, 80 per cent had suffered trauma-related symptoms, and 75 per cent suffered depression. Seventy-five per cent of respondents said that the bereavement through homicide had affected their other close relationships, 60 per cent found it difficult to manage their finances after the death, 25 per cent stopped working permanently, 25 per cent moved house, and 25 per cent gained sudden responsibility for a child or children as a result of the killing. The average cost of the homicide to each family was £37,000, ranging from probate, to funerals, to travel to court, to cleaning up the crime scene. The majority received no help with these costs and some were forced into debt. The scale of the impact is striking, and it shows that the physical and emotional effects of this particular form of bereavement, as well as the associated practical problems, can persist for many years after the death itself (Casey, 2011: 5–6).

In the case of an alleged homicide, or other unlawful death such as a fatal road traffic offence or accident at work, the circumstances which led to the death will be the central concern of the criminal trial. If criminal liability is denied, and the defendant enters a not guilty plea at the start of the trial, much of the evidence will relate to the death, the events which led up to it, and whether the defendant can be shown to have been responsible for what occurred. Every criminal case in England and Wales is brought by the Crown Prosecution Service (CPS). The task of the CPS is to prosecute on behalf of the state, and the defence advocate represents the interests of the defendant. Neither an alleged victim of the crime nor the bereaved relatives of a deceased victim is a 'party' to the case, so no lawyer is present in court to represent them. It is of course possible that a bereaved relative may be required as a witness, if he or she observed some part of the incident which caused the death, or if he or she has other important information to give. That possibility aside, a bereaved relative has no right to address the court during the course of the trial itself, and his or her role is simply that of onlooker.

Following Casey's report, further research was commissioned, and a series of changes were made (see Ministry of Justice, 2012a, 2012b).

Support during the investigation and trial

Casey (2011) found that the trauma of bereavement is often compounded by involvement in the criminal justice system, preventing the natural grieving process, and it can sometimes retraumatise relatives. Although bereaved families do not want to stand in the way of bringing a perpetrator to justice, and most have a strong desire for this to occur, families feel that they lose control over their loved ones as the Crown appropriates the body and determines when it can be returned for burial. The home may become a crime scene, and in the next weeks, months, and years, their loved one's death and who was responsible for it is likely to become the focus of their lives. Yet the bereaved family cannot determine or control any of this. The police investigation, and the trial, verdict, and sentence, all happen around them. The family is entitled to be informed and to receive explanation, but they have little voice, little influence, and little power (Casey, 2011: 6–7). A 'homicide service' is offered by Victim Support to all newly bereaved families in cases of homicide (but excluding death on the roads). This is a peer-support service, with emotional support offered by volunteers who have had a similar personal experience. There is a number of other small self-help/peer-support groups providing friendship, support, and help to families bereaved by homicide, some of which have charitable status.

One particular issue which can cause distress to bereaved relatives is the experience of arriving to attend the trial and being told by the prosecution barrister that the Crown intends to accept a guilty plea to a lesser offence (manslaughter rather than murder, or causing death by careless rather than reckless driving). In considering whether to accept a guilty plea, the prosecution is required to consider the views of the family, but families report that they feel as if they are being informed, not consulted. This change in the case may come as a huge shock, and families will not hear the evidence about what happened and why. The legal principle of encouraging defendants to plead guilty, and to do so as soon as possible, is designed in part to reduce distress for victims or bereaved relatives (Sentencing Council, 2017a). Many would prefer to have the admission of guilt, and thereby avoid having to attend court or give evidence. Some relatives, however, feel cheated by the process, and would have wished to hear everything there is to know, because they have little other access to information. The admission of guilt (which attracts a significant sentence discount when entered early) is resented by some, and leaves the family with unanswered questions (Casey, 2011: 39).

As Casey acknowledges, there are many aspects of the legal process that simply cannot be changed, such as the fact that the prosecution barrister works for the Crown and not for families, that the defence team may require a second post-mortem, or that the defendant delays entering a plea of guilty until the very last minute. If the trial does go ahead, the case will be held in public, with local or perhaps national press in attendance, and distressing details about how the deceased lost his or her life may be openly discussed in court, displayed in photographs or on-screen. Difficult questions may be put to witnesses, tending to show the deceased in a bad light – an example would be where the deceased is said by the defence to have provoked the defendant into killing him or her. And, of course, at the end of the trial the jury may decide that the prosecution has not proved its case and acquit the defendant.

Following Casey's report, amendments were made to the entitlements which bereaved relatives have under the Code of Practice for Victims of Crime (Ministry of Justice, 2013).The key points in the code have also been incorporated into a judicial practice direction addressed to all judges required to preside over a case of this kind. The main point is that the judge, the prosecution, and the defence should all have regard to the needs of the family of the victim, and ensure that the trial process does not, so far as possible, expose them to intimidation, humiliation, or distress. To that end the judge should, before the trial gets under way, consider practical arrangements such as seating for family members in the courtroom. If appropriate, that might be in an alternative area, away from the public gallery where family and friends of the defendant may be gathered. Also, warning should be given to families during the trial if the evidence on a certain day is expected to be particularly distressing (Practice Direction, 2015b).

Sentencing and the bereaved relative

If the defendant decides to plead guilty rather than to have a trial, or if the defendant is convicted at the end of a trial, the court will move from the trial to the sentencing stage of the proceedings. The sentencing stage is procedurally different from trial, with less emphasis on an adversarial contest between prosecution and defence. When it comes to sentencing the court will be concerned with gathering as much information as possible about the circumstances of the offence and the offender before deciding what sentence to pass. More is said about this process in the second part of this chapter, but it is appropriate in this part to explain the opportunity which a bereaved relative has to put information relevant to sentence before the court.

At an early stage in the investigation of a criminal offence, it is one of the responsibilities of the police to ensure that the victim (or a victim's bereaved relative) is made aware that he or she can, if he or she wishes, complete a standard form known as the 'victim personal statement', occasionally still referred to under its former name, the 'victim impact statement' (Practice Direction, 2015a). A properly formulated statement can provide real assistance to the court. It provides a practical way of ensuring that the personal impact of the offence on the victim or surviving family members is not overlooked. Crucially, however, the statement does not provide an opportunity for the victim or the bereaved relatives to suggest what form or length of sentence should be imposed. Any suggestion of that kind which by mistake has been included in the personal statement should be removed. In Perks (2001), a robbery rather than a homicide case, the husband of the victim wrote to the court and asked the judge to '[j]ail him! And make an example of him to others.' The Court of Appeal said that this document should not have been included in the case papers, and reduced the sentence passed by the judge partly because of concern that the judge may have been influenced by it. By contrast, Nunn (1996) was a case of causing death by dangerous driving (a category of case acknowledged as being one of the most difficult to sentence), where the defendant had caused a collision in which the victim, his best friend who was with him in the car, was killed. The defendant was sentenced to four years imprisonment and on appeal against sentence the mother and one of the sisters of the deceased wrote to the appeal court asking for a more lenient sentence because the sentence passed on the offender

> was having an adverse effect on their ability to come to terms with the loss and grief which they had suffered following the death of the deceased.
>
> (at para 10)

The court in Nunn said that regardless of whether the bereaved party was seeking a more severe or a more lenient outcome, the bereaved party's view could not provide a sound basis for sentence. Sentencing was a matter for the court, taking all relevant matters into account, including applicable sentencing guidelines. Otherwise very similar cases would receive disparate outcomes because of the different attitude of the victims. Whilst that statement of principle is clear, in their research, Jacobson and Hough (2007) found a divergence of views amongst trial judges on this issue (at p. 30). The position in practice seems to be that judges should never accede to a plea for vengeance and should only give weight to pleas for mercy if there is evidence that a severe sentence will increase the suffering of a victim or bereaved relative. That was apparently the case in Nunn, and the sentence was reduced from four years to three years for that reason, but the difficulty of this issue is reflected in the fact that the father and brother of the deceased did not share the views of the mother and sister.

The victim personal statement is always made available to the judge along with all other material relevant to the case. In some cases, material within the statement may be referred to, or read out, by prosecution counsel in order to assist the judge with sentencing. Advocates and the court must be sensitive to the position of the victim and the need to protect the privacy of the victim. In the past, some bereaved relatives have expressed a wish to read out their victim personal statements in court during the sentencing process, and this became possible from 2013 when amendments were made to the Code of Practice (and see Criminal Practice Direction, 2015b). Judges are now told that they should normally accede to this kind of request, provided that it does not occasion delay or otherwise interfere with justice. Whatever the advantages of this process, the reading out of these statements heightens the emotions in court.

Casey (2011) found that the passing of sentence was one of the most important moments for the bereaved family in homicide cases, but that it was often difficult to absorb the judge's sentencing remarks, which can be complex and detailed, and to understand how the judge has come to the decision. Yet in the weeks, months, and years following, it may come to preoccupy families, particularly if there are issues that they do not understand or lack clarity on. So, adopting another of Casey's recommendations, the judge should now always provide a written copy of the sentencing remarks to the bereaved family after the sentence has been passed, unless there is some strong reason for not doing so. The copy should be provided as soon as is reasonably practicable after the sentencing hearing is over.

Post-sentencing

Once trial and sentencing is over, the National Offender Management Service (NOMS) operates a Victim Contact Scheme that is designed to provide information for those victims or bereaved families who 'opt in' about when offenders move prison or when they are being considered for release (NOMS, 2015: 9). A victim liaison officer (VLO) is appointed to act as the channel of communication and to assist the victim or bereaved relative in making representation, should he or she wish, concerning the release date of the defendant and licence conditions upon release, such as an exclusion zone. An updated victim personal statement may be submitted to the Parole Board, describing the ongoing effect of the crime, and the impact which the perpetrator's release would have. However, as Casey pointed out (at p. 48), the Parole Board is examining the risk posed by the offender today, rather than the harm the offender caused in the past, and so the status and purpose of the victim statement is not always clear.

Part 2

As explained previously, if the defendant is convicted at the end of the trial or a guilty plea has been entered at an earlier stage, the court will move to consider the appropriate sentence. Sentencing procedure can only be dealt with in outline here, but it is important to note that the court now moves from an adversarial contest between the prosecution and defence to a more 'problem-solving' mode, in which the judge considers a range of submissions. Almost all criminal offences now have applicable sentencing guidelines produced by the Sentencing Council, which the court must follow unless for some unusual reason it would be 'unjust' to do so. The prosecution outlines the facts of the offence (of particular relevance where there has been a contested trial) and both prosecution and defence make submissions as to where in the relevant guideline the particular offence falls in terms of its seriousness. Then the defence puts forward a plea in mitigation, designed to persuade the court that a lower-than-normal sentence ought to be imposed because of factors personal to the offender. In contrast to aggravating and mitigating factors which affect the offence's seriousness, which must always be taken into account in the sentence, the court has discretion whether to take personal mitigation into account, and what weight to give to it.

Personal mitigation

The range of material which can be adduced as personal mitigation is very wide, with judges and magistrates able to take account of any matter which appears to be relevant (CJA, 2003: s.166(1)). It is impossible to provide a comprehensive list, but the standard sentencing texts indicate those matters which are most likely to come up (Ashworth, 2015: 178–201; Wasik, 2014: 66–71; see also Walker, 1999). These include previous good character, youth, old age, remorse, other meritorious conduct, a determination to tackle addiction or other issues which underlie the offending, and so on, but none of these texts mention the impact of bereavement as a personal mitigating factor. This suggests that either it does not come up very often or that (at least taken on its own) it does not have much mitigating power. The leading empirical study on personal mitigation is Jacobson and Hough (2007). They examined 132 cases and found that in over forty of those cases the defendant avoided an immediate custodial sentence because of personal mitigation. Mitigating factors could be grouped into (1) those relevant to the defendant's past, such as good character or deprived background; (2) his or her circumstances at the time of the offence, such as financial issues, psychiatric problems, and immaturity; (3) the defendant's response to the offence, such as remorse or addressing the problems which led to the offence; and (4) the defendant's present and future situation, such as family responsibilities and his or her capacity to address underlying problems. Whilst the report considers a wide range of mitigating factors, there is no specific mention of bereavement or loss, although 'traumatic life events' is identified as a possible mitigating factor relating to the defendant's past. In a separate part of the same study, forty Crown Court judges were asked about the types of personal mitigation which they thought were important but, again, there was no mention of bereavement.

The presentence report

Defence mitigation will often rely upon the presentence report (PSR), prepared for the court by a probation officer (or, in the case of an offender under 18, by a social worker). When compiling a PSR the officer must follow national standards setting out what the report should contain and how it should be structured (Youth Justice Board, 2013: 22; NOMS, 2015: 17). The officer must always interview the defendant (at least once) and may interview other people, such as family members. As well as being clear about the seriousness of the offence and the risk of reoffending, the officer must explore the defendant's background, significant life events, circumstances which led up the commission of the offence, and the offender's attitude towards the offence (remorse, victim empathy, and so on). Report writers are, for the most part, trained in social work and it is likely that matters such as the death of a parent, sibling, or child would be mentioned in the report assuming, of course, that the offender was frank about that in the interview. The issue is reflected in protocols on report writing and in relevant training packages. The Kent Youth Offending Service (2011), for example, refers to the need to address issues of 'mental and emotional health, including separation, loss, bereavement and rejection' (at p. 31). As Denney explains, a report writer has a critical role in placing the offence in context for the court. This might mean reference to 'depression, sickness, bereavement' or characterising the offence as a temporary aberration (2016: 126).

A presentence report is not read out in court. However, the defence lawyer often refers the court to a particular part or parts of the report. If the section contains sensitive personal information, the lawyer may refer to it obliquely rather than openly in his or her argument. Examples can be found of such mitigation being advanced at trial and reported in the local press. In one recent example the *Hertfordshire Advertiser* (2016) reported the case of a 19-year-old defendant employed as a cleaner who was given a suspended sentence for stealing £3,000 of property from her clients. The personal mitigation was previous good character, together with the 'turmoil and depression' which she suffered following her father's death when she was aged 17. It is not clear whether the defendant's personal loss was a significant factor in suspending the sentence, but the judge did comment on the need for the defendant to seek 'bereavement support'. In another, more serious case a 25-year-old defendant admitted taking and driving away with a taxi, and then setting fire to it. He was sentenced to five years' imprisonment. Commenting on the information that the defendant had recently suffered a bereavement (his grandmother) which had had a 'massive effect' on him, the judge said that this could not have any bearing on the sentence – 'it's an explanation, but not mitigation' (Northampton Chronicle, 2015).

In cases where the defendant appeals against his or her conviction or sentence, or where the prosecution appeals against the sentence, the matter is considered by the Court of Appeal. In considering the appeal the appellate judges will review the evidence and reconsider salient features of the mitigation. An online search of recent appellate sentencing decisions on Westlaw throws up further examples of the relevance of bereavement as personal mitigation. In *Gould* (2011) the offences were burglary and breach of a community order, and the defendant was appealing his sentence of two years' imprisonment. The Court of Appeal noted that the appellant had expressed remorse, and that his drug use was linked to a depressive illness and to the effect of a recent bereavement. The court said that

> all those matters must be taken into account but, in our judgment, they carry little weight – the inescapable reality is that the appellant was yet again resorting to deliberate dishonesty.

The sentence was upheld in this case, as was the sentence of three and a half years' imprisonment in *Downie* (2014) for seven offences of theft. The court in that case said that the judge had given what credit he reasonably could for the mitigation – that the defendant had suffered three bereavements of close members of his family, had now become drug-free, and was remorseful. A total sentence of twelve years was upheld in *Chambers* (2016), for two separate conspiracies to smuggle drugs – one offence involving cocaine, and the other cannabis. The court said that the judge had fully taken into account the appellant's lack of previous convictions, a number of personal bereavements over the years, and a perilous financial position which had prompted the offending. All that, however, 'was not an excuse for his behaviour'. In *Ward* (2012) the PSR set out the defendant's explanation for commission of theft and breach of a suspended sentence – that he was depressed following the death of his partner and had no money to pay for food – but the writer added that the appellant's relapse into heroin use was the most direct cause of the offending. The court in this case reduced a sentence of eighteen months to fourteen months. In *Freer* (2014) the court upheld a sentence of eighteen months suspended for two years where the defendant admitted cultivation of cannabis plants. The personal mitigation was his guilty plea, the fact that he had only one previous conviction for a minor offence, and that

> he had suffered a double bereavement in the death of his mother and his grandmother within a relatively short space of time and had experienced particular difficulties in coming to terms with the death of his mother. When a friend was bereaved, he had taken the time to use his own experiences to help them through the grieving process.

A final example is *Webster* (2015), where the offender was a man with an 'appalling record' for burglary. He pleaded guilty to two house burglaries, and asked for fifteen more to be 'taken into consideration'. The Court of Appeal noted that the appellant had suffered a bereavement 'in particularly distressing circumstances', which had 'sent him off the rails'. The court observed that '[n]o judge could fail to understand and sympathise with his loss, but when he burgled people's houses he made innocent victims suffer.'

   A more detailed discussion of the circumstances of bereavement can be found in *McCann* (2011), where the defendant had been convicted of money laundering and been sentenced to two and a half years' imprisonment. In this case it would seem that the defence was so concerned about the appellant's mental state that they ordered the preparation of a psychiatric report. The court observed

> [t]he sadness in McCann's life was the fact that his son Paul committed suicide in September 2005. This would be a tragedy for any parent and, as Dr Wilson's psychiatric report makes clear, the effect on the appellant was very severe – an abnormal bereavement reaction leading to a moderate depressive episode . . . The tragic history of his son's suicide and its consequences for him were mitigation, but we cannot accept that they were such powerful

mitigation as to make the sentence excessive. The offences persisted over a number of years and the appellant clearly knew very well what he was doing.

Again, the sentence was upheld. Another case in which a psychiatric report, as well as a presentence report, was considered is *Hilton* (2015), where the defendant admitted starting a fire which had put people at risk of injury or death. The reports explained that the defendant was not mentally ill, but that following the 'stressful events' of the recent death of his father and his own children being taken into care, he had 'relapsed into drug abuse'. This time the court agreed with the prosecution that the original sentence of two years' imprisonment had been too low, and increased it to three years.

This small group of cases suggests a number of things. First, they show that issues of bereavement are sometimes identified in the reports placed before a sentencing court. It is worth repeating the point that the defendant must be willing to 'open up' and discuss this issue with the relevant report writer. In all the cases the Court of Appeal had no difficulty in recognising bereavement as personal mitigation, although its relevance and impact varied considerably from case to case. Second, it is obvious that almost all adult defendants will have experienced bereavement at some point in their lives, and so something more than what might loosely be described as the 'normal experience' of bereavement is needed to make a difference to sentencing outcome. Judges will have experienced bereavement too (indeed in Darbyshire's 2011 study of the modern judiciary she interviewed seventy-seven Crown Court judges and found that seven of them had experienced the death of one of their own children). In the aforementioned group of cases it seems that the court was more likely to be swayed by evidence of multiple bereavements, or bereavement in particularly tragic circumstances (such as the son's suicide in *McCann*), or bereavement closely linked in time with some other life-changing event (such as the removal of the children in *Hilton*), or clear evidence of an 'abnormal' psychological reaction to bereavement. Third, it is a recognised general principle in personal mitigation that it has less relevance in more serious cases. It should be borne in mind that the aforementioned cases are on appeal from the Crown Court, and are thus at the serious end of the spectrum. There may be greater scope for personal mitigation in the magistrates' court, where the offences are less serious, although empirical research would be required to see if that were true. Finally, in several of the cases, whilst the court accepted that the bereavement was a relevant part of the background to the offending, where the defendant had relapsed into drug abuse or property offending as a result, the bereavement was characterised as 'explanation, but not excuse'.

All the reported cases considered here involved adult defendants. It may well be that personal mitigation, including bereavement and loss, carries more weight if the defendant is aged under 18, where the court is under a statutory duty to consider the 'welfare' of the young offender (Children and Young Persons Act, 1933: s.44) and to focus on the defendant as an individual rather than on passing a sentence which is deserved for the offence committed (Sentencing Council, 2017b: para 1.2). For a young person, bereavement may have been more unexpected and shocking, especially if it was of a parent or sibling, or may have been particularly traumatic (such as a defendant involved in a 'joy-riding' case where a sibling or friend has been killed). Again, empirical research would have to be undertaken in the youth court to see if bereavement issues figured differently in that venue. In her research, Sharpe found that bereavement and loss was a 'recurrent theme' in the narratives of girls and young women entering the youth justice system (Sharpe, 2012: 58–61). In one sample of the population of young offenders inducted into custody, 13 per cent had experienced bereavement of a parent or a sibling (Jacobson et al. 2008). That figure may seem high, but it should be placed in the context that, of the same population, 20 per cent had self-harmed, 27 per cent had been in care, 39 per cent were on the child protection register, 54 per cent were school truants, and 76 per cent had absent fathers. This survey presents a picture of young people suffering from multiple disadvantages, of which the experience of bereavement or loss is likely to be only one aspect. The Howard League for Penal Reform (2016) has urged that some of these factors – including 'physical illness, experience of bereavement, experience of discrimination and experience of self-harm' – should be more clearly spelled out as mitigating factors in the guidelines. This has been accepted by the Sentencing Council who, in the 2017 revision of their guideline on sentencing children and young persons (Sentencing Council, 2017b: para 4.7), says that courts must be alert to issues such as the effect on young people of 'experiences of trauma or loss', along with other potential issues such as mental health problems, learning difficulties, and vulnerability to self-harm. This may be seen as a significant step in according greater recognition to the experience of bereavement as a relevant factor in sentencing.

References

Ashworth, A. (2015). *Sentencing and Criminal Justice* (6th ed.). Cambridge: Cambridge University Press.

Casey, L. (2011). *Review into the Needs of Families Bereaved by Homicide*. London: Ministry of Justice.

Darbyshire, P. (2011). *Sitting in Judgment: The Working Lives of Judges*. Oxford: Hart Publishing.

Denney, D. (2016). Probation: Rights and new agendas. In M. Vanstone and P. Priestley (eds.), *Probation and Politics: Academic Reflections from Former Practitioners*. London: Palgrave Macmillan. (pp. 119–140).

Hertfordshire Advertiser (2016). Available at www.hertsad.co.uk/news/court-watch/harpenden_cleaner_who_stole_from_her_clients_sentenced_1_4609864 (Accessed November 2017).

Howard League (2016). The Howard League for Penal Reform's response to the consultation on the sentencing guidelines specifically relating to children. 3rd August. London: The Howard League for Penal Reform.

Jacobson, J., Bhardwa, B., Gyateng, T., Hunter, G. and Hough, M. (2008). *Punishing disadvantage. A profile of children in custody*. London: Prison Reform Trust.

Jacobson, J., and Hough, M. (2007). *Mitigation: The Role of Personal Factors in Sentencing*. London: Prison Reform Trust.

Kent Youth Offending Service (2011). *Report Writing Policy: Pre-Sentence Reports, Practice Guidance*. Available at https://cpdyouthcommunity.kentcpdonline.org.uk (Accessed November 2017).

Ministry of Justice (2012a). *Getting it Right for Victims and Witnesses Consultation Document*. CP3/2012. London: Ministry of Science.

Ministry of Justice (2012b). *Getting It Right for Victims and Witnesses: The Government Response*. Stationery Office Cm 8397. London: Ministry of Science.

Ministry of Justice (2013). *Code of Practice for Victims of Crime*. London: Ministry of Science.

National Offender Management Service (NOMS) (2015). *National Standards for the Management of Offenders*.

Northampton Chronicle (2015). Available at www.northamptonchron.co.uk/news/robber-upset-over-death-of-grandmother-stole-and-torhced-taxi-in-northampton-1-7056732 (Accessed November 2017).

Practice Direction (2015a). *CPD VII Sentencing F: Victim Personal Statements*.

Practice Direction (2015b). *CPD VII Sentencing G: Families Bereaved by Homicide and Other Criminal Conduct*.

Sentencing Council (2017a). *Definitive Guideline: Reduction in Sentence for a Guilty Plea*. Available at www.sentencingcouncil.org.uk/publications

Sentencing Council (2017b). *Definitive Guideline: Sentencing Children and Young People*. Available at www.sentencingcouncil.org.uk/publications

Sharpe, G. (2012). *Offending Girls: Young Women and Youth Justice*. London: Routledge.

Walker, N. (1999). *Aggravation, Mitigation and Mercy*. London: Blackstone Press.

Wasik, M. (2014). *A Practical Approach to Sentencing* (5th ed.). Oxford: Oxford University Press.

Youth Justice Board (2013). *National Standards for Youth Justice Services*. London: Youth Justice Board for England and Wales.

Cases

Chambers [2016] EWCA Crim 1328.
Downie [2014] EWCA Crim 2630.
Freer [2014] EWCA Crim 456.
Gould [2011] EWCA Crim 2348.
Hilton [2015] EWCA Crim 1442.
McCann [2011] EWCA Crim 2038.
Nunn [1996] 2 Cr App R (S) 136.
Perks [2001] 1 Cr App R (S) 19.
Ward [2012] EWCA Crim 2534.
Webster [2015] EWCA Crim 2115.

Statutes

Children and Young Persons Act 1933.
Criminal Justice Act 2003.

8 Bereavement work in the criminal justice system

Mary Corcoran

Introduction

This chapter considers the false demarcation that operates in practice between the administration of criminal justice and the inadequacies in the system when faced with managing the personal elements of bereavement. From a criminological vantage point, the justice system appears to be indecisive in handling emotions arising from loss through death, despite the fact that acknowledging such emotions is essential to the very structures of justice. This leads to the curious neglect of bereaved people on the part of the criminal justice system. I will examine how bereavement work is sidelined from the overall process of justice, despite its essential role. The concept of secondary victimisation is central to understanding the marginalisation of the experiences of the bereaved (Walklate, 2007). Secondary victimisation occurs when the perspectives, needs or involvement of victims or bereaved people are disregarded, which compounds their initial (or 'primary') victimisation caused by the original crime. Secondary victimisation occurs because the institutional culture of the criminal justice system is primed to investigate, prosecute and sentence offenders. Victims, the bereaved and their losses are unintentionally marginalised as 'collateral' in the justice cycle (Wolhuter et al., 2009). The chapter seeks to redress the analytical gap by examining the many ways in which the voluntary sector performs vital bereavement work both at different junctures in criminal justice procedures and by crossing 'boundaries' in offering support to all parties affected by death or homicide.

Criminology and grief

Criminology as a field of study and practice is essentially concerned with harmful or lawbreaking behaviour, its consequences for individuals and society and the costs borne by harmers and the harmed. It is all the more surprising, then, that a sphere which is suffused by feelings of grief, loss, disgust, shame, outrage or anger, for example, is so inconsistent about the place of emotions in the development of our structures and concepts of justice. It is more accurate to suggest that loss, grief and bereavement hover in the background of criminological thought or they are relegated to the discrete subdisciplines of victimology (Christie, 1977) or restorative justice (Braithwaite, 1999). In this sense, emotions are constant but often unspoken influences in myriad themes relating to crime, justice, punishment and restoration.

This is not to say that criminologists ignore emotions, but that it is to observe that they are rarely a direct and explicit object of inquiry, with some notable exceptions (Karstedt, 2002; Karstedt & Farrall, 2007; Braithwaite, 1999). According to these scholars, law and criminal justice systems are tasked to 'deal with the most intense emotions and emotional conflicts, with individual as well as collective emotion' (Karstedt, 2002: 300). Susanne Karstedt (2002: 299) observed that the movement to bring 'emotions back involves profound problems that go beyond the mere instrumental use of emotions in criminal justice'.

Karstedt goes on to identify three 'core problems' which are at the root of criminological contentions about the influence of emotions on systems of crime and justice. First, there are questions about how the system deals with demands that, because emotional reactions are part of human experience, they 'should occupy a prominent place in criminal justice' (ibid: 305). Second, there are questions about how far strong emotions – such as empathy, intuition, disgust or shame – should be foundations for the moral principles of justice (ibid: 306). Third, it must be seriously asked how far punishment should be weighted (if at all) against the perceived 'authenticity' of remorse or shame on the part of the perpetrators, or in relation to the victim's emotional injuries and losses. In this vein, Karstedt asked, how should the criminal justice system deal with emotions that are invisible? At root, there is a tension between the sociological appreciation of emotions as integral to structures of justice in its social and human forms alongside a tendency to distance the formalities of law and legal procedures from potentially distorting or irrational influences.

From a more formal legalistic perspective, there is circumspection about this matter because of concerns that the 're-emotionalisation' of public life might unbalance justice (Bandes, 1999), prompting legal checks and balances for diffusing potentially irrational elements in otherwise 'neutral' justice systems. There are enough examples of punitive outrage expressed in political or media discourse, purportedly in the name of the victim or survivors but servicing ulterior purposes, to validate these concerns (Boltanski, 1999). Gaucher (1998: 1) summarises the dynamics whereby the arousal of strong emotional states in relation to crime can turn into vigilantism: 'In this context, the designation "victim" is selectively applied to those cases which reinforce rightwing punitive justice ideology and serve to forward that agenda.' Some public ritualisations (such as the angry demonstrations during trials of particular notoriety, such as those of Thompson and Venables or Ian Huntley[1]), have been likened to 'grief roadshow[s]' (Appleton, 2002 cited in Greer, 2004: 115). The establishment of online vigilantism in the wake of child murders, especially where there has been a sexual element, corresponds with a conception of regrouping around people's real fears and concerns about redress, which are thought to be ignored by remote professionals and the justice system (Greer, 2004: 119).

Secondary victimisation and its relevance to those bereaved by crime

The perception that the criminal justice system is distanced from the emotional losses of the bereaved has been acknowledged as a source of injustice and grievance, encapsulated in arguments that they too have been victimised *by* the system.

'Secondary victimisation' occurs when those who have been directly affected by crime are subjected to 'inadequate, insensitive or inappropriate treatment, attitudes, behaviour responses and/or practices by criminal justice and social agencies' in ways that are thought to 'compound their original trauma' (Gekoski et al., 2013: 307). In particular, those bereaved by violent crimes or harms make up a largely invisible and forgotten group (Reiff, 1979). Some victimologists and practitioners propose that the term 'secondary victimisation' implies a hierarchy of suffering which subordinates the bereaved persons' losses, arguing instead that they should be regarded as 'survivors' (Kelly, 1988) or even 'co-victims' (Armour, 2002). 'Co-victimisation' pays attention to the claim that bereavement equates with a substantial form of victimisation in its own right. For example, the stress, anguish and grief stemming from the homicide of a loved one may be 'more closely aligned to trauma reactions than to what we might term "normal bereavement"', which has led to an understanding of homicide's contribution to 'complicated mourning' (Gekolski et al., 2013: 308). Others argue that the term 'survivor' needs to be reclaimed as it conveys a more positively proactive language than the negative connotations of passivity and helplessness ascribed to 'victims' (Kelly, 1988). Either way, the range and depth of the additional suffering experienced by those bereaved by a death which comes under the remit of the criminal justice system was unmapped until fairly recently.

Once officialdom began to pay attention to this issue, they uncovered a tangled web of examples of secondary victimisation which accumulated at almost every juncture in the investigation, prosecution, sentencing and post-sentence monitoring of homicide cases.

Consider the 'Review into the Needs of Families Bereaved by Homicide' (2011) produced by Louise Casey, the first appointee to the post of Commissioner for Victims and Witnesses. Casey's findings recount the corollary harms experienced by 'families who have suffered a bereavement by homicide' in terms that resonate with definitions of secondary victimisation at the hands of the authorities. Casey remarked,

> I did think . . . [that] the system would be at its best, both in its prosecution of the offender and in its care of those *who through no fault of their own*, relied on it for justice. [However,] I found a deeply troubling mismatch between what I expected and what I found.
>
> (Casey, 2011: 5, emphasis added)

She went on to document the many ways in which 'murder is devastating for those left behind' (ibid). The wider impact on those whom homicide 'leaves it its wake' included multiple losses with 'accessing counselling . . . lack of information about their case, and stonewalling' by the justice offices (Casey, 2011). Relatives were 'doubly victimised' by exclusion from the criminal justice procedures, especially by not being informed of developments in the criminal investigation or the withholding of details about the crime itself. Denying relatives elementary information underlined relatives' perceptions that they were being 'treated insensitively and uncaringly', which 'can both produce and exacerbate already existing feelings of frustration and powerlessness in the aftermath of homicide' (Gekolski et al., 2013: 313).

The Casey review also unearthed significant, long-term difficulties faced by bereaved relatives which went far beyond the scope of procedural faults in the criminal justice system, as bereaved families reported that the death had led to 'significant debt . . . housing problems, dissolved relationships' or had blighted their lives by trauma, suicide attempts, depression or mental and physical health problems (Casey, 2011). 'Bereavement through crime is so often followed by loss of employment, the breakdown of relationships and mental health problems', with financial and practical hardships being disproportionately borne 'by those in our society who are already the least well off' (Clarke, Foreword in Casey, 2011: 5).

Casey's review was followed by a small number of official inquiries to establish how practices across the criminal justice system could be recalibrated to redress unfairness in this context. As with most systematic reviews, these inquiries produced a limited set of recommendations aimed at rectifying irregularities in the system. For example, the Northern Ireland Department of Justice's (Government of Northern Ireland, 2014) *Research on the Experiences of Families Bereaved through Murder, Manslaughter and Culpable Road Death* found that survivors had been treated insensitively by family liaison officers (FLOs, specialist police officers assigned to families) to a point of 'revictimisation'. The report found that this tended to occur to greater degrees if the FLO was inexperienced or unused to the type of criminal investigation, or if families were not informed about the temporary replacement of their assigned FLO by a colleague if taken ill or on leave (Government of Northern Ireland, Department of Justice, 2014: 29). The report confirmed the roles of FLOs, which ranged from keeping families informed to assisting the bereaved to deal with unwanted media attention. In the event of a culpable road death, FLOs were instructed to facilitate access to the accident scene 'where possible and if the family member requests it' (Department of Justice, 2014: 29). Research also found that co-victims were distressed by the use of graphic images or testimony in court, which might have been avoided if they had been forewarned.

Inquiries have also identified the bereaved's frustrations with systemic blockages across different agencies. This ranged from the length of time that it can take to issue death certificates when a post-mortem was required, to inadequate information from coroner's offices about the condition of the deceased's body or how and when the remains might be returned for interral. Other causes of distress arose through omission where an issue fell between the remits of different agencies. This was highlighted by the practice of charging families the cost of cleaning up the crime scene after the homicide of a relative. The charges included removing blood stains from carpeting and furnishing or steam cleaning homes to remove the debris of the forensic investigation itself. Victim Support lobbied for provision to be made by Parliament for a public compensation scheme for cleaning (Evening Times, January 4, 2008).

A notable point of contention arises where victims' families reported their shock on discovering that an offender was to be released from prison without their knowledge (Department of Justice, 2014: 24). Gekolski et al. (2013: 324) found that co-victims were not always given adequate guidance on court procedures or what sentences meant. As some of their research participants believed that a 'life sentence' meant a natural life term, the release on parole of the convicted person could lead to anger, frustration and disappointment. The role of informing families was added to the responsibilities of the police (Department of Justice, 2014: 24).

The adequacy or otherwise of the various recommendations of these reports cannot be dealt with in this chapter. The most significant contributions of the Casey review (2011) were that co-victims should have statutory rights enshrined in a 'Victim's Law' which was intended to both set out the rights of the victim in the criminal justice processes and ensure that they 'are actually afforded the specific services they are promised' (Gekolski, 2013: 325). It is worth noting, however, that the Code of Practice for Victims of Crime (Ministry of Justice, 2015) has the status of statutory guidance and its measures are not legally enforceable as they would be if enshrined in statute. Compliance by agencies and practitioners is voluntary, and the code cannot be used to pursue judicial review or to enforce aspects of the code (Ministry of Justice, 2015).

The 'deserving' and 'undeserving' bereaved

As the opening discussion highlighted, there are valid reasons for vigilance against selectively dividing people bereaved by crime into those deserving of public support and those who are not deservedly bereaved. The nature of sentencing is such that decisions are made according to thresholds of guilt and punishment, or innocence and exoneration, and the criminal justice system recognises individuals as 'perpetrators' (the 'guilty') or 'victims' (the 'innocent'). However, the experience of bereavement in the criminal justice system may cross the 'victim/perpetrator' polarity. For example, the homicide figures for England and Wales in 2015 showed that the number of people who died at the hands of a partner, family member or acquaintance ($n = 121$) outnumbered those killed by a stranger or unknown suspect ($n = 80$) (ONS, 2016). This is a consistent picture of homicide patterns, and for the purposes of this chapter, it indicates that loss and bereavement are also experienced by offenders whose actions may have played a role in the death of a relative. This goes against the grain of commonsensical assumptions by showing strongly that being bereaved and a defendant or convicted person are not mutually exclusive conditions. Moreover, this crossover occurs in sufficient numbers every year to make this a noteworthy phenomenon.

Meanwhile, the normative boundaries between the so-called deservedly and undeservedly bereaved are upheld in the official reviews and policies where access to, and entitlement to, supports are explicitly and consistently assigned only to those who are described as blamelessly carrying the consequences of crimes. This is understandable, as statutory authorities derive legitimacy to a significant degree by acting and being seen to act in defence of the wronged. The Casey review (2011) offered some acknowledgement that the lines between perpetration and victimisation are blurred, but this fact tended to be submerged in the presentation of data, and there was little in the way of explicitly stating the complications of grief that are presented. The likelihood that the links between being both a perpetrator and the bereaved also arises in the case of culpable road deaths (Department of Justice response, 2014).

Persons who may be grieving for the death of a person where they are later convicted for that death present an awkward anomaly which is largely glossed over in official documentation. These cases are rarely considered as 'bereaved' and are not included in the recommendations of official reports. It is not proposed to discuss in depth the representation of 'victimhood' and 'offending' as entirely separate categories of experience, except to say that there are many contexts where the assumption that they represent competing interests is complicated by reality. That complexity is often understood and encountered by voluntary-sector and bereavement service agencies who work outside the criminal justice system, as the next section explores.

Bereavement work in criminal justice: crossing boundaries

The most obvious difference between the criminal justice and bereavement support approaches is the guiding principle that all individuals need recognition for their losses which comes before considerations of public safety or criminal status. Bereavement carers proceed from a different set of first principles which holds services to focus on the universal experience of *loss through bereavement* and 'to ensure that informal and practical and emotional support is available to people who are bereaved' (Department of Health, 2013). The National End of Life Care Programme (Department of Health, 2013) recognised the universal and elementary need for people who have experienced bereavement 'to have their loss recognised and acknowledged by professionals' (Department of Health, 2013: 4). Such recognition was both intrinsic to the dignity of individuals facing death and in the care of custody of the state, but it underlined the wider costs socially and in terms of public well-being of unrecognised grief, such as 'poorer mental health and physical health'. The report, which aimed to set thresholds of practice with respect to end-of-life care and bereavement care, also acknowledged that 'the essential elements of high quality care and services for people who are bereaved must be structured around partnerships' comprising 'statutory, independent and voluntary organisations [which] will be involved in providing bereavement services and care'. It also called for the establishment of 'a bereavement forum could be used [in each locality] to identify opportunities for integrated working and share good practice', and populated by health, statutory, voluntary and criminal justice agencies including police, prison and probation agencies (Department of Health, 2013: 5). Furthermore, the report articulated a holistic model of bereavement care which should permeate all aspects of care work and crosscut occupational silos, recognising that bereavement care should be 'provided by a workforce that has the relevant skills . . . It is equally important that professionals and volunteers have access to supervision and support to undertake their role' (Department of Health, 2013: 11).

Additionally, the Care Quality Commission, the independent regulator of health and adult social care, outlined the essential thresholds of care that service users should expect, including respecting and involving service users, obtaining consent for care, cooperating with other agencies and safeguarding service users from abuse. The promotion and formalisation of standards of dignity and respect, personal integrity, the inclusion of service users and patients and their partners/ families and equality is a constructive development. Although the trend toward collaborative working is welcomed, it must be noted that important and sensitive bereavement work encounters a unique set of obstacles and challenges in custody settings, in this case prisons, secure hostels, bail hostels or police custody suites. Despite the careful scoping of potential opportunities to provide bereavement support in care institutions, prisons and places of custody do not feature a great deal in the design of bereavement care, and merit only cursory mention in the key reports.

The voluntary sector is a diverse source of bereavement services ranging from nationwide agencies such as Cruse, to more localised agencies or those with specialist expertise in services for child bereavement or for bereaved parents. Support for the bereaved is sometimes interwoven with campaigning charities which may have been formed in response to particular types of death or homicide. Examples include Victim's Voice, founded by those bereaved by knife crime; Support after Murder and Manslaughter Abroad (SAMMA); those bereaved by road deaths; by medical negligence such as Death after Medical Negligence (DAMN); or INQUEST, which campaigns and brings judicial reviews on behalf of the families and survivors of people who die in custody or mental health facilities. Large nationwide charities, such as Victim Support, provide a court-familiarisation visit to the bereaved, whom they also support throughout the trial. Victim Support has commissioned Cruse in Northern Ireland to provide its specialist homicide support service for 'those bereaved through murder, manslaughter or deaths which come under a criminal investigative remit . . . especially for the most complex cases' (Ministry of Justice, 2015: 27).

A few prison officers undertake some specialist bereavement training as one aspect of their jobs, but generally this work is either assigned to social or healthcare professionals or handed on to the voluntary/third sector. The voluntary sector has been contributing skilled and specialist service to the work of prisons by supporting prisoners and staff for decades, and continues to do so despite the obstacles placed by the current restrictions and emergencies that restrict voluntary-sector involvement in prisons (Mills & Meek, 2016: 163–166). Too often, the voluntary sector in prison is applauded by government for addressing gaps in service whilst suffering the misapprehension that it is a cheaper alternative to state provision (Jaffe, 2012: 19–28). Bereavement work is largely undertaken, therefore, by mental health nurses, prison chaplains, psychologists or clinical staff. Prisoners who are on drug and alcohol rehabilitation programmes may be referred by the Counselling, Assessment, Referral, Advice and Throughcare (CARAT) team for bereavement services if it is believed they will be of benefit. However, the severe strain on the prison system has brought it to a point of crisis. Prison psychologists have linked inadequate mental health resourcing with rising levels of violence, self-harm, suicide and homicide in custody (Guardian, May 24 2014). Social workers are seconded by local authorities to work in prisons, but their case load is under strain, whilst the outsourcing of most of the Probation Service in 2015 has created confusion amongst prisoners as to whom to approach for help. Most welfare work is the province of prison officers acting in the role of 'personal officers', but

> [i]n practice, officers and other support staff may not recognise a bereaved prisoner's needs because they have a limited understanding of the grieving process and its length.
>
> (Potter, 1999: 22)

Studies suggest that there is an increased risk of a poor outcome to a bereavement in a prison setting because emotional support required by the bereaved is not always forthcoming from internal sources (Vaswani, 2014; Wilson, 2010). In addition, the 'powerful sociocultural prescriptions' and closed nature of prison environments, as well as the distance from family or community, 'can cause the grief of prison inmates to be profoundly disenfranchised and demonstrates how this can impact hugely negatively on their coping ability' (Masterson, 2014: 56).

Cruse provides specialist bereavement care in prison settings through its volunteers and paid staff. The primacy of security considerations and the shortage of prison staff (who are required to escort prisoners or volunteers to meeting places) have led many organisations to customise their one-to-one and group supports structure to the particular demands of secure environments. Cruse, for example, also offers access to bereavement materials to prisoners on the prison intranet (where that is available) and have developed specialist training modules for volunteers to work within the difficult demands of secure environments (Pritchett & Wilson, 2013). It is also less well known that prisoners act as a source of support to other prisoners, including those grieving and bereaved. The Samaritans operate a listener scheme in almost every prison in England and Wales. Listeners are trained Samaritans who are also prisoners, providing the confidential support according to the Samaritans model as far as possible in the conditions of confinement (Jaffe, 2012). Evidence in non-prison settings suggest that peer support can benefit individuals by alleviating anxiety or depression (Pfeiffer et al., 2011), improving attitudes and behaviour related to substance misuse (Black, Tobler & Sciacca, 1998), reducing bullying and fostering an environment of care (Naylor & Cowie, 1999). More research is needed to see how mentoring might apply specifically to alleviating distress from bereavement.

The voluntary sector takes on the bereavement needs of those who are left behind by crime or disaster or are caught in the tailwind of the criminal justice process. In important respects, the justice system has outsourced the difficult work of channelling loss and grief towards healing or reconciliation to the care system and civil society agencies. There is considerable crossover between the voluntary sector and the complicated experiences of the bereaved, whether they are offenders, their victims, communities or survivors (families or loved ones). Most bereavement services are available to the whole community. The invitation to offenders to access these services is often tacit; whilst victims and survivors are openly invited, few services that work with the criminal justice system explicitly state that their services are for offenders. This may be a response to punitive beliefs that offenders, who have committed harm have forfeited their claim to civic privileges and are therefore ineligible or undeserving of the right to grieve. Nevertheless, this indispensable facet of criminal justice work, whilst not widely publicly recognised, continues unassumingly.

Note

1   Robert Thompson and Jon Venables were convicted of murder in Liverpool in 1993 for the murder of Jamie Bulger (aged 2 years). Ian Huntley was convicted of the murders of Holly Wells (aged 10 years) and Jessica Chapman (aged 14 years) in 2003.

References

Armour, M. (2002). Experiences of co-victims of homicide: Implications for research and practice. *Trauma, Violence and Abuse*, 3 (2): 109–124.

Bandes, S. (1999). *The Passions of Law*. New York: New York University Press.

Black, D. R., N. S. Tobler & J. P. Sciacca (1998). Peer helping/involvement: an efficacious way to meet the challenge of reducing alcohol, tobacco, and other drug use among youth? *Journal of School Health Mar*, 68 (3): 87–93.

Boltanski, L. (1999). *Distant Suffering: Morality, Media and Politics*. Cambridge: Cambridge University Press.

Braithwaite, J. (1999). Future where punishment is marginalised: Realistic or utopian? *UCLA Law Review*, (46): 1727–1750.

Casey, L. (2011). *Review into the Needs of Families Bereaved by Homicide*. London: Ministry of Justice.

Christie, N. (1977). Conflicts as property. *British Journal of Criminology*, 17: 1–15.

Department of Health (2013). *When a Person dies: Guidance for Professionals on Developing Bereavement Services*. London: Department of Health.

Evening Times (2008). Don't make families pay over murder. January 4th. www.pressreader.com/uk/evening-times/20080104/281925948685263 (Accessed September 2017).

Gaucher, B. (1998). Punitive justice and the victims' movement. *Journal of Prisoners on Prisons*, 9 (2): 1–8.

Gekoski, A., J. R. Adler & J. M. Gray (2013). Interviewing women bereaved by homicide: Reports of secondary victimization by the Criminal Justice System. *International Review of Victimology*, 19 (3): 1–23.

Government of Northern Ireland, Department of Justice (2014). *Research on the experiences of families bereaved through murder, manslaughter and culpable road death: Department of Justice Response*. https://www.justice-ni.gov.uk/sites/default/files/publications/doj/bereaved-research-the-department-of-justice-s-response-paper.pdf

Greer, C. (2004). Crime, media and community: Grief and virtual engagement in late modernity. IN: J. Ferrell, K. Hayward, W. Morrison and M. Presdee (eds.). *Cultural Criminology Unleashed*. London: Cavendish. (pp. 109–121).

Guardian (2014). We are recreating bedlam: The crisis in prison mental health services. May 24th.

Jaffe, M. (2012). *Peer support and help-seeking in prisons: A study of the Listener scheme in four prisons in England.* Unpublished doctoral thesis. Staffordshire: University of Keele.

Karstedt, S. (2002). Emotions and criminal justice. *Theoretical Criminology*, 6 (3): 299–317.

Karstedt, S. & S. Farrall (2007). *Law-Abiding Majority? The Everyday Crimes of the Middle Classes.* Briefing 3. London: Centre for Crime and Justice Studies.

Kelly, L. (1988). *Surviving Sexual Violence.* Cambridge: Polity Press.

Masterson, J. (2014). A confined encounter: The lived experience of bereavement in prison. *Bereavement Care*, 33 (2): 56–62.

Mills, A. & R. Meek (2016). Voluntary work in prisons: Providing services in the penal environment. IN: A. Hucklesby & M. Corcoran (eds). *The Voluntary Sector and Criminal Justice.* Basingstoke: Palgrave MacMillan. (pp. 143–169).

Ministry of Justice (2015). *The Code of Practice for Victims of Crime and Supporting Public Information Materials.* London: Ministry of Justice.

Naylor P. & H. Cowie (1999). The effectiveness of peer support systems in challenging school bullying: the perspectives and experiences of teachers and pupils. *Journal of Adolescence*, 22 (4): 467–479.

Office for National Statistics (ONS) (2016). *Findings from the Homicide Index Recorded by the Home Office.* London: Office for National Statistics.

Pfeiffer, P. N., M. Heisler, J. D. Piette, M. A. M. Rogers & M. Valenstein (2011). Efficacy of peer support interventions for depression: A meta-analysis. *General Hospital Psychiatry*, 33 (1): 29–36. doi: 10.1016/j.genhosppsych.2010.10.002. Epub 2010 Nov 13.

Potter, M. (1999). 'Inside' grief: Bereavement in a prison environment. *Bereavement Care*, 18 (2): 22–25.

Pritchett, S. & M. Wilson (2013). Bereavement behind Bars. *Cruse Bereavement Care Conference.*

Reiff, R. (1979). *The Invisible Victim: The Criminal Justice System's Forgotten Responsibility.* Chicago: University of Michigan Press.

Vaswani, N. (2014). The ripples of death: Exploring the bereavement experiences and mental health of young men in custody. *Howard Journal*, 53 (4): 341–359.

Walklate, S. (2007). *Imagining the Victims of Crime.* Maidenhead: Open University Press.

Wilson, M. (2010). 'This is not just about death: It's about how we deal with the rest of our lives': Coping with bereavement in prison. *Prison Service Journal*, 190: 10–16.

Wolhuter, L., D. Denham & N. Olley. (2009). *Victimology: Victimisation and Victims' Rights.* London: Routledge-Cavendish.

9 'Sympathy to the offender'

The Hobbesian account and the sympathy to the offender as an issue in end-of-life care (part B)

Sue Read and Sotirios Santatzoglou

Introduction

In the first part, chapter 3, it was argued that the public moral view of the offender is shaped by the lenses of crime and criminality, which deprive the offender of the human dimension (i.e. as a person with needs). In chapter 3, the Hobbesian perspective was seen as the established account regarding public sentiments towards the offender. In this chapter, the emphasis will be on the professional context, especially the end-of-life care setting, where the question will be whether professional attitudes differ with respect to the needs of the offender.

Social distance and the choice to be 'uninterested'

The Hobbesian account of non-sympathy to the offender, which was discussed in chapter 3, regards the criminal as the 'undeserved distant other' and promotes public adiaphorisation, namely denial of the offender's needs as a person. Therefore, the Hobbesian account constitutes the *established* public morality on the issue of the sympathy to the offender. In Devlin's words, an *established* public morality represents 'the moral judgment of society' which is embodied in the 'viewpoint of the man in the street' (1965: 15). Importantly, 'his judgment may be largely a matter of feeling' (Devlin, 1965: 15), namely, not primarily a matter of experience. Therefore, the Hobbesian public morality which justifies adiaphorisation (the social indifference to the offender's needs) partly arises from the existing social distance and, therefore, the lack of any experience with respect to the offender as a person with complex needs. The degree of social distance is, however, critical in the shaping of compassion. This is clearly inferred from de Waal's statement that '[h]uman sympathy is not unlimited . . . It is offered most readily to one's own family and clan, less readily to other members of the community, and most reluctantly, if at all, to outsiders' (1996: 88). Indeed, as the study of Cialdini *et al.* showed, 'as relationship closeness increased, so did empathic concern for a needy other' (1997: 490).

With respect to social attitudes to criminalisation, Christie pointed out that in our understanding of the concept of crime, 'social distance is of particular importance' (1993: 23). Christie used the family paradigm to argue about the impact of social distance on public attitudes towards crime:

Think of children . . . Most children sometimes act in ways that according to the law might be called crimes . . . But still we do not apply categories from penal law. We do not call the child a criminal and we do not call the acts, crimes. Why? It just does not feel right. Why not? Because we know too much. We know the context . . . And the son himself; we know him so well.

(1993: 23)

Christie's point regards social closeness as the mechanism which generates an experiential process of engagement, allowing the development of an understanding of the wrongdoer as a person beyond the wrongdoing: '*because we know too much*'. Hence, furthering Christie's thesis, the question is whether the effort to know the *other* can reduce the social distance and the preconceptions arising from the *otherness* and therefore foster emotions of sympathy towards the offender. *Is* there a choice, especially for the various professionals who are involved in the criminal context directly or indirectly? According to Jerome Miller, head of juvenile justice systems in Massachusetts, Pennsylvania and Illinois in the 1970s, probably yes.

Miller indicated that a wide number of administrators of youth correctional systems 'knew the inmates in their institutions only dimly' (Miller, 1991). Miller indicated how this 'dim' knowledge clearly underpinned and also fuelled amongst the administrators the development of the criminal myth of violent delinquents filling their correctional institutions (Miller, 1991). Importantly, Miller's account pointed to the lack of interest from the side of the administrators, 'uninterested', as he said, in approaching the young offenders and finding out about their stories rather than relying on the 'incomplete and usually inaccurate' accounts of the offence files (Miller, 1991). They were *uninterested*; they did not choose to find out more about these young persons and reconstruct their perceptions and emotions.

The policy environment can be an influence in shaping professional choices. With reference to prison governors in England and Wales, Faulkner and Burnett (2012) argued that from 'the 1970s onwards, people were selected for governor grades more for their ability as managers than for their interest in changing prisoners' lives'. As Faulkner and Burnett further argued, the governors 'attached more importance to performance and efficiency, and to fairness, due process and objectivity, than to care or compassion . . . they were not inclined to be sympathetic towards prisoners' (2012). Arguably, the policy/professional emphasis on '*performance and efficiency*' seemed to have deepened the distance of those professionals from the offender and deprived professional knowledge from the experience of the offender as a person, driving in this way organisational ethos away from ideas of compassion: 'they were sceptical about how far people were capable of changing . . . more comfortable than their predecessors would have been with the view that prisons should be places of punishment' (Faulkner & Burnett, 2012). With reference to the contemporary Probation Service, Worrall indicates that 'there is plenty of personal altruism still around'; however, the contemporary general consensus is that 'organisational altruism is harder to find' and its concept 'now appears rather weak' (2015). Worrall's statement is a reference to the influence of successive policies which transformed the probation role into a crime control mechanism.

The accounts of community palliative care nurses regarding experiences with offenders in the community or in the context of hospitals or hospices provides a useful insight about the formation (or non-formation) of compassionate attitudes towards the offender. The accounts were provided during the course of a focus group which was part of an empirical study (see endnote in chapter 1).

The case of a team of community palliative care nurses and a carer who *'had a long history with the police'*

The carer as a problem case: 'so it did stand in the way of that'

The interviewee, a community palliative care nurse, who is identified as PN1, offered an account about a person who *'had a long history with the police'* and was the main carer of his terminally ill mother. The practitioners saw him as a problem. As PN1 put it, he *'was preventing us from doing our job, which was to offer the palliative care to his mum, so it did stand in the way of that'*. PN1 indicated that he interfered with the administration of medication:

> he was withdrawing drugs, he wasn't allowing us to use the anticipatory medication, which she needed, . . . it was a lack of understanding on his part . . . that he couldn't get his head around what we were trying to do.

According to PN1, communication was difficult:

> He didn't like the use of long words, he didn't like people in a position of authority as he saw, such as GP, social workers, the CNS. He wasn't happy with that, he wanted everything sort of at ground level that he could understand, . . . that's when the lines of communication were opened.

When communication failed, PN1 indicated that the experience turned threatening: *'but if you went in using big words that he didn't understand, that's it then, he just fired up, and that's when he became quite threatening, quite abusive, and physical at times.'* PN1 stressed that *'he did understand the threat, and he understood how he appeared and how he came across.'* The experience of a threatening environment clearly informed PN1's account: *'you were . . . needing to go in twos for safety and, talking about exits, that's what you clocked as soon as you went in, but, unfortunately, there was only one exit and he locked it every time.'* His interference with their tasks, the problematic communication and his threatening attitude all informed PN1's account of him as a problem standing in the way of the nurses' job.

The carer as a person with needs: his 'bereavement process hadn't been resolved'

At the same time, PN1 also pointed to his needs, especially his unresolved needs arising from loss and bereavement – a rather deeper account of this person's profile:

we could understand why he was feeling the way he was feeling, because he'd lost his dad twelve months previously – dad had died, he'd made himself the head of the household. He hadn't coped with that . . . that bereavement process hadn't been resolved, it hadn't even been touched upon before his mum became terminally ill. Then he'd got his mum to deal with, then he'd got his sister – his sister had got mental health problems so he was looking after his sister's mental health as well. So really with him, I think his behaviour was a reaction to his anxieties and his frustrations and the fact that he hadn't grieved properly for his dad. And he did mention that quite a few times when we went round there.

As PN1 further mentioned, '*now he was losing his mum and he couldn't come to terms with that.*'

A difficult environment to work: 'so you were up against this brick wall day after day after day'

However, PN1's overall account did not demonstrate any further sympathy. As said previously, in PN1's view he '*was preventing us from doing our job, which was to offer the palliative care to his mum, so it did stand in the way of that*'. Indeed, for the community palliative practitioners, this person as well as his overall household environment constituted a set of daily '*distractions*', '*a brick wall*':

> when you went in the house, you'd got Mum, who you'd gone to see for palliative care, then you'd got him and you were trying to control his outbursts by watching what you were saying and treading on eggshells, then you'd got his sister who you were considering because she was having some sort of meltdown in the corner, so you'd gotta deal with her. So you'd got all these issues going on, when you've actually gone in there just to see Mum and offer support to Mum, keep Mum pain-free. And it was really, really difficult because she was what you were there for but you'd got these other things going on, and in order to get to that point, you had to deal with these other distractions as well, and you couldn't have got to Mum without dealing with that. And that was really quite difficult because . . . you were visiting her daily, so you were up against this brick wall day after day after day and it was teamwork, . . . How we were gonna deal with the situation.

The team was therefore faced with a dilemma: should they keep providing care in the community, or withdraw it?

Making a rather not-compassionate decision: 'move this lady from the house'

As PN1 said, in order to deal with this '*situation*' of '*distraction*' the team decided that '*it was appropriate, under police escort, to move this lady from the house, and in the end he agreed to it.*' In other words, the community palliative care team restructured their relationship with their client from a community-based one to a hospital-based one. In this way, the team placed their focus on the needs of the terminally ill patient. However, at the same time, through the new structure, they kept the needs of the carer-son (and the needs of the sister as well) clearly outside their scope of care. In this case, the potential of a holistic model of the end-of-life care did not look attractive to practitioners, and the bereavement needs of both the career-son and his sister were left unmet. The practitioners did not make the discretionary decision to address the complicated grief. They were 'uninterested' in bridging the distance and remained 'uninterested', despite the fact they became aware of and understood his loss and bereavement problems – as PN1 said, he '*did mention that quite a few times*', which was arguably a cry for help. In the eyes of the practitioners, the carer-son was and remained a Hobbesian *other*.

Street-level bureaucrats and the conditionality of compassion

The feelings and the consequent choices of the palliative community nurses reflect Lipsky's analysis of professional attitudes and practices. Lipsky argues that street-level bureaucracy embraces a professional *contradiction:* the conflict between a service 'model of human interaction, caring, and responsibility' and a bureaucratic 'model of detachment and equal treatment under conditions of resource limitations and constraints' (2010: 75). With respect to the end-of-life care practice, Mosoiu, both academic and palliative care trainer, also indicated the significance of the 'working environment' where practitioners need to '*balance*' their compassion against the 'administrative aspects of the work' (2016: 167). According to Lipsky, the latter makes 'care and responsibility conditional' to the extent that Lipsky further argues of 'a myth of service altruism' (2010). In other words, practitioners narrow the discretionary limits of their 'altruistic' care practice as resource issues set *limits* and *constraints* against the demands of compassionate and helping practice. Indeed, within a context of limited resources, a bureaucratic model of practice which is based on *detachment and equal treatment* (the practice model could be called a *principled detachment*) can be more attractive to professionals because it can control demand, namely workload. Lipsky (2010) indicates that 'routinization rations services' enforce professional rules of regularity and accountability, and 'insulate workers from having to deal with the human dimensions of presenting situations', namely situations which tend to increase workload.

By moving '*this lady from the house*' to a hospital, the team brought their end-of-life care practice back to their normality, and also *insulated* themselves from the '*presenting situation*', namely from having to address the complex and '*unresolved*' loss and bereavement issues of the carer-son, or even the further needs which arose daily within the particular household setting. At the same time (and this is very important), their decision also encapsulated ethical considerations, which, in turn, provided a justification for the abandonment of compassionate discretion. Indeed, PN1 indicated that in dealing with the carer-son, in order to avoid outbursts, they also '*had to make sure that* [they] *were placating* [him] *and just agreeing'*, but some of the things they *'were agreeing to wasn't in the patient's best interests, it was in his best interest, and that was a real conflict of interest'*. As PN1 put it, *'I felt I was bending rules and doing things to placate him.'* In this way, PN1 not only indicated some of the problems the team had to deal with, but also justified as professionally ethical their decision to move the mother to a hospital setting, where the normality of end-of-life practice procedures (and routines) could be easily reinforced. From this point of view, it can be seen why it was so important for PN1 to indicate that their professional task was to *'keep Mum pain-free'*. The demands of this particular task, which was their most important task, provided the key ethical justification in controlling both the pace of their work and its input, namely the scope of their work against 'the human dimensions of presenting situations'.

Lipsky argues that practitioners tend to work only on *segments* of their work (e.g. *'keep Mum pain-free'*) and tend to *control the work pace* or tend to *control the input* (e.g. moving *'Mum'* to hospital and avoiding holistic practice involving unresolved bereavement). Lipsky calls these interrelated patterns the phenomenon of the *alienated* practice work, 'a concept summarizing the relationship of workers to their work' (2010: 75), a concept which summarises the nature of their work: 'Street-level bureaucrats' work is alienated work . . . [which] affects their commitment to jobs and clients' (Lipsky, 2010: 75). In other words, street-level bureaucrats, in particular PN1's team, were engaged in a work of particular limits and therefore it was part of their task to retain those limits. Therefore, their aforementioned practices (which fall within Lipsky's concept of *alienated practice work*) reflected their concern to preserve the limits, the scope, of their work. PN1's claims about the carer-son standing *'in the way'* or about the *'distractions'*, which functioned as *'a brick wall'* obstructing daily practice, all indicated the team's concern to retain their professional scope within its prescribed limits: *'keep Mum pain-free'*. From this point of view, new experiences, however they are recognised (e.g. the unresolved grief of the carer-son which was recognised by the team), cannot be easily accommodated unless they are part of the existing work scope. This is something which Lipsky's account also recognises when he argues that it is in the nature of the *alienated practice work* to 'affect the quality of [the professionals'] vocational experiences' (Lipsky, 2010: 75). This is because of the exclusion of experiences, which fall outside the particular *segment* of work scope.

Therefore, arguably, it was the job scope which defined the context which directed the abandonment of compassionate practice discretion and led PN1 and the team to become *uninterested* professionals and preserve their distance from the carer-son. Managing the *'distractions'* mattered more to PN1's team than the carer's criminal record, or his *'long history with the police'*, or even his threatening behaviour. The latter things only reinforced their attitude towards bureaucratic *detachment*. Indeed, their professional attitude was mostly informed by *the* question of how to keep daily practice in a state of normality. As PN1 said, working in that household was *'frustrating and scary'*, namely *first* 'frustrating' and only then 'scary'. Overall, it was clear that beyond the household, the totality of the local setting constituted a problem for the community palliative nurses.

PN2, another focus group participant, also shared and supported PN1's views regarding the atmosphere of this local setting:

> especially in this sort of area, it is quite the norm to be that aggressive, to be that strong-minded, and 'I'll eff and blind at you and I'll swear at you and I'll do this and I'll do that and I'll get what I want.'

These accounts do not reflect the Hobbesian account about crime and criminals, but rather the practitioners' frustration from having to work in a social context which lacks conditions of 'normality' as in a hospital environment. From this point of view, their lack of altruism towards the son (and the daughter) of the terminally ill patient should be better seen as part of the failings of social policy in end-of-life care, rather than as an individual reflection of a Hobbesian morality of non-sympathy to the offender and his social context.[1]

The significance of the work scope

As Lipsky says, a problem that street-level professionals have to confront is that 'their work is their master' (2010: 79). The definition of their work constitutes the contextual element which sets the limits of their discretion and therefore defines the scope of their compassion. Indeed, as Madden *et al.* (2012) argue, 'organizational capacity for compassion can emerge under the right set of conditions', meaning work-set conditions. As Atkins and Parker (2012) also indicate, 'encouraging people to become more compassionate, without considering the associated self-regulatory demands' can lead to serious implications on the psychological well-being of these professionals. Sawbridge and Hewison stress (2015) that 'the emotional labour involved in sustaining kindness and compassion can exact an immense toll on nurses – in whatever setting they are employed.' Therefore, the work scope can become the significant factor in the emergence (or non-emergence) of compassion. The study of Slocum-Gori *et al.* indicated that part-time palliative care nurses experience 'a higher level of Compassion Satisfaction, and lower levels of Compassion Fatigue . . . than full-time ones' (2011: 176). Compassion fatigue means 'the emotional "cost of caring" for others', which leads to 'compromised' practice (Slocum-Gori *et al.*, 2011). Therefore, the part-time contract can be assumed as a defining work element which facilitates the compassionate care practice. Apparently, part-time nurses would be more prepared to be compassionate without compromising their care practice. However, when the work conditions are not 'right', the practitioners will have to compromise or otherwise defend or negotiate their work scope and, therefore, as Dunn and Rivas argue, 'protect themselves from the experience of the patient by distancing self from the perceived vulnerability of suffering' (2014: 48). Indeed, as Atkins and Parker argue, 'developing psychological flexibility is a way of achieving more complex differentiation and integration of the self and emotions, ultimately enabling a focus on others that at the same time preserves a distinct sense of self' (2012: 540). The work set or otherwise *alienated practice work* is a defining factor in adjusting 'psychological flexibility'.

The work set is a significant 'value' of the 'social architecture' which 'constrains' or 'enables' professional action in general, and compassion in particular (Dutton *et al.*, 2006: 74). From this point of view, the novel question is not whether professionals will show sympathy to the offender, but rather how the offender is placed within the 'social architecture' of their work. As one of the participants, palliative care professional PN6, said, '*I think there's two ways you see* [offenders]*: you see them both as patients and . . . as the relatives of patients, and it's different depending on how you're seeing them.*' In other words, it depends on how they are placed within the work scope. This becomes particularly evident in the accounts of those palliative care nurses who experienced offenders as palliative patients rather than as relatives of dying patients.

Palliative care nurse PN3 shared the experience of nursing a '*convicted paedophile and rapist*'. PN3 indicated that this patient '*was in his late 50s/early 60s*' and '*he had got learning difficulties*'. PN3 said that

> his family had all completely disowned him so, as far as we were concerned, there was nothing we could do to support the family . . . his only other friends were his drinking buddies . . . he adopted us as his family and actually came back to us to die with us because he regarded the hospital we'd worked in as his home.

PN3 saw this experience as '*a very different sort of bereavement situation*', (and indeed it was), but the matter is that their attitudes towards the '*convicted paedophile and rapist*' are not actually influenced by this dimension and, instead, a sympathy to the *person* is evident. This does not mean that these professionals excused the crime, but only that they chose to deal with the person as a patient involving sympathy in their practice. A further participant, palliative care nurse PN4, recalled a further case of a dying offender in the hospital context:

> We had one person as part of a hospital team . . . who was a prisoner with a known malignancy, became acutely unwell and got admitted to hospital and constantly had prison guards next to him in the bed, his condition was deteriorating and he was not responding to treatment and entering that terminal phase of his illness.

PN4's account demonstrates the team's sympathy and compassion towards an offender patient who in the last phase of his life was restricted by security rules:

> the amount of effort, through time and phone calls and letter-writing, to try and actually allow that person to have a bit more dignity and time with his family at that final stage was incredible. And it got to the point where he was in a side room and, towards the end, the prison guards were outside the door, they weren't in the room with him, but when you're having very sensitive, difficult conversations with perhaps him and his family and there's a prison guard there, it does, I think, have an impact on your ability to do that and

I think also on that family's situation. And he, unfortunately, sadly died in hospital.

PN4's account shows how their work scope defined the offender primarily as a patient rather than as an offender. Indeed, the arising frustration was triggered by the security rules which precluded them from conducting their compassionate job towards a patient appropriately. As PN4 said, dealing with a prisoner '*can be quite challenging, I think*', but this would not be because of Hobbesian moral perceptions but because of the rules which construct the daily life of a prisoner even in the last days of his life.

No doubt the accounts of PN1 (regarding the carer-son) and PN4 (regarding the dying prisoner) are different in terms of sympathy, but they also show that they are both defined by the same 'value' of the 'social architecture': their work scope. They were both frustrated because they could not provide their intended compassionate care to their *main* focus of their job, the *dying patient*. No doubt, professionals certainly have their own independent perceptions of the limits of sympathy. Some may be Hobbesian prone, whilst others more altruistic. However, what is argued here is that the work focus provides the borders which define whether professional experiences can enter the professional self and facilitate the triggering of compassion. As PN6 said,

> when we've had offenders who are relatives of patients, it's almost easier because they're in prison and you know they can't actually come and visit unless you contact the prison . . . And then they come for the visit and then they go, and they don't actually touch your radar in any other way . . . Offenders who are patients are much, much harder because the prison is always with you, the prison comes in to the hospice and that's a very, very different way of working to how the hospice normally works.

PN6's account clearly demonstrates that the bereaved offender is an outsider to those professionals not because he is an offender but because he is outside their scope. In the case the of carer-son with the long history with the police, this border was violated, and the bereaved offender was no longer an 'easy' case but actually a frustrating one. Similarly, the dying offender who is in the centre of the job is a 'harder' case not because he is an offender but because *the prison is always with* him. In this case, sympathy or compassionate attitudes can arise towards this patient and his complex needs, which are conditioned and overburdened by security priorities and alien to palliative practice.

Therefore, when the bereaved offender *is* the focus of the work scope, there is a greater possibility that sympathy or compassion will arise. This can be evident in bereavement counselling. Despite the non-judgemental professional culture of bereavement counselling, Hobbesian reservations can be shared between practitioners. Indeed, under the telling subheading 'The Right Kind of Client?' Ferrera-Pena (2010) indicates this experience:

When I started offering bereavement counselling in HMP Lewes, a colleague expressed absolute bewilderment and disbelief about the appropriateness of undertaking such work: 'But you will be counselling criminals. Are you sure that is the right thing to do?' Behind that presumably protective comment lies a very damaging belief, quite commonly held, that an offender (ie. 'a criminal') doesn't deserve the attention and painstaking work that we put into helping individuals who enjoy freedom of movement. It also tacitly supports the commonly held belief that a criminal should be punished rather than rehabilitated.

However, as the offender becomes the work focus of the professional, the experiences of the bereaved offender as a person with needs can influence professional perceptions. Indeed, this is what Diane Schetky indicated in her paper titled 'Mourning in Prison: Mission Impossible?':

> The author learned much about herself through this group including her ability to suspend judgment and care for these men despite the brutal acts that had brought them to prison. This was not easy for one who has spent much of her professional life working with and advocating for victims. Each member of the group had something of value to offer and demonstrated a capacity for change. Treating them with kindness and respect, along with setting firm limits, helped catalyze the group.

(1998: 390)

Schetky's account is characteristic of the impact of experiences which arise within a well-set work scope and trigger *sympathy to the offender*.

Conclusion

Within the professional sphere, and in particular the palliative care context, '*the relationship of self and other*' is not necessarily conditioned by perceptions of crime and criminals. The professional dilemma between *sympathy* or the Hobbesian adiaphorisation is primarily shaped by the lenses of the work setting and the needs of the professional to preserve an alienated, namely precise, work scope. It is this professional need, and not so much moral perceptions of criminality, which significantly evaluate the experiences of the offender as person and trigger (or not) compassionate feelings and care. Therefore, the original Aristotelian observation can still be seen as holding: 'it is true . . . that "the difficulty is not to praise the Athenians at Athens but at Sparta"' but, as it has been argued, this is not because the person in need is an offender.

Note

1 It is not in the aims of this paper to discuss the impact of social care policy on professional compassion, in particular the current problems of social care policy. However, it

should be noted the research indication about the austerity driven restraints on community care and its impact on the high mortality rate (Watkins *et al.*, 2017).

References

Atkins, P.W.B. & Parker, S.K., (2012), 'Understanding individual compassion in organizations', *Academy of Management Review*, Vol. 37, No. 4, 524–546.

Christie, N., (1993), *Crime Control as Industry* (Routledge, London and New York).

Cialdini, R.B., Brown, S.L., Lewis, B.P., Luce, C. & Neuberg, S.L., (1997), 'Reinterpreting the empathy-altruism relationship', *Journal of Personality and Social Psychology*, Vol. 73, No. 3, 481–494.

Devlin, P., (1965), *The Enforcement of Morals* (Oxford University Press, Oxford).

de Waal, F., (1996), *Good Natured: The Origins of Right and Wrong in Humans and Other Animals* (Harvard University Press, Cambridge, MA).

Dunn, D.J. & Rivas, D., (2014), 'Transforming compassion satisfaction', *International Journal for Human Caring*, Vol. 18, No. 1, 45–50.

Dutton, J., Worline, M.C., Frost, P.J. & Lilius, J., (2006), 'Explaining compassion organizing', *Administrative Science Quarterly*, Vol. 51, 59–96.

Faulkner, D. & Burnett, R., (2012), *Where Next for Criminal Justice?* (Policy Press, Bristol).

Ferrera-Pena, M.A., (2010), 'Bereavement counselling in a prison setting', *Bereavement Care*, Vol. 29, No. 3, 37–40.

Lipsky, M., (2010), *Street-Level Bureaucracy: Dilemmas of the Individual in Public Service* (Russell Sage Foundation, New York).

Madden, L.T., Duchon, D., Madden, T.M. & Plowman, D.A., (2012), 'Emergent organizational capacity for compassion', *Academy of Management Review*, Vol. 37, No. 4, 683–708.

Miller, J., (1991), *Last One over the Wall: The Massachusetts Experiment in Closing Reform Schools* (Ohio State University Press, Columbus).

Mosoiu, D., (2016), 'Compassionate Love', in P. Larkin (ed.), *Compassion* (Oxford University Press, Oxford).

Sawbridge, Y. & Hewison, A., (2015), 'Compassion costs nothing: The elephant in the room?', *Practice Nursing*, Vol. 26, No. 4, 194–197.

Schetky, D.H., (1998), 'Mourning in prison: Mission impossible?', *Journal of the American Academy of Psychiatry and Law*, Vol. 26, No. 3, 383–391.

Slocum-Gori, S., Hemsworth, D., Chan, W. W., Carson, A. & Kazanjian A. (2011), 'Understanding compassion satisfaction, compassion fatigue and burnout', *Palliative Medicine*, Vol. 27, No. 2, 172–178.

Watkins, J., Wulaningsih, W., Da Zhou, C., Marshall, D. C., Sylianteng, G. D. C., Dela Rosa, P. G., Miguel, V. A., Raine, R., King, L. P. & Maruthappu, M. (2017), 'Effects of health and social care spending constraints on mortality in England: A time trend analysis', *BMJ Open*, Vol. 7, 1–9.

Worrall, A. (2015), 'Grace under pressure: The role of courage in the future of probation work', *The Howard Journal*, Vol. 54, No 5, 508–520.

10 Working in the shadows

Reflections on counselling in prison and hospice settings

Alison Soulsby

Introduction

This chapter is a personal reflection of a person-centred counsellor whose experiences include working with both prisoners on a voluntary basis and people at the end of their lives. It explores the author's personal experience of counselling those people experiencing many forms of loss within both settings. This exploration will seek to highlight the similarities and differences between the two client groups and to draw out how these affect the counsellor's experience of counselling in these client groups. It then explores those differences that are specific to the criminal justice system, rather than arising from the differences in the populations themselves. It will argue that such differences arise due to the practical constraints placed on individuals within the criminal justice system. The chapter then makes explicit the limitations of the discussion before ending with some broad conclusions.[1]

The person-centred approach views people as principally functional with an innate desire towards personal growth, a principle known as 'the actualising tendency' (Rogers 1951, p. 487). The basis of this is that it is the sense and meaning people place on their experiences that determines their personalities. The client develops 'conditions of worth' (Rogers 1959, p. 224) which collectively help to form a concept of the self. The client modifies and interprets his or her phenomenological world through the filter of this self-concept. This process enables clients to deny, delete or distort their own experiences. Where the self-concept is at odds with the real or organismic self, incongruence occurs, which needs to be resolved if the actualising tendency is to realise its full potential. The principal proponent of this approach was Carl Rogers. He theorised that if, in the context of the therapeutic relationship, an individual was offered congruence (genuineness, honesty), unconditional positive regard (acceptance, without judgement) and empathy (an accurate understanding of the client's awareness of his or her experiences), then constructive personality change would follow. He believed these conditions were both 'necessary and sufficient' (Rogers 1957). As Mearns (1995) states,

> The person centred approach emphasises the importance of the therapeutic relationship between counsellor and client and the active use of that

relationship to highlight and explore aspects of the client's social and emotional functioning which are manifested in the therapeutic relationship.

(pp. 64–65)

Similarities and differences

Person-centred counselling is founded on a 'contract' between the counsellor and the client, which defines the boundaries for the relationship: for example, setting the time limits for sessions, defining what is confidential but what disclosures are not, outlining the basis on which sessions can be arranged, making payment arrangements and outlining the nature of person-centred counselling (Wilkins, 1999). Contracting with both prisoners and hospice patients presents complexities, for example in agreeing session timings or clarifying the boundaries of confidentiality, especially about what needs to be disclosed if revealed (i.e. criminal offences). With prisoners, the counsellor does not know why the prisoner is there and does not need to know (unless it is linked in some way to his or her bereavement) but obviously knows the prisoner has committed an offence. If a prisoner then discloses a criminal act, the counsellor would not know whether this has previously been disclosed. With patients, it can feel impossible to be congruent whilst seeking to contract in the normal manner. For example, it can feel wrong to inform hospice patients in an enfeebled state and quite clearly not capable of being a danger to anyone that if they reveal they may harm themselves or others, or have committed criminal offences, then this must be disclosed, when it is obvious that they are in no position to carry out such activities.

One aspect of contracting is to agree session timings by agreeing a prescribed time for each session, usually fifty minutes or an hour. In both prisons and hospices, practicalities can intervene. In a prison delays may occur between arrival and getting to see the prisoner: there may be no prison officer available to escort the counsellor to the room; prison officers may be unaware that the counsellor is visiting and have to fetch a prisoner; prison officers may need to cut short the session or may not return when planned, leaving the counsellor unsure when to terminate the counselling session. This can impede the effective use of counselling time, and extra care is needed to ensure that the prisoner is not left in a vulnerable position. A similar situation can occur with patients. The counsellor may find that a patient is too tired to complete a full session, or there may be an acute problem during the session (e.g. the patient becomes cyanosed), or a patient is unable to start at the intended time due to other therapeutic interventions being in progress. In the aforementioned cases the counsellor needs to be flexible within the differing institutional constraints that arise.

Another phenomenon in counselling these two groups is the environment. In a typical counselling relationship, the counsellor is often able to control or manage the counselling environment – for example in a counselling room the welcome, introduction, physical environs and privacy are relatively straightforward issues. This is not the case in prisons or in hospices.

A first experience of attending a high-security prison setting is, in many ways, unnerving. A personal search is made of you and your belongings on each occasion. There is a very real sense of entering into another community – one that is undesirable. Doors are opened and locked as you pass through the different areas – the uniformed escort carries jangling keys on a belt. The comfortable but cold counselling room which offers privacy has a green panic button on the wall, making the need for safety abundantly clear. It is not unusual for a prison officer to knock on the door and check that all is well, and a five-minute warning of the end of the session may be given. Angry voices can sometimes be heard passing the door when other prisoners are returned to their wings, another intrusion into the counselling setting. The client is brought to you, so the welcome and introduction to the session is, in part, out of the counsellor's hands. Sometimes it may not be possible to utilise the designated room and another, less private area is provided where it is difficult to speak confidentially, but it is important not to miss an opportunity; otherwise it may be several weeks before another appointment can be made. It is, therefore, incumbent upon the counsellor to adapt to these circumstances and to become inured to the potentially negative aspects of the prison environment.

The hospice setting could not be more different – calm and relaxed with a warm welcome. Spacious corridors and single rooms with comfortable furnishings offer privacy and space for family and friends, and bedded hospice bays offer communal spaces for patients. Most areas open out onto the tranquil garden with an abundance of seating in shaded and sunny areas to suit everyone. Although tinged with sadness when losses occur, the hospice offers quality of life and a real sense that life is for living and nourishment for the spirit. Sessions held in the inpatient unit may experience interruptions from health professionals and friends or relatives arriving to visit. Times of silence may be hampered by others in proximity behind closed bay curtains and the noise of equipment. However, a quiet therapeutic space where there are no interruptions can be utilised for those patients who are mobile, and for the bereaved.

The social environment in both settings differs from the 'normal' context for most clients. Hospice patients are surrounded by people who are caring, perhaps sometimes overly so, which creates an abnormal social context: patients can choose to access food and drink or personal hygiene and care whenever required, whilst friends, family and therapists can visit whenever it is convenient. The counsellor may come into contact with friends and family members, and counselling is accepted by staff as a therapeutic intervention. Prisoners have very structured regimes with little choice, for example when they can see people; visiting is restricted, and counsellors can only access prisoners at set times, prescribed well in advance. Counsellors are not so naturally understood by prison officers (although they have always been universally pleasant to me). The counsellor would never come into contact with friends and family members. The culture of hospices is caring and compassionate. It feels much more harsh and unsupportive for prisoners than for patients. The implication of this for the counsellor is that sometimes prisoners are consumed with ill feeling towards prison officers or the criminal justice system when they believe that they have been treated unfairly. It is sometimes necessary for the counsellor to allow a short period for the prisoner to vent his feelings before refocusing attention on issues arising from his bereavement.

Another issue for these two client groups is the much greater prevalence of multiple and cumulative losses. It has been my experience that prisoners have multiple and more traumatic losses, primarily the loss of freedom due to their convictions, although there are other losses such as identity; little or no peer support; and personal relationships with family and children, which, however chaotic previously, are now limited to infrequent visits (if at all). Prisoners are told when to wake, eat, work and sleep, leaving very few personal choices, and they have few material possessions. These observations resonate with those of Schetky (1998) and Vaswani (2015). I have also noticed that self-esteem is poor amongst prisoners and they feel little or no hope. James (2013) states that following a prolonged period of incarceration, '[h]ope may be exhausting and dangerous, but one thing I did learn in prison is that there is no such thing as false hope – there is only hope'.

There may also be multiple issues of unresolved grief – many prisoners are overwhelmed with the thought that upon their release they must face losses that have occurred during incarceration. Some may not be able to see or speak to the person prior to his or her death, view the body at the funeral home, attend the funeral or even visit the grave following release if they are prohibited from certain geographical areas. It is only with listening and exploring experiences, thoughts and feelings over time that clients can achieve some acceptance, closure and peace. However, on occasion a recent bereavement can trigger suppressed emotions arising from a loss that may have been buried for years, and feelings and emotions can emerge. For most prisoners, counselling sessions can be the first time they have explored these issues within a safe psychological environment. It sometimes feels that just being there and giving them an opportunity to talk can make a real difference. Hospice patients can also face multiple losses, but in different ways. They are losing their health sometimes in a slow, declining and potentially painful manner, one which takes away their future, mobility, dignity, hope and control. Family are left traumatised by images of the slow decline. Some patients decline quickly, leaving no time to reach understanding, acceptance or peace for themselves or their families. Some patients are too poorly or die too quickly to sort out practical issues, leaving the family not only bereft but also not knowing what their relative wanted. It can feel that the counsellor's role sometimes becomes more supportive than therapeutic in nature.

These two client groups also experience to a greater degree than normal significant incongruence between their internal and external worlds. The prison environment does not appear to be conducive to grieving. In many cases prisoners are unable to show emotions to other prisoners or prison officers without the fear of being seen as vulnerable. Trust issues within their social environment present a real challenge for them, as any disclosure may be passed on to others and highlight a vulnerability which may then involve them being subjected to verbal and physical assaults from other prisoners. Doka (2002) describes disenfranchised grief as 'grief that is experienced when a loss cannot be openly acknowledged, socially sanctioned, or publicly mourned' (p. 160), the outward face being that of strength and bravado whilst the inward face that of vulnerability and despair. Prisoners may have historically adopted a position of trusting no one as a defence throughout their entire lives as a result of childhood emotional, verbal, physical or sexual abuse. Many prisoners have low self-esteem and poor problem-solving capabilities, which makes them unable or unwilling to accept responsibility for their actions and the subsequent consequences. They may also adopt negative self-destructive coping strategies such as self-harm. A far higher proportion of clients from the prison setting experience mental health issues, perhaps due to their chaotic home environment, the use of illegal substances or the many forms of neglect and abuse they have experienced.

Patients from a hospice setting may present a stoic exterior for relatives and friends whilst tussling with anxiety and fear. Patients, overwhelmed by the process of dying, can appear to be imprisoned in their failing bodies where, for some, death is a welcome outcome as an end to their suffering, but for others there is reluctance and fear in the face of death. Belief systems may provide some acceptance and peace that this life must end and a new, better life is to follow. Likewise, relatives and friends present a strong and positive face to maintain hope and to provide support to the patient and each other, whilst inwardly wrestling with anticipatory grief. My experience suggests that it is much easier for patients experiencing losses and for relatives of hospice patients to openly acknowledge the grieving process (usually after death has occurred) than it is for prisoners. In particular, there is a social context that expects patients and their relatives to be grieving – both because those around them know of the (impending) death and there is an anticipation of the potential need for counselling support. Bereaved prisoners often face a situation in which those around them are unaware of the bereavement, and if the death is known, the social expectation is that the prisoner will manage without counselling support. This latter facet of the prison environment is changing, for example with prison governors accepting the need for bereavement support.

The last issue considered is intrusive factors. In counselling both these client groups, there is a noticeable increase in the intrusion of extraneous issues within the session than would be experienced in a usual counselling session. In the prison setting, very often issues of bereavement are overshadowed by complaints about the conditions experienced, the lack of purposeful activities, the amount of time locked in cells and concerns around transfer, parole and release. These factors, being of importance to prisoners, may make it harder for the counsellor to focus the prisoner's thoughts on the issues arising from his or her bereavement. For hospice patients, there can often be concerns about issues within their families – often only peripherally to do with the patients. These can be very real personal issues. Who will care for someone? What will happen to something? Or the issues may concern interfamily dynamics that do not directly relate to patients, but which nevertheless cause them concern. Again, these immediate issues for patients make it difficult for the counsellor to engage with them in discussions about themselves. Thus sessions may seem more supportive than therapeutic in nature. Sometimes these discussions seem to be deliberate deflections by patients away from the painful issues they might originally have wished to discuss with a counsellor, impeding the counselling process. However, they often address issues that patients might feel can be resolved in the time available to them.

Specific issues in Her Majesty's prison

The grief work of prisoners is difficult for many reasons: shame over their crimes can make it impossible to address issues of grief; incarceration makes it difficult to move their lives on; their criminal history and life experiences lead to a sense of being unworthy; endless time locked in prison cells leaves time for unhealthy introspection. Prisoners are removed from their support networks to a setting where it is risky to invest in new relationships, leaving only the lost relationships to hold on to. An enormous amount of resilience is required by prisoners to develop positive coping strategies. It may be some weeks before I am able to see prisoners again, so I have discussed the writing of poems or letters as a form of therapy with prisoners; however, a lack of motivation, perhaps emanating from mental health issues and basic writing skills, can hamper prisoners in doing this.

When prisoners have been responsible for the death of loved ones, there can be a sense of overwhelming loss and guilt, together with a feeling of being further punished by a period of incarceration. Many of the deaths are traumatic, with murder, suicide (which is highly stigmatised) and drug- and alcohol-related experiences being recalled. Prisoners have in some situations been the people to discover the deceased and are left with traumatic images but unable to speak about the experiences. Bereavements occurring immediately prior to or during incarceration leave prisoners unable to take part in rituals such as spending time with the person prior to death, being with the person at the time of death, making arrangements and attending the funeral and thus being unable to grieve. Due to communication difficulties between chaotic families and the Prison Service, it may be some time after the event before a prisoner is informed of a loss. On some occasions, the inability to attend the funeral appeared to have made the death more difficult to acknowledge. Prisoners may only be able to attend the funeral of their parents, siblings, spouses or offspring and further restrictions may be in place for those who have committed a sexual offence. For many prisoners, families are extended from past and new relationships, and sometimes the people closest to prisoners are not necessarily immediate family members: they may be grandparents, aunts, uncles and even friends, and prisoners would not be able to attend these funerals. A prisoner recently stated that the family intended to videotape the service in order that he might watch it at a later date, but in the meantime there remains a lack of closure. For those who are able to attend the funeral, the experience may involve being shackled to a prison officer, causing embarrassment for the prisoner and other family members. They may not be permitted to stay for the wake or to talk to family members and friends, resulting in feelings of isolation and not being part of the bereavement process.

My introduction to providing bereavement counselling for mainstream offenders was humbling, as never before had I come into contact with so many people who have had such poor life experiences. They were never nurtured, listened to or guided – with many different forms of neglect and what, to me, were awful and unusual experiences, which now seem to be the norm within the prison population I have counselled. Why would anyone be interested in trying to understand their world, let alone discuss their multiple losses, experiences, thoughts and feelings? Physically, sexually and emotionally abused in the most horrendous manner – this was their life experience. It can therefore be frightening for prisoners to contemplate baring their souls to a counsellor when trusting relationships have never existed, but it can also be very liberating. Providing bereavement counselling for sex offenders has proved to be challenging and caused me to carry out a great deal of soul-searching. Even now I am not sure what I have found so difficult to internalise, as I am not informed of the prisoner's crime unless this is spoken about during counselling. I do not need to know unless it is linked in some way with the prisoner's bereavement issue. Perhaps it is something to do with the fact that whilst mainstream prisoners openly accept their guilt, many sex offenders stated that they were not guilty of the crime that brought them to prison. Is this the truth or a deception? There must have been sufficient evidence for the conviction to be made. How is this thought process congruent and offers unconditional positive regard? Perhaps it is more about my own interpretation of the phrase 'sex offender' – an automatic assumption that it is a crime involving children. I am a mother and would be devastated if my child came to harm at the hands of a sex offender. I am, of course, aware that there are many sex offenders who would be equally appalled at the thought of abuses against children.

I have been privileged to hear of the losses of prisoners when they have been unable or unwilling to talk about such losses to anyone else, and perhaps it is about having an ability to withdraw from moral issues and hold onto human compassion – whatever the crime. I am working in a respectful role, but I am also human. It would be challenging to believe that a therapist could be all-accepting and all-understanding at all times, a point acknowledged by Schetky (1998) and Rogers: 'It is not necessary (nor is it possible) that the therapist be a paragon' (Kirschenbaum & Henderson 1990, p. 224). On occasion I have heard prisoners ask, 'What is to become of me?' It is difficult enough to aspire to having a job, home and family if you have not served time in prison, but when you have been labelled a sex offender will you be accepted into society? As Van Ginneken (2015) states, 'Sex offenders also tend to face more challenges in living a normal life, due to the additional stigma that society attaches to their offences' (p. 10–15).

Prison counsellors access their own supervision separate from other counsellors in the charity. This is considered necessary given the traumatic nature of the issues raised within the prison setting, which may be too traumatic to discuss more widely. I would concur, as I have on occasion found myself leaving the prison feeling slightly traumatised and distressed by the narrative of a client who has described a violent and frightening world that is unimaginable to me outside of films and fiction. It is, therefore, important not to hold on to words and to try not to form images in my mind. Rothschild (2006) suggests trying 'sometimes to attend only to words' as 'it is not necessary to picture a client's situation to understand it . . . producing traumatic pictures in the mind's eye' (p. 205). Further training and continuous reading of relevant literature can be valuable, but more important is to take care of myself – taking time to consider my own situation, as this is not my narrative. It is also important that I do not take on too many traumatic cases and have balance in my work.

Limitations

This exploration of the similarities and differences in counselling bereaved people in two different settings has some clear limitations. It represents only one person's perceptions in two specific settings. It is, however, noticeable that in supervision, both group and individual, that others who have been in one or other or both settings frequently reflect the majority of observations made in this chapter. The sample of prisoners counselled is relatively small and is only bereaved or post-bereaved males, whilst the hospices include many more clients of both genders, both dying and bereaved. There was no intention to carry out a prior assessment of clients in different settings, thus the observations set out what is a personal reflective assessment. There has been no attempt to systematically categorise the similarities and differences and carry out a prospective assessment of these within the two populations. The themes raised in this chapter may not be specifically generalised to other settings, although the exploration of these issues may accord with others' views.

Conclusion

The impetus for writing this chapter stems from the personal observation that the two client groups – prisoners and hospice patients – reflect a similarity absent from all other client groups I have counselled. They not only face the issues of bereavement arising from a death – or impending death – but often experience multiple losses. Prisoners have a loss of freedom; patients a lost future. Both are imprisoned: patients in a failing body; prisoners behind bars. They both experience a significant loss of control, even as to the fundamentals of their daily living. Both can become socially isolated, one due to a lack of contact with the outside word, the other through the social taboo of death. Prisoners are often unable to complete the rituals of mourning and can find it hard even to accept that death has occurred. Worden (1991) suggests that mourning is necessary following a loss and that 'there are certain tasks of mourning that must be accomplished for equilibrium to be re-established and for the process of mourning to be completed' (p. 10). Stroebe and Schut (1999), in the dual process model of orientation, suggest that the bereaved person oscillates between two processes that need to run in tandem in a healthy mourning: the first is 'loss orientation' (coming to terms with the loss) and the second 'restoration orientation' (doing new things). Prisoners may struggle with the restoration orientation, as their lives are often regimented with fewer opportunities for restorative processes. A lot of their time, spent in their cells, affords opportunity for rumination, rather than restoration. What is clear to me is that each person facing loss is unique and will deal with it in his or her own way and within his or her own environment (whether physical or social); therefore, there is no one right or wrong way to respond. The challenge that faces counsellors each time we meet a bereaved person is to find what helps the client the best.

I have found that with these two groups of clients my role as a counsellor can slip easily from therapy to support. Whilst with any other client group I have found it easy to maintain the boundaries of the therapeutic relationship, this has proved at times impossible for me with prisoners and patients. For me, time spent with clients in both the hospice and prison setting is about endeavouring to accompany clients at a human level in their grief and pain, whoever they are and whatever their circumstances. As Taylor (2012) puts it,

> Companioning is about going to the wilderness of the world with another human being; it is not about thinking that you are responsible for finding the way out . . . The goal is for all of us . . . to reinvest in life with all its joys and sorrows. Grief is not something one 'gets over'. Rather, it becomes part of one's life history.

The use of external counselling support within prisons can provide an important conduit to release the pressures prisoners face when confronting issues of bereavement in what can be an otherwise hostile and unsupportive environment.

Note

1 For clarity, clients in Her Majesty's prisons will be referred to as prisoners, clients at the end of life as patients and the term 'clients' is reserved for non-specific or other types of client.

References

Doka, K.J. (ed.) (2002). *Disenfranchised grief.* Illinois: Research Press.
James, E. (2013). Hope for a prison lifer is exhausting. *The Guardian.* Opinion Section. 7th July 2013.
Kirschenbaum, H. & Henderson, V.L. (eds.) (1990). *The Carl Rogers reader.* London: Constable & Company Ltd.
Mearns, D. (1995). *Developing person-centred counselling.* London: Sage Publications Ltd.
Rogers, C.R. (1951). *Client centred therapy: Its current practice, implications and theory.* London: Constable.
Rogers, C.R. (1957). The necessary and sufficient conditions of therapeutic personality change. *Journal of Consulting Psychology.* 21: 95–103.
Rogers, C.R. (1959). A theory of therapy, personality and interpersonal relationships, as developed in the client-centered framework. IN: S. Koch (ed.). *Psychology: A study of science.* New York: McGraw Hill. (pp. 184–256).

Rothschild, B. (2006). *Help for the helper: Self-care strategies for managing burnout and stress*. London: W. W. Norton & Company Ltd.

Schetky, D.H. (1998). Mourning in prison: Mission impossible? *The Journal of the American Academy of Psychiatry and the Law*. 26: 383–391.

Stroebe, M. & Schut, H. (1999). The dual process model of coping with bereavement: Rationale and description. *Death Studies*. 23: 197–224.

Taylor, P.B. (2012). Grief counselling in the jail setting. *American Jails*. July/August: 39–42.

Van Ginneken, E. (2015). The role of hope in preparation for release from prison. *Prison Service Journal*. 220: 10–15.

Vaswani, N. (2015). A catalogue of losses: Implications for the care and reintegration of young men in custody. *Prison Service Journal*. 220: 26–35.

Wilkins, P. (1999). The relationship in person-centred counselling. IN: C. Feltham. *Understanding the counselling relationship*. London: Sage Publications Ltd. (pp. 55–75).

Worden, J.W. (1991). *Grief counselling and grief therapy: A handbook for the mental health practitioner*. Great Britain: Routledge.

11 The evolution of change

Factors involved in the design and delivery of a therapeutic service within the confines of a custodial setting

David Pitt and Lisa Thomson

Introduction

Whilst bereavement is universally recognised as an unavoidable part of life, limited research and little consideration appears to be given to the true impact of trauma, bereavement and loss experiences upon young people within the criminal justice system across both community and custodial settings. Throughout this chapter, we will explore this phenomenon and discuss the explicit and implicit processes, both conscious and unconscious, that were taken into consideration during the creation of a trauma-, bereavement- and loss-informed service, latterly known as Barnardo's Here and Now Service, within HMP (Her Majesties Prison) & YOI (Young Offender Institution) Polmont.

The Here and Now Service was formed in direct response to research undertaken by Vaswani (2014) which highlighted the increased presence of trauma and bereavement for young men held within a custodial setting. This research forms the rationale evidencing the need for such a service and, as such, will be discussed here. The creation of Here and Now and its ethos is the 'conscious' work of the authors of this chapter, and we will describe the factors considered during the creation and development of the service, particularly at its concept but also, as new research evidence continues to emerge, in its continual development. Throughout this chapter a consideration of service evolution and change will be explored which perhaps illustrates some of the 'unconscious' processes at work, how the environment of the custodial setting exerts influence over individuals and services and how in turn the Here and Now Service has begun to subtly shift perceptions held within this environment. Challenges and successes continue to be experienced by this service and will be explored throughout this chapter.

Research and rationale for service

Research indicates that bereavement affects between 43 per cent (Highet & Jamieson, 2007) and 78 per cent (Harrison & Harrington, 2001) of UK children, with this number increasing to more than 90 per cent for young people within a custodial setting. For these young people, 77 per cent were found to have experienced traumatic bereavements, with 67 per cent experiencing four or more deaths prior to the age of 20 (Vaswani, 2014). This series of multiple bereavements, often experienced within the context of childhood developmental trauma, provides little opportunity for bereaved children and young people to process immediate difficulties before the next adversity strikes. This exposure to compound trauma and multiple bereavements can subsequently result in the development of a non-recovery process coupled with poor resilience levels which young people frequently aim to alleviate through problematic self-medication and risk-taking behaviour, which can occasionally lead to contact with criminal justice departments.

In addition to experiencing increased levels of bereavement and childhood trauma, in comparison to the UK national average, young people held within custodial settings are further impacted by experiences of bereavement as a result of exclusion and marginalisation from society. This exclusion from society frequently prohibits participation in socially recognised grieving practices, such as funerals or cremations, predominantly due to security concerns and restrictions. Additionally, a frequent observation is that the parameters constituting a 'family' as recognised by custodial settings appear to be much more reductive than those held in the wider society. The 'reconstituted family' is often less about biology and more about significant others, with the status and importance of relationships often being misunderstood or overlooked by professionals. This underexplored and often-ignored exclusion appears to significantly impact young people's processing of grief, emotional well-being and behavioural management, which not only becomes problematic for the self but also for the services and staff responsible for caring for their needs.

Following publication of the research noted previously, Barnardo's Scotland were commissioned by the Scottish Prison Service, in partnership with the Robertson Trust, to design and deliver the first direct intervention of its kind, providing cross-modal support to young men housed within HMP & YOI Polmont directly affected by childhood experiences of trauma, bereavement and loss. This service was subsequently evaluated by Strathclyde University, where its effectiveness and impact was highlighted within the paper 'Our Lives with Others: An Evaluation of Trauma, Bereavement and Loss Developments at HMP & YOI Polmont' (Vaswani et al., 2016).

Service creation

As the first service of its kind, practitioners were faced with numerous challenges during initial service development, not only from commissioners, who stipulated that a whole-prison approach must be adopted in order to minimise the experience of exclusion and marginalisation, but also from prison staff, who possessed limited awareness of the impact of adverse childhood experiences upon emotional well-being and behaviour. Additionally, staff described feeling reluctant to broach the subject of bereavement with young men due to time constraints, concerns about well-being and safety and a fear of 'making things worse'. This experience was further compounded by the challenge of engaging the non-engaging: young men who frequently attempt to go unnoticed and generally rely on masking, avoidance and violence in order to hide their true emotions and experiences. As such, a dual approach was developed, one which provided training and confidence building to staff and also provided client-focused cross-modal interventions to young men directly affected by experiences of trauma, bereavement and loss.

In order to effectively explore need, numerous focus groups were undertaken in which staff and young men were supported to share their experiences of trauma, bereavement and loss, whilst additionally providing their views and experiences of various targeted interventions within both community and custodial settings. In line with Here and Now's ethos of sharing, listening, observing and reflecting, during these focus groups young men were viewed as being 'experts of self' and were actively encouraged to work collaboratively with practitioners to design and shape the fundamental elements of the Here and Now Service, ensuring it was fit for purpose and addressed self-identified need whilst also striving to minimise service overlap and avoid replicating negative practices identified in other services.

During these focus groups, young men identified huge gaps in terms of trauma, bereavement and loss support available both in custody and in the community, describing it as being almost a taboo subject they felt the need to hide from others. Young men described frequently feeling ignored by professionals or being incorrectly diagnosed as suffering from mental health conditions following the experience of bereavement. These negative responses subsequently inhibited the development of meaningful grieving practices and further led to feelings of isolation, anger, lowered resilience and a tendency to rely upon negative coping strategies, namely substances and engagement in risk-taking behaviour, as a means of emotional control and management, seen in both community and custodial settings. From these focus groups young men clearly expressed their desire and motivation to engage with therapeutic support aimed at addressing experiences of childhood trauma and bereavement within a safe and inclusive environment, eradicating feelings of secrecy and promoting free exploration of thoughts, emotions and experiences.

Engagement in focus groups also highlighted the plight of young men held on remand. Individuals on remand face an uncertain time when they can be held in custody for anything between 7 and 366 days whilst waiting for their case to be heard in the Scottish courts, during which time individuals can be liberated at a moment's notice or subsequently found guilty and sentenced to a further period of custody. During this time these young people not only have to deal with a plethora of emotions in relation to court proceedings, wonderment about the future and settling into a custodial environment but also, presumably, have to deal with various other difficulties which may include separation from family, partner or child, or loss of home, job or community status, all of which is coupled with an increased likelihood of having experienced episodes of childhood trauma or bereavement. With the remand population, and their uncertain placement in mind, it was felt by practitioners that whilst it was important for support to be offered to this group, it was vital that the service be specifically adapted and individually tailored in order to meet the needs of this population and limit the risk of further traumatisation through non-concluded therapeutic interventions. This was vitally important given the possibility of an unexpected return to the community where frequently little or no support was available. In order to address need, practitioners' concerns were shared with commissioners and the benefits of adopting a holistic approach were recognised and subsequently achieved through implementation of sequencing and working with community partners. This was undertaken in order to ensure continuity of individually tailored support plans where risk to self and others could be continuously monitored and support adapted as required.

In order to further support this approach, extensive research is being undertaken by the Here and Now team exploring the current provision of throughcare models and practices. Throughout this research, various gaps have been identified specifically in relation to poor communication between statutory and third-sector organisations, coupled with a lack of knowledge and confidence amongst staff groups in relation to the identification and provision of trauma-, bereavement- and loss-focused support. As such, the Here and Now Service is currently piloting alternative throughcare models where communication and transparency are central to support. Additionally, modular training packages which aim to improve knowledge, awareness, understanding and confidence in addressing trauma, bereavement and loss experiences are being offered to staff groups. It is hoped that through improved communication and the upskilling of staff, more targeted and appropriate support will be available for individuals, with the ultimate focus being on the achievement of positive destinations for young people post-liberation.

Service development

As a result of information gathered throughout focus group sessions, it was felt that implementation of a cross-modal, two-tiered service would be most appropriate in the context of HMP & YOI Polmont, with Here and Now 1 and Here and Now Plus subsequently evolving. Here and Now 1 adopts a twelve-week, one-to-one psycho-educational approach which is individually tailored to client's needs and emerging themes, with common approaches to service including work around emotional understanding, awareness of emotional triggers and resulting behaviour. Through the use of topography of mind (Sandler et al., 1997), young people are supported to understand the concept of conscious and unconscious thought and how this can impact upon behaviour and subsequent life experiences. Within this work, particular attention is paid to the consideration of attachment styles, thinking styles and cognitive functioning, as well as supporting clients to develop insight into individual strengths and the development of appropriate and effective coping strategies. This is coupled with improving social awareness and promoting the establishment and maintenance of positive and meaningful relationships.

Here and Now Plus, on the other hand, takes a psychotherapeutic approach with one-to-one support being available for up to thirty weeks. Consideration of the interventions held within Here and Now 1 are important elements for Here and Now Plus, as is the notion of the therapist being viewed as a 'container', first posited by Wilfred Bion (1963). In his description of therapy, Bion described a therapist as acting as a repository for his clients difficult-to-contain, unprocessed experiences with the therapist supporting the client in working towards processing these experiences before safely accepting their return from the therapist. Clients working with Here and Now Plus have predominantly experienced environments void of safe emotional containment, a failure here of the recognition of, and active attention to, need and nurturing. The thoughtful mind of a primary carer is an essential element of an infant's environment, with the resulting developmental process being described by Fonagy et al. (2003) as mentalisation. Within this, carers not only notice and respond to the physical needs of their child, but also, through attuned responding, allow the infant to understand what it is that it is feeling, thus gradually developing an emotional literacy. These experiences of attuned caring subsequently, amongst other things, foster the development for the capacity of affect regulation. In total, mentalisation is the process of coming to know ourselves through the mind of another. Within Here and Now Plus, clients begin to experience this process of being noticed and thought about in a therapeutic setting.

Here and Now Plus also focuses on de-sensitisation in regard to client-specific traumatic incidents and the development of affect regulation and appropriate coping strategies. This is coupled with elements of a systemic approach using genograms to allow clients to safely explore their experiences of family and attachments. In order to ascertain need and ensure appropriate service allocation, Briere's trauma checklist (Briere & Runtz, 1989) was utilised, which assesses emotions, behaviour, prescriptive thoughts, intrusive thoughts and coping skills. Whilst influential in ascertaining the frequency of experiences, it was felt by practitioners that an adaption to this assessment was required in order to assess not only the frequency of experiences but also the impact of experiences. This adaptation proved significantly useful, not only by supporting appropriate assessment and service allocation but also further allowing for the tailoring of individually targeted support packages, leading to more positive outcomes for clients. Latterly, Adverse Childhood Experience (ACE) assessments devised by Felitti et al. (1998) and Adult Resilience Measures (ARM) devised by Liebenberg and Unger (2016) were also utilised by the service in order to effectively assess need and support formulation, which is particularly important within the provision of a 'time-limited' service.

As noted previously, at the outset of service commissioning, despite the apparent understanding of client need, there was an underestimation of demand versus service capacity. During service commissioning, it was estimated that approximately sixty referrals would be received within the first twelve months. As such, the service was allocated two practitioners with an availability of forty-four hours of therapeutic time per week. At the outset this seemed appropriate; however, when taking into consideration the prison regime this reduced client access to five hours per day (three clients per day) coupled with the unexpected uptake of service (167 referrals in the first twelve months). It quickly became apparent that extensive thought was required in order to manage not only commissioner expectations but also those of our clients and the extensive waiting lists which were forming.

Service evolution

In order to manage this recognised need and high demand of service, trauma, bereavement and loss training was offered to 208 Scottish Prison Service staff members across a range of settings and areas within HMP & YOI Polmont. The training aimed at increasing staff awareness of trauma, bereavement and loss symptomatology and the impact of this on individuals, with the focus being on increasing staff confidence in terms of management and engagement. During staff training, the majority of attendees were recognised as being prison officers who actively sought information and guidance on effective trauma and bereavement interventions they could apply to young men in their charge.

As more staff experienced the training, a shift in staff perception developed with a cohort of individuals beginning to show further interest in the topic and how it impacted on young men in custody. Here and Now practitioners subsequently recognised that any gains made in therapy would be further enhanced if they were consolidated with support from Scottish Prison Service colleagues outside of the one-hour-per-week therapy session currently allotted to each client. As a result, the process of consultation and co-working with some prison officers was cautiously evolved. This emerging aspect of practice, working alongside clients and prison colleagues, allowed for the safe transfer and exploration of client change experiences both within and outside the confines of the therapeutic space. Some clients were able to identify trusted members of staff with whom they wanted to share their therapeutic work, highlighting that, for many of the young men, positive relationships with prison staff were possible and fulfilling and thus went some way towards alleviating demand versus capacity and the waiting list phenomena.

As Here and Now became more involved with the internal community at HMP & YOI Polmont, through various case management meetings and training opportunities, the external profile of the service also developed, with practitioners being sought out to present their work at a series of conferences, raising the profile of the service and in turn generating further interest in the field. As a result of this interest, a continuing symbiotic loop emerged whereby the process of providing presentations encouraged the feedback of information to practitioners, allowing them to consider and notice what they offer clients and how clients can shape what is offered, further developing practice. This evolving process of defining, honing and presenting helped instil a reflective, creative and collaborative element into the working practices of the Here and Now team, with presentations and workshops becoming more fluid as confidence grew and service identity developed. This fertile micro-environment began to introduce a cross-pollination of ideas where a more integrative approach to practice emerged, one that was client centred and open to experience and individual need, rather than a static, one-size-fits-all 'programme'. Within this notion of change, the service sought to retain its essential Here and Now ethos and shape which aimed to offer its clients information regarding the impacts of trauma, bereavement and loss and moment-by-moment information noticed by the therapist about the client in the 'here and now' of the session. An example of a simple but effective intervention was the introduction of biofeedback techniques achieved using small pulse-rate monitors placed on a client's finger. During sessions clients were encouraged to practise affect regulation via simple grounding exercises, the immediate effect of which could be witnessed by the visible lowering of a rapid heart rate whilst the client noticed his own emerging feelings of calm; here the feedback loop was encouraged to be both internal and self-reflective, as well as external through observation by another.

Service review and reflection

As noted throughout this chapter, environment is recognised as a key factor in evolutionary processes. As such, the impact of the prison environment and containment cannot be ignored when considering the environmental impact upon service creation and evolution. It is widely recognised that the central function of custodial institutions is containment, with the prioritisation of risk management clearly apparent in the architecture of the building, its working practices and routines. Prison, therefore, is no place for mavericks, with breaches of convention having the potential to cause serious consequences for both those held in custody and those working in prison. The possibility of therapy, therefore, can seem daunting at first sight, with the conventions of therapy seemingly challenged at every turn. Control and order needs to be maintained, locks and keys symbolise power differentials and rooms deemed suitable for therapy have windows exposing vulnerable clients to the prying eyes of others, thus preventing privacy. Here, hierarchies are constructed for the staff and prisoners in both a formal and informal sense. Therapeutic practitioners, therefore, seemingly have only two options: either fight against the system, by making valiant attempts to mimic the therapeutic spaces experienced in the wider world and ignore the reality of the setting, or be rendered ineffective by passively adopting the hierarchical approach of the establishment.

As the Here and Now Service began using allocated therapy spaces, it was noticed that the service was operating in a different manner which allowed for an acknowledgement of setting whilst also establishing a safe space. Our service ethos of share, listen, observe and reflect was recognised as being applicable for not only our clients but also ourselves as practitioners and the wider prison population as a whole. This was most significant when noticing how the clients seemingly responded to their environment and their apparent normalisation of abnormal situations. It was subsequently recognised that clients would frequently make emotional and behavioural accommodations in order to avoid the impact of incarceration, predominantly through emotional masking or acting out. Supporting clients to understand the impact of the environment on the therapists themselves, and naming some of these 'intrusions', opened up a dialogue about differences and surviving incarceration. This appropriate sharing of phenomenological experience in 'the here and now' served to minimise any perceived hierarchy between client and therapist and nurtured the development of appropriate and trusting therapeutic relationships.

As the service continued to develop and grow we, as therapists, became aware that noticing and being noticed had many connotations for our clients. The caring noticing by a parent-carer, as experienced through mentalisation, had not always been at the fore for the majority of our clients during childhood, whereas the negative attention of the police had frequently been experienced. Being noticed in a therapeutic sense, which is perhaps equivalent to the gaze of a parent-carer, could feel unusual, hostile and threatening. Subsequently many clients would, because of adverse childhood experiences, be hyper-vigilant and quick to arouse. As a result of this, the offering of practitioner feedback in the moment, not from the position of expert, but with curiosity, allowed clients to begin to notice themselves both internally, with regard to physical sensations and feelings, and externally, with how they were behaving and interacting. As such, the phenomenological noticing of ourselves as practitioners, operating within a restrictive environment, enabled our clients to reflect on how they were feeling from within what might be thought of as the confines of complex grief and trauma within a confined and restricted environment.

Measuring change and the effectiveness of a therapeutic intervention must be central to any psychological input in order to ascertain its efficacy. This notion of change should therefore take a systemic approach so that a client's personal gains are not the sole measurement of service effectiveness. Change should be viewed within the wider context of development including client, therapist and service. This approach reduces any perceived hierarchy between client and practitioner, with all elements being subject to scrutiny as evidenced by systemic therapy's use of cybernetics, which is defined as 'a general theoretical model advocating the interrelatedness of parts within a functioning entity' (Griffen, 1993). Feedback is actively sought from Here and Now clients throughout the course of interventions, to gauge both client development and service efficacy, given that

> [t]he concept of feedback, as applied to human's systems, encapsulates the idea of *reflexivity* – a system has the capacity to monitor or reflect on its own actions . . . In human relationships the notion of a system contains the idea of assessing what the needs of a particular situation or relationship are and adjusting to deviations from attaining these.
>
> (Dallos & Draper, 2010)

If a service considers itself as being a catalyst for change and development, then that service must be fluid and able to adapt to internal and external stimuli with the onus being on noticing, measuring and scrutinising explicit development and gradual evolution, thus ensuring the service's continued relevance for its client group.

Evolution, as opposed to explicit creation, is organic and adaptive. In biological terms it is the reciprocal processes through which an environment impacts upon organisms and how these organisms in turn impact on each other and their environment, thus producing adaptations in both the environment and the organisms contained. This process is analogous to a range of social and cultural situations in which individuals and organisations interact and impact with and on each other. When focusing on the placement of young people in custody and considering the range of impacts this has on emotional and behavioural development and sense of self and well-being, this is significant. Consequently, the impact of young people on prison environments and criminal justice settings as a whole is also significant and something which would benefit from substantial thought and consideration in order to make for a nurturing and prosperous environment which supports change and encourages desistance from further offending.

Conclusion

The notion of noticing and being noticed has proven relevant to both young men and practitioners within the environment of HMP & YOI Polmont. As the Here and Now Service has developed and evolved, perceptible shifts within the prison culture have been noticed by both clients and practitioners alike, specifically in relation to prison staff's awareness and understanding of the impact of trauma and bereavement on emotions and behaviour. This shift has been attributed by staff as being influenced by their engagement in Here and Now training and by ongoing contact with service practitioners who offer additional support and consultancy when required.

As awareness of trauma, bereavement and loss has grown within HMP & YOI Polmont, coupled with information and skills garnered through training, this has supported a streamlining of referrals to the Here and Now Service due to prison staff actively recognising symptomatology and identifying interventions they can independently employ specifically in the immediate aftermath of a bereavement. Despite awareness of impact and need, confidence within the prison staff force remains limited, particularly in regard to supporting young men experiencing complex bereavement or compound harm, meaning Here and Now continues to receive a high number of referrals. This situation requires further systemic thought with the implementation of early intervention, with families, communities and schools being essential in order to avoid criminal justice settings shouldering the full responsibility for resolution. It is hoped that when considering future developments in relation to trauma, bereavement and loss services, heed be paid to previous research and findings within this field, with the need for further funding being recognised specifically in relation to the disparity between the identified level of client need and current service provision and capacity across the criminal justice setting as a whole.

Following on from the successful implementation of Here and Now within a young male custodial context, further research has subsequently been commissioned to explore the presence and prevalence of trauma and bereavement within the female custodial context, with particular attention being paid to gender, age, impact, resilience and differing experiences when compared to the male population. This process of ascertaining need will again be informed by the ethos of the Here and Now Service through sharing research, listening to clients as experts of self, observing experiences and reflecting these to clients and professionals alike in the hope of continuing to influence progression in the field of trauma and bereavement recognition within custodial settings.

References

Bion, W.R. (1963). *Elements of Psycho-Analysis*. Berkeley: University of California.

Briere, J., & Runtz, M. (1989). The Trauma Symptom Checklist (TSC-33): Early Data on a New Scale. *Journal of Interpersonal Violence*. 4: 151–163.

Dallos, R., & Draper, R. (2010). *An Introduction to Family Therapy: Systemic Theory and Practice*. London: Open University Press.

Felitti, V.J., Anda, R.F., Nordenberg, D., Williamson, D.F., Spitz, A.M., Edwards, V., Koss, M.P., & Marks, J.S. (1998). The Adverse Childhood Experiences (ACE) Study: Relationship of Childhood Abuse and Household Dysfunction to Many of the Leading Causes of Death in Adults. *American Journal of Preventive Medicine*. 14: 246–258.

Fonagy, P., Gergely, G., Jurist, E.L., & Target, E.L. (2003). *Affect Regulation, Mentalization and the Development of the Mind*. New York: Other Press.

Griffen, W. (1993). *Family Therapy: Fundamentals of Theory and Practice*. Philadelphia: Brunner/Mazel.

Harrison, L., & Harrington, R. (2001). Adolescents' Bereavement Experiences: Prevalence, Association with Depressive Symptoms, and Use of Services. *Journal of Adolescence*. 24: 159–169.

Highet, G., & Jamieson, L. (2007). *Cool with Change: Young People and Family Change*. Edinburgh: Centre for Research on Families and Relationships.

Liebenberg, L., & Unger, M. (2016). *Adult Resilience Measure*. Halifax: Resilience Research Centre.

Sandler, J., Holder, A., Dare, C., & Dreher, A.U. (1997). *Freud's Models of the Mind: An Introduction*. London: Karnac Books.

Vaswani, N. (2014). The Ripples of Death: Exploring the Bereavement Experiences and Mental Health of Young Men in Custody. *Howard Journal of Criminal Justice*. 53.

Vaswani, N., Paul, S., & Papadodimitraki, Y. (2016). *Our Lives with Others: An Evaluation of Trauma, Bereavement and Loss Developments at HMP&YOI Polmont*. Strathclyde: Centre for Youth and Criminal Justice.

12 Offenders and the challenges of palliative care in the community setting

Steve Cartwright

Introduction

The tensions of care-giving ideals and the realities of modern health systems are an acknowledged part of palliative care (Tishelman *et al.*, 2003). The layers of complexity presented by any one client can often determine outcomes of quality of life and death and may lead to a variation of end-of-life care delivery to under-represented groups (Care Quality Commission, 2016). The community palliative care nurse specialist (PCNS) is pivotal in identifying those at risk and their issues of care, support and loss. It is not unusual for patients to report a wide range of physical symptoms, social/financial hardships, relationship issues, spiritual pain and depression (Mako *et al.*, 2006). All of these aspects of care frequently over-lap, interact and repeat through the course of the illness.

As a palliative patient, the inmate of a prison may have access to a range of palliative services (Macmillan, 2015), albeit in a secure setting. Where patients are outside their usual domestic environment and in institutional contexts (be it hospital or clinic), they may also be under the supervision of specialists who give care and advice according to their perceived needs. In the patient's own home, the district nurse and general practitioner (GP) are expected to be able to treat and care for a much wider range of conditions, as well as promote health, independence and decision making. In community-specialist palliative care, the focus is on the patients with illnesses or conditions which are imminently limiting their lifespans. The subsequent assessments, therefore, tend to be wider and deeper than routine community nursing assessments. They have to be holistic, patient centred and anticipatory in terms of family, feelings, spirituality, meaning, symptoms and finances – offering a wide range of services (Hardy, 2011). This can lead to beneficial outcomes in terms of rapid symptom relief, identification of social need and appropriate management of financial need. Perhaps more importantly, a patient's supportive structures are included in the plan of care, be they family, friends or other professionals and more likely a combination of all of these.

The age of those in prison is increasing and the ageing process is recognised as impacting significantly earlier than the general population (Prison Reform Trust, 2016). Consequently, increased physical health needs and the prospect of death is also increased. However, not everyone in the criminal justice system (CJS) is in prison. Offenders can feature in a community case load either in the system prior to a case being heard, after sentence is completed or on parole. Palliative patients under these circumstances can fall between the different constructs of health and social offender care pathways and may be missed or misunderstood by health practitioners. One size fits all does not necessarily work effectively in all these cases, and the difficulties of working with national guidelines and standardised assessment methods are often brought to the fore. Differences in ways of working and, perhaps more importantly, the context of care also have to be taken into account. Practically, the challenges of assessing and caring for clients within the CJS lie in offering the core services (i.e. symptom control, benefits assessment, end-of-life care, bereavement care) and more importantly in the individualisation of the palliative approach.

In this chapter the author will discuss the challenges faced by clinical nurse specialists caring for palliative clients who are in (or who have experienced) the CJS, using direct evidence, where it exists, and related evidence from other disciplines and personal experience.

Community PCNS practice and multidisciplinary team (MDT) issues

Traditionally, the PCNS has operated within five areas of responsibility: clinical practice, management, education, consultancy and research (Newbury *et al.*, 2008). Typically, community PCNSs manage their own geographical case loads and corresponding GP practices. The underlying nursing philosophy is holistic and focused on improving quality of life via physical, psychological, social and spiritual care (Mulvihill *et al.*, 2010). The PCNS has a face-to-face role with patients and their carers. There is a high degree of nurse-to-patient personal contact leading to the formation of therapeutic relationships based on individual need. This relationship aims to be dynamic, non-hierarchical, humanistic and firmly rooted in a MDT approach. Therefore, this practice encompasses a senior nursing role which also involves bridging the gap between professional disciplines, organisations and services whilst possessing recognised and expected professional leadership and autonomy in order to meet the special needs of patients and their families. As a result, interprofessional communication is fundamental and is fostered via practice interaction including regular Gold Standard Framework (GSF) meetings where each GP practice and MDT systematically reviews all its palliative patients on a regular basis (Thomas, 2003). At the same time the fundamental roles and relationships between patients and district nurses and GPs are recognised, respected and supported.

It is possible that any palliative patients referred to a service by probation services or social workers could be on any part of not only the palliative pathway but also a general rehabilitative or drug-rehabilitative pathway. This necessitates effective MDT communication and possible referral to a palliative care medical team, either in the community or via a hospice inpatient unit, with the necessary skills and experience to enable safe management of pain and other symptoms, particularly where it is likely that controlled drugs are used, since in specialist palliative care the use of controlled drugs is very common. It is a routine part of PCNSs' workday that they will be applying their specialist symptom-control knowledge and giving advice and support on how to use, for example, opiate analgesia safely. This implies a relationship of mutual trust and shared goals.

Building trust with stigmatised clients who may feel vulnerable, socially excluded and frightened can be particularly challenging. Indeed, given the acknowledged chaotic lifestyle of the most challenging ex-offenders (Van Hout & Bingham, 2014), the management of controlled drugs and therefore pain and other symptoms in the community setting can be particularly difficult to plan without the cooperation of the local pharmacist, who is likely to be able to assist the patient with a drug-dispensing method to suit his or her particular needs (i.e. providing blister packs, dispensing to a prearranged schedule, dispensing to a nominated carer or delivering to the home). The client in particular needs to be motivated and in a trusting relationship with those practitioners. The critical role of carers and family should not be neglected in this respect. Positive, non-judgemental relationships will greatly influence how clients are seen by the wider MDT (Johnston, 2016). Working as part of a team alongside specialist palliative services is essential in a community setting – this team will certainly involve district nurses, GPs and local pharmacists, but may extend to family, neighbours, friends, CJS, the MDT and local hospice.

Community palliative care and the challenges of marginalised groups

People cared for in the palliative or end-of-life phase of their illnesses have a right to expect high-quality care at this time, delivered by knowledgeable healthcare professionals. These principles were outlined in the Department of Health's End of Life Care Strategy (2008) and have since formed the basis for all related national standards. This includes the Leadership Alliance for the Care of Dying People (2014) initiative which introduced five priorities for the care of the dying person:

- The possibility that a person may die within the coming days and hours is recognised and communicated clearly, decisions about care are made in accordance with the person's needs and wishes and these are reviewed and revised regularly.
- Sensitive communication takes place between staff and the person who is dying and those important to the person.
- The dying person, and those identified as important to him or her, are involved in decisions about treatment and care.
- The people important to the dying person are listened to and their needs are respected.
- Care is tailored to the individual and delivered with compassion – with an individual care plan in place.

The rights of marginalised patients in the community are the same as they are for any other patient, but their needs may be vastly different. The number of common issues shared between various patient groups outnumber the differences.

The practitioners themselves may need to overcome their own personal prejudices (Johnston, 2016). Non-judgemental listening is critical and exhausting to the practitioner – psychological support to both parties becomes essential (Nyatanga, 2016). Relationships and support may seem, at times, fragile and easily lost. There is a case for considering those in the CJS as exceptional and resource intensive, with a disproportionate number of men, ethnic minorities and those with learning disabilities (Macmillan, 2011). In the community, there are particular challenges for practitioners, such as the identification of these individuals and their roles (patient, friend or carer), and recognition of the level of complexity. Difficulties may also arise from practitioners' perceptions of the quality of the lives of these patients, as practitioners may perceive them leading chaotic lives or regard their support structures as fluid and deviating from the expected stable family care norms. For example, at every visit the PCNS may come across a different carer, friend or others. In the eyes of the PCNS this is a perceived problem of lack of stability, which challenges the ability to bolster the necessary support system for the patient, as the main care cannot be consistently identified or relied upon. All such issues and needs seem to be under-represented in the forums normally used for communicating palliative care (i.e. GSF meetings, GP surgeries, referral channels and systems).

The application of the knowledge, skills and principles of specialist palliative care should present no immediate problems for professionals. Similarly, the national guidance should apply to all patients regardless of their circumstances. However, there are challenges of referral pathways, recognition of specialist need, awareness of what the service has to offer disenfranchised groups and practitioners' recognition of the issues for these individuals, their families and the MDT, which include

- the patchy medical history of referred patients;
- multiple previous encounters with health and social services leading to a perception of complexity or chaos;
- the potential for poor symptom control when living at home without support;
- psychological issues arising from having served time in gaol;
- the level of support and monitoring needed to maintain safety and ensure medication is taken properly;
- issues of trust, for example, in following advice on how to take analgesia;
- patients' perceived over-reliance on informal carers such as friends, neighbours and acquaintances;
- the potential for ex-offenders to be vulnerable when in possession of prescribed opiates;
- patients using medication (prescribed and other) inappropriately to control or blot out stress and anxiety;
- challenges to the wider MDT, including the GP, pharmacist, district nursing and any home-visiting service;
- communication problems such as not being at home, not answering the phone and problems with literacy and numeracy (e.g. reading labels on drug boxes);

- multiple emergency admissions to the acute sector;
- the complexity of end-of-life issues around beliefs, regret, guilt, fear of the afterlife and what it may mean to someone who has served time in prison;
- the effect of feelings of powerlessness on the patient which can be exacerbated in these circumstances; and
- overall problems with self-management.

Chaos and complexity

Patients with a criminal record will sometimes present as unusually complex and chaotic for a number of reasons, and practitioners should be prepared for this, not only from a medicines-management perspective, but also from the point of view of the patient concerned. There is a strong case for health services to recognise the uniqueness of these individuals and the chaotic normality and complexity of their lives – notwithstanding their diagnosis of a life-limiting condition. This in itself is sometimes viewed as the patient's least-problematic issue, as those who refer to specialist services are often compelled by a set menu on the paperwork to request certain actions (i.e. 'symptom control' and so on). Where previsit communication takes place, issues around offenders are often not discussed, either because health services are not aware, or because the offender is not the subject of the referral itself.

Keeping the structure of care in the chaos will become critical and often challenging; simultaneously, so will a willingness to adapt to a frequently changing situation. It may well be argued that the chaos and complexity of a patient's destabilised life under all these circumstances requires extra commitment and ends in more resources being allocated to this individual than others on any given case load (Nyatanga, 2012). This can be said of any patient with a high degree of complexity, and this fact should, therefore, not be allowed to undermine the rights of any individual to access this care. Therefore, the full weight of any given group of local palliative care resources may be anticipated and prepared for. In particular, practitioners themselves will recognise a point where more help will be needed more acutely – including staying at the local hospice where intense support can be delivered twenty-four hours a day until the situation is resolved or under control.

Anticipating and preventing problems becomes even more important for this group of patients. Often the PCNS can anticipate in good time the triggers that will lead to deterioration of the situation. This makes professional self-care and teamwork critical, as well as a sharing of these perceived burdens possibly leading to different solutions which will progress or resolve any given problem. Sometimes, when the issues for the patient and carers seem overwhelming, the PCNS can facilitate admission to hospice, a nursing home or other appropriate care centre for twenty-four-hour care until the patient's situation is stabilised or the person deteriorates and dies. All the same, the MDT approach will continue; quite often this proves to be the best solution after patients' fears of leaving home have been allayed.

The indeterminate and variable length of the palliative phase of a person's illness will eventually give way to end-of-life care. Enabling seamless transition from one phase to another, and at the same time dealing with the potentially over-whelming social, psychological and spiritual states of that individual, can be one of the most challenging aspects of care.

Loss or change of faith may also become an issue, particularly if the patient has been through the CJS. Whatever the practitioner's personal values or beliefs, this area of care should not be overlooked. Hand in hand with physical pain, the presence of spiritual hardship should be acknowledged and this part of holistic care addressed. Being unable to give clear answers to patients, let alone those living chaotic lifestyles, is one of the many challenging aspects of palliative nurs-ing. Ultimately, patients have the right to be themselves (Stoter, 1994), whatever the circumstances, and it is the community PCNS's role to uphold that right and provide high-quality supportive care.

Conclusion

Meeting the total needs of patients approaching the end of life is challenging at the best of times. Caring for a person who is (or has been) through the CJS requires a MDT-led, patient-centred, holistic approach. It also requires a practitioner who is not necessarily constrained by traditional interdisciplinary boundaries. Practi-tioners must be willing and able to help the dying person to come to terms with his or her situation in an individual way knowing that this may not be achieved.

As a palliative patient in the CJS, high-quality care should be expected towards the end of life either in a prison inpatient unit, a local hospital, hospice or at home. Nevertheless, release to anywhere outside the prison to die is not guaranteed by the authorities (Macmillan, 2015). In the community the experience is somewhat different, as discussions around preferred place of care are part of the normal assessment by specialist and community nurses, as are discussions centred around anticipatory care in the form of advance care planning. It is more likely that the offender or ex-offender as a patient is a direct referral from a GP or local hospital. It is also possible for members of marginalised groups to be revealed on fam-ily assessment not as patients but as carers, friends or relatives who have loss, bereavement or coping issues related to the patient or feelings from poor experi-ences recalled by current events. The referral process itself may be fraught with eligibility issues for services, relying on diverse issues such as family attitudes and knowledge, the experience of the referrer, post-code lottery and the disad-vantages of under-representation when the patient is classified by more than one characteristic (i.e. economically disadvantaged, homeless, ex-offender, learning disability, psychiatric history and so on) (Ahmed *et al.*, 2004).

The evidence for palliative care working in the community with anyone in the CJS (be they patient, family or carer) is very limited. The overall feeling is of a constituency that not only falls between pathways but also needs to be recognised in its own right and prioritised. This constituency certainly seems to need inter-ventions by agencies from across the health and social care spectrum and from the CJS – not just in prisons themselves. Support for non-custodial sentences for vulnerable groups (including those with a primary-care responsibility) has been recognised (Prison Reform Trust, 2012), as has the counterproductive effects of essentially punitive sentencing in marginalised groups. It could be argued that this 'care not custody' approach is wholly appropriate for those at end of life and those who are carers of these patients. Palliative care services need to be more aware of their local constituents' needs to face these challenges and be part of the future care strategies that will unfold. Agencies involved in the care of such clients will welcome the intervention and different approach of such specialised input, be it educational, supportive or interventional.

Relying on aspects of Lipsky's (2010) street-level bureaucracy may be too informal to begin to grow the necessary experience to address the fundamental care and rights issues briefly discussed here. Certainly, more research and a higher profile are called for, as well as new ways of working when engaged within communities where there is a greater likelihood of caring for people in these circumstances. More integrated ways of working and a multidisciplinary approach to those with unmet need are called for. The training of custodial staff on social and healthcare would be beneficial, as well as workforce development for social and healthcare workers, including collaborative development of services where need is identified (i.e. transition from prison to home) (Prison Reform Trust, 2016). Here, palliative care services can interact with mental health, probation and voluntary-sector services to assess needs in vulnerable populations, provide support to those who need it and continue utilising their well-established MDT approach to support and care with professionals, carers, families and patients.

Community PCNSs may have to engage with services unusual to their everyday practice – probation workers, specialist social workers and voluntary-sector support organisations. Local services may seem hidden or difficult to access, but the caring process should not be impeded by the view that palliative care is a speciality that cannot contribute to their support. Creative thinking becomes paramount for effective holistic care to be delivered. The risk is that care can be delivered in parallel pathways, with one group of practitioners never talking to or aware of the other. This makes communication and involvement with multiple MDTs essential and alternative ways of working especially important.

References

Ahmed, N., Bestall, J.C., Ahmedzai, S.H., Payne, S.A., Clark, D., and Noble, B. (2004). Systematic review of the problems and issues of accessing specialist palliative care by patients, carers and health and social care professionals. *Palliative Medicine* 18: 525–542.

Care Quality Commission (2016). *Addressing inequalities in end of life care: Overview report*. Newcastle-Upon-Tyne: Care Quality Commission.

Department of Health (2008). *End of life care strategy*. London: Department of Health.

Hardy, B. (2011). Palliative care in the community: The complexity of service provision. *British Journal of Community Nursing* 16: 574.

Johnston, B. (2016). Moving on from patient labelling in palliative care. *International Journal of Palliative Nursing* 22: 523.

Leadership Alliance for the Care of Dying People (2014). *One chance to get it right*. London: Department of Health.

Lipsky, M. (2010). *Street-level bureaucracy: Dilemmas of the individual in public services.* New York: Russell Sage Foundation.

Macmillan Cancer Support (2011). *Palliative and end of life care in prisons conference report.* London: Macmillan Cancer Support.

Macmillan Cancer Support (2015). *Dying: A guide for prisoners in England and Wales.* London: Macmillan Cancer Support.

Mako, C., Galek, K., and Poppito, S.R. (2006). Spiritual pain among patients with advanced cancer in palliative care. *Journal of Palliative Care* 9: 1106–1103.

Mulvihill, C., Harrington, A., and Robertson, A. (2010). A literature review of the role of the specialist palliative care community nurse. *International Journal of Palliative Nursing* 16: 163–169.

Newbury, J., de Leeuw, W., and Newton, C. (2008). What do community palliative care nurses do? An activity analysis. *International Journal of Palliative Nursing* 14: 264–271.

Nyatanga, B. (2012). Is there room at the inn? Palliative care for the homeless. *British Journal of Community Nursing* 17: 473.

Nyatanga, B. (2016). Challenges of loss and grief in palliative care nursing. *British Journal of Community Nursing* 21(2): 106.

Prison Reform Trust (2012). *Response to the ministry of justice consultation, punishment and reform: Effective community sentences.* London: Prison Reform Trust.

Prison Reform Trust (2016). *Response to improving health within criminal justice Northern Ireland.* London: Prison Reform Trust.

Stoter, D. (1994). Spiritual care. IN: J. Penson, and R. Fisher. *Palliative care for people with cancer.* London: Edward Arnold.

Thomas, K. (ed.) (2003). *Caring for the dying at home: Companions on the journey.* Abingdon: Radcliffe Medical Press.

Tishelman, C., Bernhardson, B., Blomberg, K., Börjeson, S., Liselotte Franklin, L., Johansson, E., Leveälahti, H., Sahlberg-Blom, E., & Ternestedt, B.M. (2003). Complexity in caring for patients with advanced cancer. *Journal of Advanced Nursing* 45: 420–429.

Van Hout, M. and Bingham, T. (2014). Service stakeholders' perspectives on methadone maintenance treatment, Special Community Employment schemes and client recovery pathways. *Journal of Vocational Rehabilitation* 40: 49–58.

Section 3

Insights to inform reflections for ongoing support

13 Sorrow, loss and the transition of chronic disease to end-of-life care in prisons

Sue Ashby

Introduction

This chapter identifies the significance of chronic disease (CD) management in prisons, explores the role of healthcare professionals (HCPs) and recognises the challenges they face in supporting prisoners with the diagnosis, treatment and progression of CD to end-of-life care. In this circumstance, prisoners and their families have the potential to experience multiple losses and feelings of chronic sorrow, as highlighted throughout the chapters in this book.

CD and custody

Similar to other developed countries, prison healthcare in the United Kingdom aims to provide the same level of provision as for the general population (United Nations 1991), reinforced by the move from the UK Ministry of Justice to the Ministry of Health in 2002 for the commissioning and provision of prison healthcare, completing the move to National Health Service (NHS) England and Public Health England in 2012 (Health and Social Care Act 2012). The equivalence of health outcomes to that of the general population was advocated alongside process (Charles and Draper 2012). However in 2015 the UK prison population was acknowledged as having 'a disproportionately higher burden of disease' and 'poorer access to treatment and prevention programmes compared to their peers in the community' (NHS England 2015a: 8). A shift to outcomes was recognised in 2016, as care was commissioned to be improved by aligning it with the five domains of the NHS outcome framework:

1 Preventing people from dying prematurely
2 Enhancing quality of life for people with long-term conditions
3 Helping people to recover from periods of ill health or following injury
4 Ensuring that people have a positive experience of care
5 Treating people in a safe and caring environment and protecting them from avoidable harm

(Department of Health [DH] 2016)

Domain 2 identifies overarching indicators for successfully supporting individuals in the management of chronic conditions:

- ensuring people feel supported to manage their condition;
- improving functional ability in people with long-term conditions;
- reducing time spent in hospital by people with long-term conditions;
- enhancing quality of life for carers;
- enhancing quality of life for people with mental illness;
- enhancing quality of life for people with dementia; and
- improving quality of life for people with multiple long-term conditions.

(DH 2016)

Whilst viewed as a benchmark for prison healthcare, there remain significant challenges in achieving equivalence between processes and outcomes for prison health and the healthcare of the general population. Her Majesty's (HM) Inspectorate of Prisons Report (2016) identified issues specifically relating to male prisoners due to staffing levels, which impacted on the accessibility of healthcare and treatment, resulting in underperformance against health targets. Examples related to 'late or missed appointments, cancelled external health appointments, curtailed inpatient therapeutic activities, and lack of supervision of prisoners at medicine times, with the potential for bullying and trading of medications' (HM Inspectorate of Prisons Report 2016: 35). However, it was acknowledged that most women had prompt access, with the exception of waiting too long for mental health.

Imprisonment, CD and complicated loss

Imprisonment restrains the personal liberty of an individual, removing autonomy with the effect of reducing self-esteem (Stevenson and McCutchen 2006). At a time when family connections are stressed by separation, the prisoner's ability to cope can also be hampered by bullying, exclusion and boredom (World Health Organisation [WHO] 2017). For prisoners with CD, there is also the impact of living with the condition or multiple conditions from a physical and psychological perspective, influenced by pain, fatigue, physical disability, depression and anxiety (Bruneau 2011; Jackson 2014). People with CD are reported to have higher psychological distress than those without (Shih and Simon 2008). Clinical symptoms can be debilitating at any age. For older adults, a decline in cognitive ability may also add to the challenges of achieving activities of everyday living (Bruneau 2011). The very nature of CD implies periods of adjustment, as continued changes throughout the trajectory of the disease process requires individuals to come to terms with changes in health and functioning to achieve mental well-being (Thompson 2011). This combination of imprisonment and trajectory of decline has the potential to lead to multiple components of loss. Additionally, in an already-challenged environment, prisoners with CD may be reluctant to discuss their psychological state for fear of being judged as not coping and drawing attention to vulnerability. The resulting feelings of sadness or grief are described as chronic sorrow (Ahlström 2007). Similar to the trajectory of chronic conditions with exacerbations and periods of stability, chronic sorrow fluctuates, as highs and lows are experienced. Figure 13.1 illustrates the potential impact on this prisoner population.

HCPs are key in providing sensitive and timely support to prisoners and their families with these complicated losses. There is opportunity for coping strategies to be assessed and supported across interfaces of care within the criminal justice system and community.

The transition of CD to end-of-life care

The National Health Service Outcome Framework (DH 2016) and the National Institute for Health and Care Excellence (NICE) pathway and guidance for prisoner healthcare (NICE 2016a; NICE 2016b) provide benchmarks for prison healthcare; however, there are issues in the general population relating to CD management. There is a plethora of literature debating the lack of coordination of healthcare services, resulting in a lack of continuity and delayed care with the potential for late diagnosis, exacerbation and deterioration of condition (Coulter et al. 2013; Goodwin et al. 2010). A lack of continuity in care impacts on HCPs being able to observe trends in the fluctuation of the condition. This can be problematic when making decisions surrounding active treatment and palliative approaches as chronic conditions progress. Cancer-based palliative care services are based on an ability to determine when individuals are entering the last twelve months of life, supported by diagnostic tools which have now extended to indicate predictors for chronic conditions (Gold Standard Framework [GSF] Centre 2011; NHS Scotland 2016). The Prisons and Probation Ombudsman for England and Wales (2013) reported that the location of death for prisoners reflected similarities in the community for patients with cancer. There were four themes linked to the quality of end-of-life care and achieving preferred place of death and dignity – having palliative care plans in place, appropriate use of restraints, mechanisms in place to achieve early release and family involvement – all of which require forward planning. It is these changes indicating last years, months, weeks and days that afford the individual, family, friends and HCPs the ability to plan a pathway of supportive care recognising the potential for and impact of chronic sorrow (Figure 13.2).

The aim of the pathway is to avert crises and achieve timely referrals to support physical, psychological, social and spiritual needs. These are all quality indicators identified by the NICE Quality Standard for End of Life Care (NICE 2011). The National Palliative and End of Life Partnership (NPELP) (2015: 17), responding to issues recognised in the general population, identified eight foundations on which quality for those that are living with dying, death or bereavement depend:

1   Personalised care planning
2   Education and training
3   Evidence and information
4   Co-design
5   Shared records
6   24/7 access

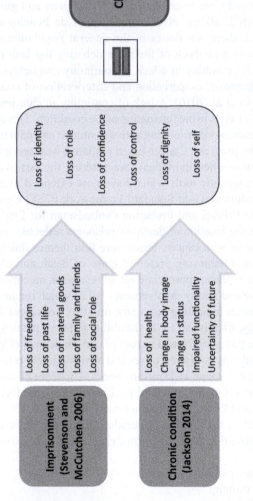

Figure 13.1 Potential impact of imprisonment and living with a chronic condition

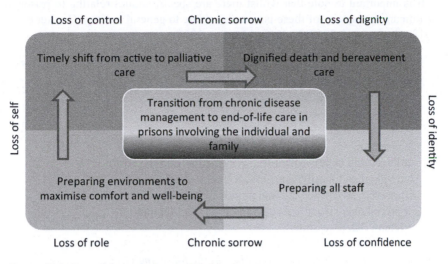

Figure 13.2 Care pathway and potential chronic sorrow

7 Those important to the dying person
8 Leadership

Applying a positive language, this partnership launched from these foundations six ambitions to drive forward quality care:

1 Each person is seen as an individual
2 Each person gets fair access to care
3 Maximising comfort and well-being
4 Care is coordinated
5 All staff are prepared to care
6 Each community is prepared to help

(NPELP 2015: 11)

Considering these foundations and ambitions, the remainder of this chapter explores the challenges for HCPs working with prisoners in the context of the transition of chronic condition to palliative and end-of-life care and the potential for chronic sorrow.

Challenges for HCPs

There are a number of investigations into prison deaths which indicate common issues in the management of CD which are publicly accessible via the UK Prisons and Probation Ombudsman Independent Investigations webpages (i.e. www. ppo.gov.uk/). Three cases are utilised to illustrate these issues, acknowledging the Open Government Licence, version 3.0 (www.nationalarchives.gov.uk/doc/ open-government-licence/version/3/).

It is important to note that whilst there are specific issues relating to prisoner healthcare, a majority of these issues also relate to general society (Coulter et al. 2013; Naylor et al. 2012; Nolte and McKee 2008):

- timely diagnosis;
- access to diagnostics;
- coordinated care plans;
- multidisciplinary working;
- integrated care;
- leadership;
- attitudes and beliefs (of staff, the individual and the family);
- individual and family/carer involvement and choice;
- emotional, psychological and practical support;
- appropriate environments to support end of life; and
- ongoing risk assessment.

These issues are highlighted in bold text in the following cases.

Case 1

A Prison Ombudsman Report of Northern Ireland (2015) investigated the death of a 34-year-old male following early release on licence due to an inoperable brain tumour. The investigation identified four missed opportunities for the diagnosis of an inoperable brain tumour, which constituted a combination of issues around prison leadership, medical management, healthcare professional knowledge, issues with coordination of care, lack of care planning, delays in care, intermittent non-compliance with medications and refusal by the man on one occasion to attend an accident and emergency department, all of which resulted in fifteen recommendations for improvement. The report states that 'while multi-disciplinary fora were not as effective as they should have been in delivering an appropriate care plan, residential staff were appropriately concerned about him and worked hard to monitor his well-being' following 'manifestation of symptoms'; however it was also stated that 'an unnecessary level of security and bureaucracy was also applied to his hospital visitors' (Prison Ombudsman Report of Northern Ireland 2015: 6). The findings indicated that had the prisoner's diagnosis been determined earlier, there would have been opportunity to reduce distress and prepare for palliative care sooner.

Case 2

A Prisons and Probation Ombudsman Report (2014a) investigated the death of a 50-year-old female from sepsis due to bronchopneumonia and neutropenia. The woman had experienced poor health for several years prior to imprisonment and now used a wheelchair. She had multiple chronic conditions, including atrial fibrillation and myotonic dystrophy. The female disclosed at her first health assessment that she used heroin and was depressed following the death of her partner (the cause of her imprisonment as a result of her dangerous driving). She was seen by an in-reach bereavement counselling service. The overall level of care this woman received was reported as unsatisfactory (i.e. not being equivalent to care expected in the community). The report stated that there was

> no evidence that the care plan agreed at the woman's initial reception assessment was followed up and there was no evidence of any proactive planning of her medical care e.g. no monitoring of respiratory function with no opportunity for healthcare staff to proactively manage care observing for signs of deterioration. Where records indicated nutritional issues there were incomplete records and a validated screening tool was not used. There was no record of multidisciplinary meetings between the agencies involved in her care or that they shared relevant documentation between them.
>
> (Prisons and Probation Ombudsman Report 2014a: 12)

Despite records indicating a decrease in mobility, opportunities were missed to investigate and treat this person. Issues were raised in relation to restraints and two escorts which were used when this woman attended an emergency admission to hospital authorised by an operational manager, despite earlier records which indicated that this woman had left the prison unrestrained and without escort on several occasions for overnight unaccompanied family visits, as her sentence progression gave eligibility for release on a temporary licence. The officer making decisions about restraints reported not having this information available at the time. It was a doctor who requested the removal of handcuffs a few hours after hospital admission which resulted in escorting officers obtaining this permission.

Case 3

A Prisons and Probation Ombudsman Report (2014b) investigated the death of an 84-year-old male from chronic myeloid leukaemia and end-stage kidney failure. The clinical reviewer of this case reported that 'overall, the level of clinical care the man received was equal to that he could have expected in the community' (Prisons and Probation Ombudsman Report 2014b: 3). The report had been adjusted following the family raising issues that whilst initially overall care was reported as equal, this was not the case. Good practice was acknowledged in relation to communication and medicines management as the man moved location between two prisons. It was however reported that there was an absence of a care plan at one prison, which would have been expected due to the man's age and chronic conditions. Restraints were used when this man attended hospital, which did not take into account the level of frailty considering age and medical conditions, which were reported as unjustified. There had been previous recommendations for one of the prisons involved in this man's care about management of risk and the 'inappropriate use of restraints for elderly and infirm prisoners' (Prisons and Probation Ombudsman Report 2014b: 8).

Resulting recommendations

The three cases in total identified nineteen recommendations (case 1, $n = 14$; case 2, $n = 3$; case 3, $n = 2$). These related to training, recording of information, accessibility of healthcare, multidisciplinary working, accurate recording of reasons for missed appointments, timely referrals for further investigations, robust follow-up procedures for patients who refuse accident and emergency attendance, identifying and addressing all healthcare concerns raised by prisoners on assessment, applying discretion relating to number of visits/visitors prisoners who are gravely ill may have and achieving continuity of care when returning to the community. All the cases raised issues relating to the active monitoring of coordinated care plans by all staff and to a standard statement relating to all staff understanding the legal position relating to risk assessment for prisoners taken to hospital taking into full account prisoner health at the time.

Holistic management of CD in prison

Healthcare is complex in prisons with prisoners often presenting with no traceable healthcare records, having not been registered with a general practice. This can be complicated by homelessness, making interaction with primary healthcare systems difficult (Norman and Parrish 2002). The initial healthcare assessment is therefore significant, requiring knowledge, skills and expertise in gathering, recording and establishing often the first baseline on which to determine deterioration of CD. The individual may not be aware of or fully understand the management of his or her condition. Prisoners therefore have the potential to present with unstable conditions which can accelerate overall deterioration in physical and mental health. Chronic pain and fatigue are common complications of living with chronic conditions (DH 2012; Whitehead et al. 2016). Within a prison environment they raise additional challenges directly relating to basic human needs (e.g. debilitating circumstances may reduce opportunity for prisoners to achieve adequate nutrition and hydration with food and drink that is provided via self-service means, personal hygiene may be compromised and the need for specialist equipment to support activities of daily living may be difficult to achieve where space is limited).

The HCP supporting effective management of pain has many factors to consider. A high prevalence of mental health and substance misuse and histories of physical and emotional trauma, including the anxiety of coming into prison, can intensify existing pain (Public Health England 2013). Pain is subjective, which makes prescribing both pharmacological and non-pharmacological treatment difficult. HCPs now have access to evidence-based protocols and drug tariffs to assist pain management for prisoners (NHS England 2015b). The relationship between pain, fatigue and depression is complex, influenced by characteristics of the presenting symptom and the individual's thoughts and behaviour developed over time and how the individual has been positively or negatively supported (Caltabiano et al. 2008). When considering the chaotic lives that prisoners present with, it is significant to note that the psychological and physical distress of living with CD interacting with individual and social vulnerability may trigger an episode of chronic sorrow. It is important to recognise the psychological state of individuals in these circumstances when commencing a holistic plan of care. For some this may already necessitate the need for social care.

The first point of contact with a HCP in prison is significant both to the HCP and the prisoner. The HCP has to consider the custodial and security issues that can affect the provision of care (Perry et al. 2010a). Where conditions are already known, there remain challenges in monitoring conditions to determine the subtle changes and the provision of timely interventions. However, such monitoring gives opportunity to review complex physical and mental health needs and coping strategies. The prisoner is required to disclose information which may be difficult to verbalise, relating to situations which have impacted on health and well-being (e.g. being in care, exclusion from school, unemployment, debt, abuse, and substance misuse) implicating long-standing psychological problems (Williamson 2007). It can be time-consuming to gain the relevant healthcare information, both from previous providers and from the prisoner. These situations have the potential to delay appropriate pathways of care for prisoners whose CD is already nearing or at the transition of active to palliative treatment. Murray et al. (2017) debate the need for integrated early palliative care within ongoing CD management, recognising the greatest barriers as late identification of people who may benefit and missed opportunities whilst waiting for a physical decline in health. Supportive conversations should be ideally aligned to prisoners' presenting states and where possible involve those closest to them.

The involvement of the individual and family

Coming to terms with the diagnosis of a chronic condition and the uncertainty of how this will be managed whilst imprisoned is a double sentence for the individual and family. There are implications for chronic sorrow as the impact of imprisonment and health status may psychologically affect the prisoner and his or her family (Figure 13.1 and 13.2). Recognised treatments involve cognitive behaviour therapy (Blenkiron 2013), exposure therapy (Grohol 2016) and meaning therapy (Wong 2015). The components of these therapies are not as easy to achieve for those imprisoned (i.e. due to a loss of freedom, and for their families, adapting to loss at a distance from their loved ones).

HCPs need to have a raised awareness of how prisoners and their families may experience interrupted or obstructed grief and loss related to the trajectory of CD to end-of-life care and experiencing chronic sorrow. Whilst the National End of Life Care Programme (NHS 2014) is a useful guide to support HCPs in the implementation of high-quality end-of-life care, further education and training is required to avoid hindering, disapproving or at worst prohibiting feelings of loss and grief in these circumstance.

Staff

Several staff may be involved in the care of the prisoner with CD: HCPs working across or within primary- and secondary-care settings, prison staff and a number of ancillary staff (e.g. porters, ward clerks). There is the potential for what is accepted as societal norm relating to the management of CD (i.e. empowerment, choice, shared decision making) to be challenged by some people who may express that prisoners are less deserving (Royal College of Nursing [RCN] 2017), and with growing concern that equivalence of care is 'underserved in relation to their high unmet and complex needs' (RCN 2017: 9). People with CD require proactive management to maximise quality of life (by providing timely support to identify, recognise and minimise debilitating symptoms) and prevent premature decline in functionality. Working with prisoners, HCPs are fundamental in both maintaining the stability of conditions and recognising trends in deterioration. In 2016 a guideline was published specifically for prison healthcare (NICE 2016a). Within this guideline, the management of chronic conditions is redirected to NICE pathways for the general population, focusing on person-centred care and individuals taking ownership of their own conditions (NICE 2016b). When providing prisoners with equal healthcare opportunities (e.g. empowerment and choice), there are conflicting philosophies where there is control by and a dependency on prison staff. HCPs are directed by these guidelines to work with prison staff to frequently monitor prisoners with CD. However, this is dependent on prisoners agreeing that HCPs share relevant confidential healthcare information (NICE 2016a). This is further challenged by the potential for frequent movement between prisons. Situated within this context, prisoners with CD are faced with the psychological effect of both imprisonment (Prison Reform Trust 2017) and living with a chronic condition (Bruneau 2011). This can be further complicated by the presence of drug or alcohol misuse. Hampered by an acknowledged shortage in prison staff, conflicting philosophies of care and potential issues with information sharing, HCPs face many challenges when psychologically supporting prisoners. It is imperative that staff do not become blinkered to the psychological needs of prisoners and their families and to the consequences of denying supportive human interaction by actions that disempower, marginalise and display a lack of compassion. Staff attitudes and behaviour that limit communication and promote avoidance and delayed care foster loss and chronic sorrow.

Quality versus risk

The focus of prison care is not healthcare. There is a constant awareness of security when operationalising care and minimising risk both to the prisoner and to others. The very nature of chronic condition management requires timely access to diagnostics supporting decision making relating to the diagnosis or changing stages of the condition and treatment. The increasing use of telemedicine (i.e. the remote diagnosis and treatment of patients by means of telecommunications technology) supports timely management and in turn the avoidance of unnecessary hospital admissions. There are many examples of good practice emerging, for example NHS Airedale NHS Trust (2012), who have telemedicine equipment installed across the hospital site, achieving rapid access across a range of specialities to over ten prisons. Allied health professionals (e.g. physiotherapists, tissue viability nurses and dieticians) are also linked via this service. This service has reported several benefits, including but not limited to improving prisoner health and addressing health inequalities, minimising disruption to the wider community and empowering the prison-based healthcare teams. Although not reported, it can be debated that the impact on the prisoner is likely a reduction in the stress and stigma of being escorted, often handcuffed, whilst enduring ill health, which possibly supports continuity of timely care as more familiar prison-based healthcare staff communicate treatment regimes. This gives opportunities to sustain effective relationships through informational and emotional support, particularly where there may be a reluctance to seek assistance (Bruneau 2011).

Conclusion

This chapter has drawn attention to CD management in prison illustrated by responses from the UK Ministry of Justice and Ministry of Health to address inequality in healthcare provision. The significance of the role of HCPs to maximise quality of life and prevent premature decline was detailed in the context of achieving this for the prison population. Examples of serious incidents were drawn on to show common challenges for HCPs supporting prisoners with the diagnosis and management of chronic conditions and the transition to palliative and end-of-life care, which were also compared to that of the general society. Loss is experienced in multiple ways throughout the trajectory of living with a chronic condition. The relationship between imprisonment, CD and the experience of multiple losses was established, determining the factors contributing to chronic sorrow. HCPs who are able to recognise and respond sensitively to these presenting circumstances will be better placed to support prisoners and their families.

References

Ahlström, G. (2007). Experiences of loss and chronic sorrow in persons with severe chronic illness. *Journal of Clinical Nursing* 16: 76–83.

Airedale NHS Foundation Trust (2012). *Telemedicine services for HMP Wandsworth.* Airedale: Airedale NHS Foundation Trust.

Blenkiron, P. (2013). *Cognitive behavioural therapy.* Royal College of Psychiatrists Public Education Editorial Board. www.rcpsych.ac.uk/mentalhealthinformation/therapies/cognitivebehaviouraltherapy.aspx (Accessed 31 May 2017).

Bruneau, B. (2011). Psychological effects of long term conditions. IN: Meerabeau, L. & Wright, K. (Eds.), *Long-term conditions nursing care and management.* Chichester, UK: Wiley-Blackwell.

Caltabiano, M., Byrne, D., & Sarafino, E.P. (2008). *Health psychology: Biopsychosocial interactions.* Brisbane: John Wiley and Sons.

Charles, A., & Draper, H. (2012). Equivalence of care in prison medicine: Is equivalence of process the right measure of equity? *Journal of Medical Ethics* 38: 215–218.

Coulter, A., Roberts, S., & Dixon, A. (2013). *Delivering better services for people with long term conditions*. London: The King's Fund.

Department of Health (2012). *Long term conditions compendium of information*. London: Department of Health.

Department of Health (2016). *NHS outcomes framework: At-a-glance*. London: Department of Health.

Gold Standard Framework Centre (2011). *The GSF prognostic indicator guidance*. The Gold Standards Framework Centre in End of Life Care.

Goodwin, N., Curry, N., Naylor, C., Ross, S., & Duldig, W. (2010). *Managing people with long-term conditions*. London: The King's Fund.

Grohol, J. (2016). What is exposure therapy? *Psych Central*. https://psychcentral.com/lib/what-is-exposure-therapy/ (Accessed 31 May 2017).

HM Chief Inspector of Prisons for England and Wales (2016). *Annual report 2015–16*. HM Chief Inspector of Prisons.

Jackson, K. (2014). Grieving chronic illness and injury: Infinite losses. *Social Work Today* 14: 18. www.socialworktoday.com/archive/070714p18.shtml (Accessed 16 April 2017).

Murray, S.A., Kendall, M., Mitchell, G., Moine, S., Ambl s-Novellas, J., & Boyd, K. (2017). Palliative care from diagnosis to death. *BMJ* 356: j878.

National and End of Life Care Partnership (2015). *Ambitions for palliative and end of life care: A national framework for local action 2015–2020*. National and End of Life Care Partnership.

National Institute for Health and Care Excellence (2011). *Quality standard 13 end of life care for adults*. www.nice.org.uk/guidance/qs13 Last updated March 2017. (Accessed 12 March 2017).

National Institute for Health and Care Excellence (2016a). *Physical health of people in prison NICE guideline NG57*. www.nice.org.uk/guidance/ng57 (Accessed 11 March 2017).

National Institute for Health and Care Excellence (2016b). *Managing the physical health of people in prisons and young offender institutions*. http://pathways.nice.org.uk/pathways/health-of-people-in-the-criminal-justice-system (Accessed November 2016).

Naylor, C., Parsonage, M., McDaid, D., Knapp, M., Fossey, M., & Galea, A. (2012). *Long-term conditions and mental health: The cost of co-morbidities*. London: The King's Fund.

NHS England (2015a). *Health and justice commissioning intentions 2015/16*. Publications Gateway number: 02104.

NHS England (2015b). *Pain management formulary for prisons: Implementation guide. Version number: 1*. Gateway Number: 04243. Health and Justice Clinical Reference Group NHS England.

NHS National End of Life Care Programme (2014). *Capacity, care planning and advance care planning in life limiting illness a guide for health and social care staff*. NHS Improving Quality. Available in the online link https://www.england.nhs.uk/improvement-hub/publication/capacity-care-planning-and-advance-care-planning-in-life-limiting-illness-a-guide-for-health-and-social-care-staff/

NHS Scotland (2016). *Supportive and palliative care indicators tool*. www.spict.org.uk/ (Accessed 12 March 2017).

Nolte, E., & McKee, M. (2008). *Caring for people with chronic conditions: A health system perspective*. England: Open University Press.

Norman, A., & Parrish, A. (2002). *Prison nursing.* Oxford: Blackwell Science.

Perry, J., Bennett, C., & Lapworth, T. (2010a). Nursing in prisons: Developing the specialty of offender health care. *Nursing Standard* 24: 35–40.

The Prison Ombudsman for Northern Ireland (2015). *Investigation report into the circumstance surrounding the death of Mr H aged 34 on 21st September 2014 following his release from Maghaberry Prison on 30th September 2014.* Prison Ombudsman Report of Northern Ireland.

Prisons and Probation Ombudsman for England and Wales (2013). *Learning from PPO investigations.* Independent Investigations. End of life care.

Prisons and Probation Ombudsman for England and Wales (2014a). *Investigation into the death of a woman in April 2014 while in the custody of HMP Styal.* Prisons and Probation Ombudsman Report.

Prisons and Probation Ombudsman for England and Wales (2014b). *Investigation into the death of a man at HMP Preston in March 2014.* Prisons and Probation Ombudsman Report.

Prisons Reform Trust (2017). *Prisons can seriously damage your mental health.* London: Prison Reform Trust.

Public Health England (2013). *Managing persistent pain in secure settings.* PHE publications gateway number: 2013106.

Royal College of Nursing (2017). *Supporting nursing staff caring for patients from places of detention.* London: Royal College of Nursing.

Shih, M., & Simon, P.A. (2008). Health-related quality of life among adults with serious psychological distress and chronic medical conditions. *Quality of Life Research* 17: 521–528.

Stevenson, R.G., & McCutchen, R. (2006). When meaning has lost its way: Life and loss "behind bars". *Illness, Crisis & Loss* 14: 103–119.

Thompson, A.R. (2011). Adaptation in long-term conditions: The role of stigma particularly in conditions that affect appearance. IN: Randall, S. & Ford, H. (Eds.), *Long-term conditions a guide for nurses and healthcare professionals.* Chichester, West Sussex: Wiley-Blackwell.

UN General Assembly. (1991). *Basic principles for the treatment of prisoners: Resolution/ adopted by the general assembly.* 28 March. A/RES/45/111. www.refworld.org/docid/ 48abd5740.html (Accessed 11 March 2017).

Whitehead, L.C., Unahi, K., Burrell, B., & Crowe, M.T. (2016). The experience of fatigue across long-term conditions: A qualitative meta-synthesis. *Journal of Pain and Symptom Management* 52: 131–143.

Williamson, M. (2007). Primary care for offenders: What are the issues and what is to be done? *Quality in Primary Care* 15: 301–305.

Wong, P. T. P. (2015). Meaning therapy: Assessments and interventions. *Existential Analysis* 26: 154–167.

World Health Organisation (2017). *Prisons.* www.who.int/topics/prisons/en/ (Accessed 4 March 2017).

Statutes

The Health and Social Care Act 2012.

14 The impact of loss on mental health

Implications for practice in criminal justice settings

Alexis Warrilow

Introduction

Many people within the criminal justice system have experienced loss in many forms and bereavement at some point in their lives. Individuals' ability to cope with such life experiences often relies on their ability to be resilient. Mental health practitioners in prisons may support individuals suffering from loss and bereavement and attempt to treat the symptoms; however, they are often not equipped to provide interventions for the root cause. This chapter will explore the impact of loss and bereavement on mental health and allow practitioners working in a criminal justice setting to:

*   develop an awareness of (and monitor for) the potential adverse effects on an individual's mental health;
*   identify risk factors that may make an individual vulnerable to loss- or bereavement-related complications; and
*   make informed decisions when exploring available treatment pathways.

Prevalence of mental health problems in prisons

Before the impact of loss and bereavement on mental health is explored in this chapter, it is important to understand the prevalence of mental health problems in the context of criminal justice settings. In a 1997 survey of psychiatric morbidity amongst prisoners, Singleton *et al.* (1998) found that more than 90 per cent of the prison population in England and Wales had one or more diagnosable mental health problems. Male prisoners were identified as fourteen times more likely to have two or more diagnosable problems than men in general, and women prisoners, despite only representing 5 per cent of the prison population, were found to experience higher rates of mental health problems (Singleton *et al.*, 1998). For young offenders, the prevalence was higher, at 95 per cent of the population presenting with a diagnosable mental illness and 80 per cent having more than one (Lader *et al.*, 2000). In comparison with the general population, the prevalence of mental health and substance misuse problems are considerably higher amongst the prison population (Singleton *et al.*, 1998, 2001). (See Table 14.1.)

Table 14.1 Prevalence of mental health problems amongst prisoners compared to the general population

Mental health problem	Prison population 1997	General population 2000
Personality disorder	66%	5.3%
Common mental health disorder (depression/anxiety)	45%	13.8%
Drug dependency	45%	5.2%
Alcohol dependency	30%	11.5%
Psychosis/delusional disorder	8%	0.5%
	Singleton *et al.* (1998)	Singleton *et al.* (2001)

Adapted from Bradley (2009).

More recently, in a survey with newly sentenced prisoners in England and Wales, Stewart (2008) found that 36 per cent reported significant symptoms of depression and anxiety, 61 per cent were identified as likely to have a personality disorder and 10 per cent psychosis.

However, caution should be taken when interpreting Stewart's (2008) findings, as they are not representative of the total prison population and did not include any clinical diagnosis data (Prison & Probation Ombudsman, PPO, 2016b). It also evident that some of the representative data is now nearly twenty years old; however, it is still widely referenced in current literature concerning prison mental health today. It is recognised that there is a need for a more up-to-date comprehensive study given the rise in the prison population over the last two decades (MOJ, 2007, 2015). Lord Bradley (2009, p. 1), in his powerful review of mental health care in the criminal justice system, was concerned with the ever-growing prison population, and concluded that

> while public protection remains the priority, there is a growing consensus that prison may not always be the right environment for those with severe mental illness. Custody can exacerbate mental ill health, heighten vulnerability and increase the risk of self-harm and suicide.

Bereavement and challenges to mental health in the criminal justice system

It is recognised that bereavement can be a highly stressful life event that may require significant social readjustment (Holmes & Rahe, 1967). Studies have shown bereavement to be associated with increased mortality and adverse mental and physical health outcomes (Stroebe *et al.*, 2007; Zisook *et al.*, 2014). In an extensive review of pertinent bereavement literature, Zisook *et al.* (2014) found that bereavement is associated with an increased risk of depression; anxiety disorders, such as post-traumatic stress disorder (PTSD) and generalised anxiety disorder (GAD); and a complicated grief reaction. Research supports the notion, however, that most bereaved people can recover from their losses emotionally and physically over time due to resilience (Boerner *et al.*, 2005; Bonanno, 2004; McCrae & Costa, 1993). Resilience reflects an individual's ability to maintain a stable equilibrium of psychological and physical functioning when faced with adverse life events. It can be thought of in terms of protective factors that promote the development of coping mechanisms needed for healthy functioning and positive life outcomes (Bonanno, 2004). Resilience can be conceptualised as the opposite of vulnerability and described in terms of protective factors such as coping resources, personality traits and interpersonal skills that can reduce the damaging effects of life stressors (Ingram & Price, 2001). Vulnerability in this context refers to a range of predispositional biopsychosocial factors that can make a person susceptible to emotional pain and increase the likelihood of mental illness when an individual is faced with adversity (Ingram & Luxton, 2005). Resilience and vulnerability therefore represent opposite ends of a stress-vulnerability continuum whereby little life stress is needed to trigger mental illness at the vulnerability end, and a great amount of stress is needed before psychopathology develops at the resilient end (Ingram & Luxton, 2005). Stroebe *et al.* (2006, 2007) have identified several vulnerability factors that can impact upon an individual's ability to cope with a bereavement. (See Table 14.2.)

Trauma, stress and anxiety

When exploring resilience, stress and trauma within the context the criminal justice system, evidence suggests that individuals within it are more likely to have experienced many traumatic events throughout their lives. In a qualitative review with ninety-eight UK prisoners, Durcan (2008), found the prison population to be composed of individuals who come from disadvantaged backgrounds and already have a low resilience to stress. He discovered that the majority of prisoners came from deprived areas, had experienced disrupted childhoods related to parental

Table 14.2 Bereavement outcome vulnerability factors

Biological	Psychological	Social
Gender	Mental health problems	Social support/isolation
Age	Intellectual ability	Family dynamics
Physical health problems	Religious beliefs/other belief systems	Religious practices
	Substance abuse	Cultural setting/resources
	Personality style	Economic/material resources (e.g. money, services)
	Emotion regulation	Preceding multiple/childhood losses
	Cognitive/behavioural processes	
	Attachment style	

Adapted from Stroebe *et al.* (2006, 2007).

separation, had disrupted schooling, had spent time in local authority care and had a personal or family history of substance misuse (Durcan, 2008). Many prisoners reported experiencing traumatic events in their lives, including physical/sexual abuse, torture and rape in both childhood and adulthood and deaths of significant others, such as parents, siblings and grandparents, often at critical stages during their development (Durcan, 2008). He found that very few interviewees reported receiving counselling/support for the losses or trauma despite these experiences having an impact on their lives, and some described symptoms of post-traumatic stress such as emotional numbness, anxiety, vivid/intrusive thoughts about the past and difficulties in relationships (Durcan, 2008). Maschi *et al.* (2015), in a study involving imprisoned older adults, found that 70 per cent of the sample reported experiencing some type of traumatic or stressful life event, such as being involved in a serious accident, physical/emotional/sexual abuse, neglect and exposure to violence. Participants also reported experiences of grief, loss and separation, as 60 per cent had experienced the unexpected death of someone close to them, and 70 per cent not unexpectedly, 28 per cent reported forced separation from a child and 53 per cent had experienced separation/divorce. All of these were associated with high levels of distress experienced by the individual at the time, with between 60 and 70 per cent reporting that they had been moderately/extremely affected by these events in the past year (Maschi *et al.*, 2015).

When considering the implications for practice within the criminal justice system, there is the possibility that the symptoms of loss and bereavement within this population could be intertwined with symptoms of other trauma, loss or stress reactions. The symptoms of anxiety or PTSD may be easily identified during mental health assessment; however, determining the most effective treatment could prove difficult if the cause of the stress or trauma is related to many traumatic life events including bereavement. With this in mind, bereavement counselling alone, for example, may not be the most effective intervention due to the complexity an individual's symptoms and presentation. Evidence-based treatment approaches for anxiety/PTSD, as recommended by NICE (2005, 2011), would need to be explored in the first instance alongside any bereavement interventions that may be available.

Grief and depression

The link between bereavement and depression has long been established, as research conducted on spousal bereavement suggests that the death of a loved one can expose the bereaved individual to a higher risk of developing depressive symptoms or a major depressive disorder (Jacobs *et al.*, 1989; Zisook *et al.*, 1994; Stroebe & Stroebe, 1993). However, the point at which a normal bereavement reaction could manifest into a major depressive disorder, warranting a clinical diagnosis, has been much debated over the years. Initially the *Diagnostic and Statistical Manual* (DSM) 4 of mental health disorders (APA, 1994) cautioned clinicians against diagnosing major depression during the first two months following a bereavement. It advised psychiatrists to only consider a diagnosis of major depression if the symptoms persisted after this period and were characterised by signs of clinical depression, such as suicidal ideation and marked psychomotor retardation (APA, 1994). However, the DSM 5 (APA, 2013) has since removed the two-month watchful-waiting period from the diagnostic criteria and a diagnosis of major depressive disorder can now be made after two weeks of the bereaved individual experiencing depressive symptoms. This change has occurred as a result of recent studies that discovered that there is no difference between depression as a result of other losses/life stressors and bereavement-related depression (Zisook & Kendler, 2007; Kendler *et al.*, 2008; Flaskerud, 2011).

The removal of the bereavement exclusion has generated much discussion about what is considered a socially appropriate length of time for a bereaved individual to grieve (Bandini, 2015). Many are concerned that the recent changes in the DSM 5 are promoting a 'medicalisation of grief' (Wakefield *et al.*, 2007; Frances, 2010; Wakefield & First, 2012). Fears are that this could lead to the overdiagnosis and overtreatment of depression, which could create opportunities for an expanded market for pharmaceutical companies and result in a loss of traditional and cultural methods being used to cope with loss (Bandini, 2015). The DSM 5 (APA, 2013) does however identify how grief can be distinguished from a major depressive episode and requests that clinicians exercise their clinical judgement to evaluate the individual's history and cultural norms in the context of loss. (See Table 14.3.) With this in mind, there should be no difference in the diagnosis and treatment of depression as a result of bereavement compared to other life stressors. When considering the implications for practitioners within the criminal justice system, this suggests that the NICE clinical guidance for depression (NICE, 2009) would need to be referred for the management and treatment of depression irrespective of the cause.

Table 14.3 Differences between a major depressive episode and grief (DSM 5)

Depression	Grief
Persistent depressed mood (not tied to specific thoughts/preoccupations) with an inability to anticipate pleasure/ happiness	Dysphoria likely to decrease in intensity over time (days to weeks) occurring in waves (pangs) associated with thoughts/ reminders of the deceased
Pervasive unhappiness and misery	Painful emotions possibly accompanied by positive emotions and humour
Self-critical, pessimistic thoughts and ruminations	Preoccupation with memories and thoughts of the deceased
Feelings of worthlessness and self-loathing	Self-esteem usually preserved; derogatory thoughts associated with perceived failings in relation to the deceased
Thoughts of suicide linked to feelings of worthlessness, unworthiness of life and an inability to cope with the pain of depression	Thoughts of death and dying focused on the deceased and about joining the deceased

Adapted from the DSM 5 (APA, 2013).

Identifying complicated grief

Bandini (2015) highlights that there has also been much debate about whether complicated grief (CG) should have been included in the DSM 5 as a medical diagnosis. Zisook *et al.* (2014) state that CG is a category of intense, prolonged chronic grief where the bereaved individual feels stuck in the mourning process and does not recover in time. Like normal bereavement, some symptoms of CG are similar to those seen in depression and anxiety; however, CG does have a unique pattern of symptoms (Zisook *et al.*, 2014). These include intense longing and yearning and recurrent intrusive thoughts of the deceased, inability to accept death, excessive guilt and anger and avoidance of reminders of the deceased (Zisook *et al.*, 2014). The DSM 5 (APA, 2013) has identified CG as persistent complex bereavement disorder, and despite not including it in the main criteria, it has been highlighted as a condition for further study with proposed criteria. Research shows that specific vulnerability factors for developing CG include history of or current diagnosis of mood/anxiety disorders, insecure attachments developed in childhood, lack of social support and multiple losses and concurrent life stressors (Shear & Mulhare, 2008; Shear & Shair, 2005). It is estimated that only 7 per cent of bereaved individuals will suffer from CG (Shear & Shair, 2005); however, there is a possibility that the risk of developing CG could be higher for those in the criminal justice system due to being predisposed to many of the vulnerability factors highlighted in Table 14.2 and the ongoing exposure to life stressors in a prison environment. Zisook *et al.* (2014) also highlights that CG often co-occurs with the aforementioned mental health conditions and is associated with suicidal attempts and ideation. Practitioners within the criminal justice system therefore need to have an awareness of the differences between normal grief, CG and mental health conditions such as depression and PTSD to ensure that appropriate evidence-based interventions are offered and accurate diagnosis is made.

Increased risk of suicide

Stroebe *et al.* (2007) also highlight several longitudinal studies that indicate an increased risk of suicide for bereaved individuals. Some studies found that bereaved parents of children who had died were at a raised suicide risk (Li *et al.*, 2003; Qin & Mortensen, 2003). Agerbo (2005) found that the risk of suicide increased for bereaved widowers and parents if the cause of death was suicide, and Erlangsen *et al.* (2004) found an increased risk of suicide during the first year of bereavement amongst men over the age of 50. This has clear implications for the criminal justice population when considering the impact of loss and bereavement on mental health, as the risk of suicide and self-harm is much higher for those in custody, with 114 per 100,000 taking their own lives in prison compared to 8.3 per 100,000 for the general population (Ministry Of Justice, MOJ, 2008). More recently the Prison and Probation Ombudsman (PPO, 2016a) reported a shocking 34 per cent rise in self-inflicted deaths for the period of 2015–2016, with a record 114 prisoners taking their own lives in 2016 alone (INQUEST, 2017). Self-harm also reached a record high of 41,103 incidents in the twelve months prior to June 2017, which is an increase of

12 per cent from the previous year (MOJ, 2017). The risk of suicide is deemed to be heightened during the first seven days of entering prison (Shaw *et al.*, 2004) and in the days following release from prison (Pratt *et al.*, 2006). Most of those who take their lives are found to have a history of mental illness (Pratt *et al.*, 2006), with 70% per cent being identified as having mental health needs between 2012 and 2014 (PPO, 2016b). The Prison Service Instruction Number 64 (National Offender Management Service, 2011) provides guidance for all staff on the management of those who are at risk of suicide/self-harm within custody and for those who are due for release. Alongside other suicide risk factors, it also clearly highlights bereavement of a family member or close friends (including exposure to suicide) as a trigger that may increase the risk of suicide, self-harm and violence. Similarly, a recent PPO report (2014) that reviewed the risk factors in self-inflicted deaths in prisons found bereavement to be a possible trigger for suicide in custody. All staff members should adhere to the Assessment, Care in Custody and Teamwork (ACCT) process as advocated by the National Offender Management Service (NOMS), which is a prisoner-centred, flexible care-planning system designed to the reduce risk of suicide and self-harm (National Offender Management Service, 2011). It is evident that practitioners working within the criminal justice system clearly need to have an awareness of the heightened risk of suicide for those within their care, particularly in relation to loss and bereavement. If symptoms of mental health conditions, in particular depression, have also been identified during assessment, the practitioner should always consider the possibility of this heightened risk of suicide and complete the necessary risk-screening tools available to adequately identify the risk in order to manage this appropriately within this setting.

Conclusion

This chapter has explored the impact of loss and bereavement on mental health and outlined the importance of resilience when coping with loss. It has been identified that individuals within the criminal justice system are at higher risk of having experienced traumatic life events and developing mental health problems and are at an increased risk of suicide when compared to the general population. This chapter should inform the thinking of practitioners in criminal justice settings, who may have an awareness of the potential adverse effects that loss and bereavement can have on an individual's mental health and can apply this to the criminal justice setting. Practitioners will also be able to identify the many risk factors that may make an individual vulnerable to loss- or bereavement-related complications, such as diagnosable mental health problems or CG. This will enable practitioners to make informed decisions when exploring available interventions in conjunction with local and national clinical guidelines to provide equivalent care.

References

Agerbo, E. (2005). Midlife suicide risk, partner's psychiatric illness, spouse and child bereavement by suicide or other modes of death: A gender specific study. *Journal of Epidemiology and Community Health.* 59: 407–412.

American Psychiatric Association (1994). *Diagnostic and statistical manual of mental disorders* (4th ed.). Washington, DC: American Psychiatric Association.

American Psychiatric Association (2013). *Diagnostic and statistical manual of mental disorders* (5th ed.). Washington, DC: American Psychiatric Association.

Bandini, J. (2015). The medicalization of bereavement: (Ab)normal grief in the DSM-5. *Death Studies*. 39: 347–352.

Boerner, K., Wortman, C. B., & Bonanno, G. A. (2005). Resilient or at risk? A 4-year study of older adults who initially showed high or low distress following conjugal loss. *Journal of Gerontology: Psychological Sciences*. 60: P67–P73.

Bonanno, G. A. (2004). Loss, trauma, and human resilience: Have we underestimated the human capacity to thrive after extremely aversive events? *American Psychologist*. 59: 20–28.

Bradley, K. (2009). *The Bradley report*. London: Department of Health.

Durcan, G. (2008). *From the inside: Experiences of prison mental health care*. London: Sainsbury Centre for Mental Health.

Erlangsen, A., Jeune, B., Bille-Brahe, U. & Vaupel, J. W. (2004). Loss of partner and suicide risks among oldest old: A population-based register study. *Age Ageing*. 33: 378–383.

Flaskerud, J. (2011). Grief and depression: Are they different? *Issues in Mental Health Nursing*. 32: 338–340.

Frances, A. (2010). Opening Pandora's box: The 19 worst suggestions for DSM-5. *Psychiatric Times*. 27: 1–10.

Holmes, T. H. & Rahe, R. H. (1967). The social readjustment rating scale. *Journal of Psychosomatic Research*. 11: 213–218.

Ingram, R. E. & Luxton, D. D. (2005). Vulnerability-stress models. IN: B.L. Hankin & J. R. Z. Abela (Eds.), *Development of psychopathology: A vulnerability stress perspective*. Thousand Oaks, CA: Sage Publications Inc.

Ingram, R. E. & Price, J. M. (2001). *Vulnerability to psychopathology: Risk across the lifespan*. New York: Guilford Press.

INQUEST (2017). *Working for Truth Justice and Accountability: Statistics: Deaths in Prison*. http://inquest.org.uk/statistics/deaths-in-prison (Accessed 20 March 2017).

Jacobs, S., Hansen, F., Berkman, L., Kasl, S., & Ostfeld, A. (1989). Depression of bereavement. *Comprehensive Psychiatry*. 30: 218–224.

Kendler, K. S., Myers, J., & Zisook, S. (2008). Does bereavement-related major depression differ from major depression associated with other stressful life events? *American Journal of Psychiatry*. 165: 1449–1455.

Lader, D., Singleton, N. & Meltzer, H. (2000). *Psychiatric morbidity amongst young offenders in England and Wales*. London: Office for National Statistics.

Li, J., Precht, D. H., Mortensen, P. B. & Olsen, J. (2003). Mortality in parents after death of a child in Denmark: A nationwide follow-up study. *Lancet*. 361: 363–367.

Maschi, T., Viola, D., Morgen, K. & Lindsay, K. (2015). Trauma, stress, grief, loss and separation among older adults in prison. *Journal of Crime and Justice*. 38: 113–136.

McCrae, R. R. & Costa, P. T. (1993). Psychological resilience among widowed men and women: A 10-year follow-up of a national sample. *Journal of Social Issues*. 44: 129–142.

Ministry of Justice (2007). *Lord Carter's review of prisons: Securing the future: Proposals for the efficient and sustainable use of custody in England and Wales*. London: The Stationery Office.

Ministry of Justice (2008). *Deaths in prison custody 2007*. London: MOJ.

Ministry of Justice (2015). *Prison population projections 2015–2021 England and Wales*. London: MOJ.

Ministry of Justice (2017). *Safety in custody statistics, England and Wales: Deaths in prison custody to September 2017, assaults and self-harm to June 2017*. London: MOJ. www.gov.uk/government/statistics/safety-in-custody-quarterly-update-to-march-2017 (Accessed 9 November 2017).

National Institute for Clinical Excellence (2005). *Post-traumatic stress disorder: The management of PTSD in adults and children in primary and secondary care.* CG26. NICE: London. www.nice.org.uk/guidance/cg26

National Institute for Clinical Excellence (2009). *Depression in adults: Recognition and management.* CG90. NICE: London. www.nice.org.uk/guidance/cg90

National Institute for Clinical Excellence (2011). *Generalised anxiety disorder and panic disorder (with or without agoraphobia) in adults: Management in primary, secondary and community care.* CG113. NICE: London. www.nice.org.uk/guidance/cg113

National Offender Management Service (2011). *Management of prisoners at risk of harm to self, to others and from others (Safer Custody)*. PSI/64. London: MOJ.

Pratt, D., Piper, M., Appleby, L., Webb, R. & Shaw, J. (2006). Suicide in recently released prisoners: A population-based cohort study. *The Lancet.* 368: 119–123.

Prison and Probation Ombudsman (2014). *Learning from PPO investigations: Self-inflicted deaths of prisoners on ACCT.* London: PPO.

Prison and Probation Ombudsman (2016a). *Independent investigations: Annual report 2015–2016.* London: PPO.

Prison and Probation Ombudsman (2016b). *Learning from PPO investigations: Prisoner mental health.* London: PPO.

Qin, P. & Mortensen, P. B. (2003). The impact of parental status on the risk of completed suicide. *Archives of General Psychiatry.* 60: 797–802.

Shaw, J., Baker, D., Hunt, I. M., Moloney, A. & Appleby, L. (2004). Suicide by prisoners: National clinical survey. *British Journal of Psychiatry*, 184: 263–267.

Shear, K. & Mulhare, E. (2008). Complicated grief. *Psychiatric Annals.* 38: 662.

Shear, K. & Shair, H. (2005). Attachment, loss, and complicated grief. *Developmental Psychobiology.* 47: 253–267.

Singleton, N., Bumpstead, R., O'Brien, M., Lee, A. & Meltzer, H. (2001). *Psychiatric morbidity among adults living in private households, 2000.* London: HMSO.

Singleton, N., Meltzer, H., Gatward, R., Coid, J. & Deasy, D. (1998). *Psychiatric morbidity among prisoners.* London: The Stationery Office.

Stewart, D. (2008). *The problems and needs of newly sentenced prisoners: Results from a national survey.* London: MOJ.

Stroebe, M., Folkman, S., Hansson, R. O. & Schut, H. (2006). The prediction of bereavement outcome: Development of an integrative risk factor framework. *Social Science Medicine.* 63: 2446–2451.

Stroebe, M. S., Schut, H. & Stroebe, W. (2007). Health outcomes of bereavement. *Lancet.* 370: 1960–1973.

Stroebe, M. S., & Stroebe, W. (1993). The mortality of bereavement: A review. IN: M. S. Stroebe, W. Stroebe, & R. O. Hansson (Eds.), *Handbook of bereavement: Theory, research, and interventions.* New York: Cambridge University Press.

Wakefield, J. C., & First, M. B. (2012). Validity of the bereavement exclusion to major depression: Does the empirical evidence support the proposal to eliminate the exclusion in DSM-5? *World Psychiatry.* 11: 3–10.

Wakefield, J. C., Schmitz, M. F., First, M. B., & Horwitz, A. V. (2007). Extending the bereavement exclusion for major depression to other losses: Evidence from the national comorbidity survey. *Archives of General Psychiatry.* 64: 433–440.

Zisook, S., Iglewicz, A., Avanzino, J., Maglione, D., Glorioso, S., Zetumer, K., Seay, I., Vahia, I., Young, B., Lebowitz, R., Pies, C., Reynolds, N., Simon, M., & Shear, K. (2014). Bereavement: Course, consequences, and care. *Curr Psychiatry Rep.* 16: 482.

Zisook, S. & Kendler, K. S. (2007). Is bereavement-related depression different than non-bereavement-related depression? *Psychological Medicine.* 37: 779–794.

Zisook, S., Shuchter, S. R., Sledge, P. A., Paulus, M. & Judd, L. L. (1994). The spectrum of depressive phenomena after spousal bereavement. *Journal of Clinical Psychiatry.* 55: 29–36.

15 Mourning in custody
Dealing with sudden death

Jane Jervis

Introduction

The aim of this chapter is to consider the nature, context and impact of sudden death within the criminal justice system. Witnessing or being bereaved by a sudden death is a particularly traumatic experience for any member of society, but those experiencing it within the confines of the criminal justice system have additional complexities for which there is very little research or evidence base. Case studies have been sensitively introduced to help the reader to reflect upon the complexities involved, the risk of disenfranchised grief and the support required when offenders are affected by a sudden death.

Defining the nature of sudden death

Bereavement is one of the most distressing emotional experiences encountered and it is widely recognised that one of the most traumatic crisis events that can be experienced is bereavement due to a sudden death (Wright, 1996). Sudden deaths are unexpected and unanticipated and so give families and friends no time to prepare for the loss.

Natural sudden deaths usually occur due to an acute disease, such as a heart attack. They may be the result of known illnesses, such as epilepsy and asthma, but where death at that time was unexpected, or the result of undiagnosed conditions, such as cardiac dysfunction leading to sudden cardiac death in the young, the cause of a sudden death may remain unexplained, which can be a feature of sudden infant death syndrome. Unnatural causes of sudden death are associated with accidents or acts of violence. Suicides, murder, road traffic collisions, combat and acts of terrorism fall into this category. Although many sudden deaths, whether due to natural or unnatural causes, are not the result of an act of violence, the manner of the death could still feel violent or traumatic to the surviving friends and family. Some may have been involved in or witnessed the events. They may have witnessed or started resuscitation attempts and many people are shocked by the brutality of these interventions. Relatives or friends may have found the body of the deceased, such as in cases of suicide and deaths through substance misuse. The nature of all sudden deaths (occurring without warning, with no time to prepare for the loss and in some cases due to a perceived prevent-able cause) often leaves a legacy of unanswered questions and uncertainty for the bereaved.

Breaking news of a sudden death

The irreversibility, perpetuity and negative impact of a death make this news one the most difficult to hear and accept. The way that the circumstances of the death are communicated is crucial and when performed badly can affect the person adversely for years to come (Fallowfield & Jenkins, 1994). Sensitive commu-nication is crucial with great importance placed upon training and guidelines for delivering bad news related to sudden death. Healthcare staff and the police receive extensive (although variable) training around this complex arena of care. However, competing priorities determine to what extent training is delivered and guidelines are followed. What is known is that the words and actions of emer-gency department staff and police officers have a huge impact on the bereavement process following a sudden death, with families often remembering what was said for the rest of their lives (Wright, 2015).

Best practice for breaking bad news about a sudden death involves several cru-cial considerations. The professionals involved must be prepared, the news given in person, in good time, in clear language and in an appropriate environment. Telephone notification is avoided where possible, as it can cause extreme distress to both the relative receiving the news and to the caller (Wright, 1996). Where possible, two people should deliver the bad news. Within the emergency depart-ment, one should be the professional who greeted the family on arrival and liaised with them during interventions such as resuscitation. For the police, this may be two police officers although, in some circumstances, one police officer may be accompanied by another professional, such as a doctor or traumatic bereavement support worker. Of extreme importance is that the person breaking the bad news must be skilled in delivering such news, be able to provide comfort and be able to answer any questions the family may have. It is well recognised that in cases of sudden bereavement, families highly value honest and direct information about the sequence of events leading to the death (Wright, 1996: 23), needing not only to reconstruct the events leading to the death but also to understand the patho-physiological processes involved (Worden, 2001; Merlevede *et al.*, 2004) and any investigative processes with relevant timescales (Wright, 2015).

The shock of receiving news of a sudden death means that families often do not ask all the questions they ultimately need to, and so questions may arise over time as families try to understand and reconstruct the events surrounding the death (Merlevede *et al.*, 2004). Following the killings in Norway in 2011, Dyregrov, Dyregrov and Kristensen (2016) found that many of the parents of the deceased chose to visit the location of the death and listen to difficult recol-lections in court. The reconstruction and need to understand events can be pro-tracted in some circumstances due to the need for formal identification, criminal or health and safety investigations and court proceedings. Incidents such as the

Hillsborough disaster and Grenfell Tower fire have provided an insight into the torment of families and friends as they try to make sense of a sudden death whilst dealing with a protracted wait for formal information that provides answers to their questions.

News of a sudden death should be delivered in a timely manner. This can be difficult, as the hospital or police try to identify the deceased and the family, but timing is a significant issue with delays being hugely stressful for bereaved families (Wright, 2015). Modern communication has intensified this problem principally relating to traumatic deaths. News and photographs of events appear on both social media and mainstream media channels as they unfold. This has increased the probability of deceased individuals being identified by the media before formal notification can be made to families by the authorities. The long-term effects on bereaved relatives and friends of this mode of uncontrolled notification are yet to be fully realised.

Consideration is given to the environment where news of a sudden death is given. Relatives often describe the time waiting in the relative's room as frightening and isolating (Wright, 1996: 16). In emergency departments, relative's rooms should be comfortable, private and close to the resuscitation area. This avoids bereaved families having to walk through busy departments in view of the public. For the police, the bereaved person's home may be most appropriate. If this is not possible, locating a private space is crucial, and if in a police facility significance is given to not leaving bereaved people alone in rooms which could cause feelings of isolation (College of Policing, 2014).

It is a common ritual after sudden death to view the body of the deceased and this is considered important in confronting the reality of the loss, dispelling any fantasies about how the deceased will look, helping with the grieving process, making a final goodbye and confirming that the person is truly dead (Wright, 1996; Merlevede *et al.*, 2004; Wright, 2015). Viewing the body is especially valuable to those relatives not present at the time of death, and the viewing taking place where the death occurred seems to afford closeness for the relatives to the event (Wright, 1996). Not seeing the deceased has been associated with a deep sense of regret (Wright, 2015) and feelings that there was no opportunity to confirm the death had really happened (Johnsen & Dyregrov, 2016). Being prevented from touching the body of the deceased due to protocols such as the preservation of forensic evidence is distressing for relatives and has a long-lasting impact as they are not able to take leave of the deceased in the way that they wish (Victim Support, 2006). Like the delivery of the news itself, the opportunity to view the body of the deceased should be offered in a timely manner and with careful preparation of the family and the deceased. Families may need time to regain composure prior to making this visit, whereas others may need to see the deceased as soon as possible. Taking leave of the deceased is an intensely emotional event, and for some families being able to do this whilst the deceased body was still warm holds great meaning and bodies which were not laid out cause painful memories (Merlevede *et al.*, 2004). Care must be taken to observe where possible any religious or cultural death rituals, such prayers and washing the body.

Reactions to sudden death

When any death occurs, there are a number of factors which have been identified which affect how the relatives of the deceased will cope with the death.
These include the manner of the death; the age of the deceased; whether the
death involved violence, was unexpected or avoidable; and if it was made public (Worden, 2001; Machin, 2009). Grief reactions and coping methods following traumatic deaths are variable with individuals and families finding their own
approaches and pace (Dyregrov, Dyregrov & Kristensen, 2016). Sudden and violent deaths are often followed by a difficult bereavement pathway (Kristensen,
Weisæth & Trond, 2012) and involve additional grief responses which can be both
intense and frightening, such as overwhelming shock, denial, avoidance, anxiety,
panic attacks, irrational thoughts and actions, extended periods of crying and sob-
bing, yearning to see the deceased again and social withdrawal, survivor's guilt,
self-blame, a sense of the continued presence of the deceased, intrusive images
and nightmares (Dying Matters, 2017).

When violence or blame is involved, additional emotions, such as fear, anger,
vengeance, blame, guilt and confusion, can be distressing to the bereaved. There
may be difficulty separating the loss from the traumatic event which caused the
death or a preoccupation with how the death or events could have been prevented (Johnsen & Dyregrov, 2016). Those bereaved by an act of murder describe
changes in their own personalities and the way in which they view the world, of a
strengthening or deterioration in their relationships and of the significant impact
it has on their ability to function in the world (Englebrecht, Mason & Adams,
2016). Anger and guilt are common reactions to bereavement, but for those experiencing a sudden bereavement this anger may cause additional stress. There may
be anger towards the deceased for dying and leaving the family, for contributing
to the cause of death or for guilt for being unable to protect them from harm
(Englebrecht, Mason & Adams, 2016). Where the death is related to risk-taking
behaviours, such as drug and alcohol use, dangerous sports or criminal activities,
feelings of anger, guilt and stigma may be paramount. In these cases, ensuring
that initial contact by healthcare workers or the police is respectful, empathetic
and non-judgemental is of paramount importance. Research has shown that initial police contact creates a lasting impression on families bereaved by homicide
and sudden death, with the views of the officers the families met first cementing
the foundation for the entire experience (Wright, 2015). In some circumstances,
such as murders and terrorism, there may be media attention where deaths may
be politicised, which can feel intrusive, and the media attention can result in the
funerals no longer feeling private (Johnsen & Dyregrov, 2016). This may also be
evident for those bereaved through suicide or road traffic collisions, where media
attention and publicity may increase feelings of isolation and stigmatisation.

Whilst most suddenly bereaved people will eventually adjust, a significant
number will suffer from mental distress in the aftermath of their loss, including
post-traumatic stress disorder (PTSD), major depressive disorder, prolonged grief
disorder/complicated grief (Kristensen, Weisæth & Trond, 2012) and risk-taking

coping behaviours such as alcohol misuse (Englebrecht, Mason & Adams, 2016). All of these issues remain fundamentally important, so when they are translated across into the criminal justice context, they cause immeasurable complications for the survivor in prison and numerous challenges for those professionals caring for them.

Sudden death in the criminal justice system

When considering the factors associated with sudden death in the complex and intense arena of the criminal justice system, it is clear that there are additional challenges to be addressed. Young offenders experience loss more often than the general public, particularly in relation to parental, traumatic and multiple deaths (Vaswani, 2008, 2014), and those who reported difficulty in coping were more likely to have been bereaved due to sudden or violent deaths or suicide (Finlay & Jones, 2000). Those in custody have the same (if not higher) risks of experiencing sudden bereavement. What is an expected death of a relative to the family at home could be experienced by those in prison as a sudden unexpected death. They may be unaware of the illness or recent deterioration in health. The family may not be in regular contact, may be estranged or may have sought to protect the offender by withholding news of an illness. The distance associated with imprisonment causes a lack of physical contact which during an illness can reduce a person's exposure to the natural deterioration associated with an illness or advancing age. This can result in reducing the anticipation of a death, and so even if the offender knew about a serious illness, the death could still be unexpected and a shock (Ferszt, 2002).

Within the criminal justice system, the mode and environment of the delivery of bad news relating to a death is variable, and the previously identified principles of good practice may not always be adhered to. An offender may be informed of a sudden death by a prison officer or chaplain, who ideally is already known to the offender, in his or her cell or an office. At times the news may be delivered by an officer unknown to the offender or in an open environment such as the admission hall (Masterson, 2014). The news may be given by a member of the family during a telephone call (Potter, 1999), which is a practice avoided whenever possible by healthcare staff and the police. Notification in these circumstances with no private space to take in the news may exacerbate grief reactions in the 'dominant macho culture' of prison where there can be no display of vulnerability or weakness (Vaswani, 2014). Offenders describe how they cannot cry or show emotion as they may be branded a weakling, wimp or psycho (Masterson, 2014). There is no personal space or privacy (Harner *et al.*, 2011) where offenders can remove themselves as they would in the outside world to perhaps go somewhere private to cry or to regain composure. Those in custody have the same needs to establish details of the death and be with their families (Potter, 1999; Masterson, 2014), but it is highly likely that they receive only limited details and they may remain unsure of the cause of death, receiving 'bits and pieces' over the telephone (Ferszt *et al.*, 2009). Whatever the circumstance, it may be difficult for offenders to accept the reality of a death and the situation may not feel real due to their detachment from home, thereby prolonging the grieving process (Vaswani, 2014).

The loss of a friend can lead to a more traumatic grief response than the loss of a non-close relative (Holland & Neimeyer, 2011; Johnsen & Dyregrov, 2016), but this may not be recognised in the criminal justice context. For fellow prisoners who have become close friends over time, maybe in adversity, the impact of that person's death or suicide can be equally as powerful as that of anyone on the outside, incorporating the same reactions of shock, guilt, blame, and self-scrutiny (Snow & McHugh, 2002). The Harris Report (2015) found that the death of someone with whom young adults were living had a profound impact on some of them even after release, particularly when there had been a self-inflicted death. Exposure to suicide-related behaviours and self-harming include those by friends, cellmates, acquaintances and non-acquaintances, with incidents of offenders witnessing incidents, finding the body, calling for help and providing assistance high in prison (Hales *et al.*, 2015). Offenders may recall traumatic events, such as seeing or hearing the deceased wounding themselves, dying or failed resuscitation attempts (Hales *et al.*, 2003). These types of events could have profound effects upon other offenders, including increasing their own suicide or self-harm risk. Witnesses to suicide can suffer post-traumatic symptomology and those with pre-existing psychopathology or exposure to suicides could be predisposed to intensifying their own suicidal ideation (Cerel *et al.*, 2014).

In cases of unnatural sudden death, the offender may have been involved in the accident or may be considered a perpetrator of the events leading to the sudden death of a relative or friend. Additional complexities will exist in these cases which often remain unacknowledged and could lead to disenfranchised grief (Doka, 1999). Whilst in custody they would be isolated from family and friends and cut off from immediate death rituals. Such isolation from family and friends can cause challenges for the survivor, as it is acknowledged that grief can feel intensified when offenders feel completely alone with it (Masterson, 2014; Ferszt, 2002). The denial of involvement in death rituals can be protracted if family and friends blame them for the death. The offender may also feel that they should not be 'entitled to grieve, because they are being punished for breaking society's laws' (Olson & McEwen, 2004) and that any painful feelings associated with the bereavement are well deserved and therefore should remain hidden.

Dolman (1997) introduces the perspective of domestic murder from the viewpoint of the offender, highlighting that in some cases offenders will have killed a member of their family whilst suffering from an acute episode of a mental illness. In some of these cases, knowledge of the death may therefore only be realised once the acute episode is in remission. This type of sudden death situation presents enormous challenges for the offender and increased risks of association with disenfranchised bereavement. For example, it may be difficult for offenders to publicly acknowledge their grief, due to feelings of guilt and shame. The offender's status as bereaved and grieving may not be recognised by society. In addition, they may need to deal with the loss of their mental health which could affect their ability to cope and to come to terms with the death. Such issues are likely to align themselves with disenfranchised grief, where survivors may not be allowed to publicly mourn their loss, or may not be cognitively able to process their grief, because of a mental health issue and because of incarceration. Those that have committed an offence during an acute mental health crisis will likely have missed the usual death rituals, such as the funeral, due to being held in custody, which can cause further delusion states, preventing them from believing that the person they have killed is really dead (Dolman, 1997).

References

Cerel, J., McIntosh, J.L., Neimeyer, R.A., Maple, M. & Marshall, D. (2014). The continuum of "Survivorship": Definitional issues in the aftermath of suicide. *Suicide and Life-Threatening Behavior*, 44 (6): 591–600.

College of Policing (2014). Public protection: Responding to sudden death. College of Policing Ltd.

Doka, K.J. (1999). Disenfranchised Grief. *Bereavement Care*, 18 (3): 37–39.

Dolman, K. (1997). Domestic killing: The perpetrator's need to grieve. *Bereavement Care*, 16 (3): 29–31.

Dying Matters. Supporting someone who has experienced sudden or traumatic loss. www.dyingmatters.org/page/dealing-sudden-or-violent-death (Accessed 1st November 2017).

Dyregrov, K., Dyregrov, A. & Kristensen, P. (2016). In what ways do bereaved parents after terror go on with their lives, and what seems to inhibit or promote adaptation during their grieving process? A qualitative study. *OMEGA Journal of Death and Dying*, 73 (4): 374–399.

Englebrecht, C.M., Mason, D.T. & Adams, P.J. (2016). Responding to homicide: An exploration of the ways in which family members react to and cope with the death of a loved one. *OMEGA Journal of Death and Dying*, 73 (4): 355–373.

Fallowfield, L. & Jenkins, V. (1994). Communicating sad, bad, and difficult news in medicine. *Lancet*, 363: 312–319.

Ferszt, G.G. (2002). Grief experiences of women in prison following the death of a loved one. *Illness, Crisis and Loss*, 10 (3): 242–254.

Ferszt, G.G., Salgado, D., DeFedele, S. & Leveillee, M. (2009). Houses of healing: A group intervention for grieving women in prison. *The Prison Journal*, 89 (1): 46–64.

Finlay, I.G. & Jones, N.K. (2000). Unresolved grief in young offenders in prison. *British Journal of General Practice*, 50: 569–570.

Hales, H., Davison, S., Misch, P. & Taylor, P.J. (2003). Young male prisoners in a young offender institution: Their experience of suicide attempts by others. *Journal of Adolescence*, 26: 667–685.

Hales, H., Edmondson, A., Davison, S., Maughan, B. & Taylor, P.J. (2015). The impact of contact with suicide-related behavior in prison on young offenders. *Crisis*, 36 (1): 21–30.

Harner, H.M., Hentz, P.M. & Evangelista, M.C. (2011), Grief interrupted: The experience of loss among incarcerated women. *Qualitative Health Research*, 21 (4): 454–464.

The Harris Review (2015). Changing Prisons, Saving Lives. Report of the independent review into self-inflicted deaths in custody of 18–24 year olds. http://iapdeathsincustody.independent.gov.uk/harris-review/harris-review-research-2.

Holland, J. & Neimeyer, R. (2011). Separation and traumatic distress in prolonged grief: The role of cause of death and relationship to the deceased. *Journal of Psychopathology and Behavioural Assessment*, 33 (2): 254–263.

Johnsen, I. & Dyregrov, K. (2016). "Only a friend": The bereavement process of young adults after the loss of a close friend in an extreme terror incident: A qualitative approach. *Journal of Death and Dying*, 74 (1): 16–34.

Kristensen, P., Weisæth, L. & Trond, H. (2012). Bereavement and mental health after sudden and violent losses: A review. *Psychiatry*, 75 (1): 76–97.

Machin, L. (2009). *Working with loss and grief: A new model for practitioners*. London: Sage.

Masterson, J. (2014). A confined encounter: The lived experience of bereavement in prison. *Bereavement Care*, 33 (2): 56–62.

Merlevede, E., Spooren, D., Henderick, H., Portzky, G., Buylaert, W., Jannes, C., Calle, P., Van Staey, M., De Rock, C., Smeesters, L., Michem, N. & Heeringen, K. (2004). Perceptions, needs and mourning reactions of bereaved relatives confronted with a sudden unexpected death. *Resuscitation*, 61: 341–348.

Olson, M. & McEwen, M. (2004). Grief counseling groups in a medium security prison. *The Journal for Specialists in Group Work*, 29 (2): 225–236.

Potter, M. (1999). "Inside" Grief: Bereavement in a prison environment. *Bereavement Care*, 18 (2): 22–25.

Snow, L. & McHugh, M. (2002). The aftermath of a death in prison custody. IN G. Towl, L. Snow, & M. McHugh (eds.). *Suicide in prisons*. Oxford: BPS Blackwell.

Vaswani, N. (2008). Persistent offender profile: Focus on bereavement. Criminal Justice Social Work Development Centre for Scotland (Briefing Paper 13).

Vaswani, N. (2014). The ripples of death: Exploring the bereavement experiences and mental health of young men in custody. *The Howard Journal*, 53 (4): 341–359.

Victim Support (2006). *In the aftermath: The support needs of people bereaved by homicide: A research report*. London: Victim Support National Office.

Worden, W.J. (2001). *Grief and grief therapy: A handbook for mental health practitioners*. London: Routledge.

Wright, B. (1996). *Sudden death: A research base for practice*. London: Churchill Livingstone.

Wright, M. (2015). *The experiences of bereaved family members contact with Greater Manchester police during the investigation into homicide and sudden death*. England: Manchester Metropolitan University.

16 Freedom to grieve

A child and parent perspective

Gill Clifford and Kevin Benson

Introduction

When a child dies or is diagnosed with a life-threatening condition the shock waves inevitably reverberate across the whole family and their wider social networks. The unfamiliar territory of the medical world; the necessity for decision making on a level never previously experienced; the confusion, despair, anger and loss of control conspire to tip a family into a tumult of emotions which can quickly overwhelm and threaten even the most steadfast of family units.

The loss, or potential loss, of an individual family member at a time of crisis can place an unbearable burden on the remaining members. The inability to share the emotional journey and the highs and lows inherent in the process of navigating the path through the shock, confusion and practical issues of caring for a child with a life-threatening condition will inevitably impact on an already impossibly difficult situation.

The impact will also be experienced by a missing parent, particularly where the situation is one of incarceration. The inability to act autonomously, to seek support and offer support to family, to attend meetings and to take an active part in the decision-making processes inevitably involved can leave the parent feeling isolated and disconnected. The subsequent impact on the grieving process, emotional well-being and mental health of the missing family member can be substantial.

The bewildering effect on the child when a parent is absent can have a detrimental effect on his or her development (Rodriguez & Margolin, 2015; Flouri *et al.*, 2015). The development of resilience in children is dependent on the love and support of significant relationships in their lives. The negative impact on the ability of a child to manage the pain and stress of living with not only the loss of a parent through incarceration but also a serious medical condition can have physical, emotional and psychological sequelae of a long-lasting nature (Kerker *et al.*, 2015).

This chapter aims to explore and reflect on these issues and to pose questions to challenge the caregivers across the criminal justice system to consider the impact that these situations can have on children and their parents and encourage them to reflect on how they can support individuals experiencing such loss.

The hidden victims

Nearly 6,000 children under the age of 19 died in the United Kingdom in 2014 (ONS, 2016) and death rates vary according to specific age groups and the causes of death within those age groups. A child's likelihood to survive and flourish can be linked to wider societal influences, for example poverty and social inequalities and their impact on health and well-being (Wolfe *et al.*, 2014).

Official statistics (gov.uk, December 2016) cite a prison population of over 85,000, and it is estimated that there are around 200,000 children in England and Wales who have a parent in prison. This group, however, remains largely unrecognised as no official record is made when a parent is arrested or sentenced to prison (Barnardos, 2014). In contrast, the number of children in local authority care, for example, is officially known to be 70,440, as of 31 March 2016, nearly three times lower than the estimated number of children who have lost a parent to imprisonment (Department for Education, 2016). The process of taking a child into care involves careful consideration from a range of professionals, an obligation to listen to the child's wishes and regular review of the child's general well-being. When a child is separated from a parent as a result of arrest or imprisonment, however, it can be a sudden, abrupt and unexpected event, experienced by the child as a grief which is unacknowledged or unrecognised as such by family and community members (Glover, 2009). A range of negative outcomes for these children and young people have been identified, from social isolation and stigmatisation, antisocial and delinquent behaviour, to physical and mental ill health (Henshaw, 2014; Glover, 2009).

This is further compounded by the effects of poverty. An evaluation of a time-limited project aimed at supporting offender's families highlighted the severe levels of economic deprivation experienced by offenders (Barnardos, 2015). A study undertaken by the Joseph Rowntree Trust (JRF, 2016) cited poverty as a factor leading to involvement in risky activities and criminality, along with health problems, drug and alcohol abuse, child abuse and neglect and family breakdown. The same study also addressed the challenges for families of children with disabilities, facing additional financial costs, further compounding poverty and its effects.

Serious illness or the death of a child elicit the rawest of emotions and are a subject largely avoided by the communities in which we live. However, for those involved in the criminal justice system, where risk factors are so prevalent, it cannot be ignored. The children of prisoners, along with their parents, are a particularly vulnerable and largely unsupported group, more likely to experience multiple losses and adverse outcomes than those in the general population (Barnardos, 2014).

Navigating loss from a distance

Incarcerated parents experience multiple losses, not least the losses associated with their inability to generate an income and to be physically present to parent their children. The remaining parent, often a mother, can experience a deep and intense emotional response to the loss of the co-parent, exacerbated by loss of income, social isolation and stigmatisation and deteriorating physical and mental health (Barnardos, 2015). This is further compounded by the necessity to consider and manage the emotional response to the incarceration experienced by their children (Smith *et al.*, 2007). High rates of depression and physical illness as a result of loss and separation can have a negative impact on parenting behaviour, potentially resulting in erratic and unsupportive care to the children (Hardy & Snowden, 2010). This increases the vulnerability of children impacted by the criminal justice system itself to experience neglectful parenting, potentially leading to impaired health and well-being. When a child has, or develops, a life-limiting or life-threatening condition, this can become a treacherous path to navigate.

A life-limiting condition in childhood is defined as one where "there is no reasonable hope of cure and from which children or young people will die," and a life-threatening condition in childhood as "one for which curative treatment may be feasible but can fail" (Together for Short Lives, 2017). The palliative care journey that such children and their families undertake begins at the point of diagnosis and can last for days, weeks, months or even years. Together for Short Lives (2017) define Children's Palliative Care as

> an active and total approach to care, embracing physical, emotional, social and spiritual elements. It focuses on enhancement of quality of life for the child and support for the family and includes the management of distressing symptoms, provision of respite, and care following death and bereavement.

This time is punctuated with periods of relative stability and episodes of crisis and sudden deteriorations, alongside times of joy at small achievements and anguish at a child's failing physical and cognitive development. It is a relentless, physically tiring, emotionally draining life of uncertainty, grief and loss, where the child and the family simultaneously hope for the best and plan for the worst.

The range of symptoms experienced by children with life-threatening and life-limiting conditions is vast. For many there will be long-term disabilities which render them physically dependant on others to meet their care needs. Children will experience seizures and acute health conditions requiring close and frequent monitoring, hospital and therapy treatments and appointments with a range of professionals delivering information which may be difficult to receive and which require a decision to be made.

Research has shown that meeting the developmental and psychological needs of children with complex needs is more likely to be achieved in the home setting than in the hospital environment (Boosfeld & O'Toole, 2000; Neufeld *et al.*, 2001). These children are likely to be dependent on technology to maintain their basic physical requirements for nutrition, respiration and elimination (Hewitt-Taylor, 2005), placing considerable strain on their carers and rendering everyday family activities complicated and time-consuming. It is recognised that parents of children with complex needs experience greater psychological distress and economic hardship than the parents of children who are well (Hatton & Emerson, 2009). When this is considered alongside the research previously stated describing the negative impact on the family when a member is incarcerated in the criminal justice system, the extent of the difficulties faced by families enduring both of these situations reveals itself. The experience of caring for a seriously ill child impacts on the whole family, the severity depending on the physical, emotional and financial resilience of its members and the resources available to them.

Under the United Nations Convention on the Rights of the Child (UNCRC), ratified by the United Kingdom in 1989, articles 5, 7 and 8 relate to the child's right to maintain relationships with his or her parents. Yet more children are separated from a parent due to imprisonment than are in care. Researchers argue that children should be supported in maintaining contact with a parent, even where the separation is due to an intervention of the state, which respects their rights to a family life, where it is in their best interests to do so (Morgan *et al.*, 2013). This is supported by research which illustrates that programmes and strategies aimed at maintaining and strengthening family ties can reduce reoffending, be a positive force in rehabilitation and enable stronger reintegration into society (Evans, 2015; Gill & Jacobson Deegan, 2013).

In spite of this, very few prisons offer opportunities for children to enjoy meaningful interactions with an incarcerated parent, provide toys or play activities or an environment in which they can feel safe and supported. Children can find searches by guards and sniffer dogs frightening and intimidating, the effects of which can be long-standing (Henshaw, 2014). Prisoners are often incarcerated many miles from home, leading to children spending long and tiring hours travelling to and from parental prison visits, whilst the costs of these visits add an additional financial burden to the family's finances. When a child is seriously ill the need for contact with an incarcerated parent becomes all the more urgent and yet so much more difficult. Long and arduous journeys with a sick or disabled child requiring therapeutic interventions, medications and the availability of cumbersome but vital equipment can turn a difficult situation into an impossible one. Requirements to search a child in a wheelchair, in pain, fatigued, with reduced immunity or otherwise unwell may be enough to render the visit contrary to the child's best interests. These difficulties will also impact on other children in the family as they, too, are unable to visit their parent and receive the reassurance of their parent's presence, invaluable contact time and an opportunity to experience a family occasion. A child with a life-limiting or life-threatening condition, and his or her family, live with the ever-present knowledge that time is limited and are collectively grieving for what they have already lost and what is to come. Loss is a fact of life but is multifaceted and more than simply bereavement. Those experiencing the effects of loss as a result of the criminal justice system, the innocent victims and the offenders, but also coping with serious illness, are stuck in a mire of despair which requires the most compassionate support we can offer.

Disconnected parenting

Parents of children who may die are frequently faced with the need to make decisions with regard to their child's care and treatment and, ultimately, as partners in the shared decision-making process at the end of life. This can be presented in various scenarios, maybe following a long illness as a result of a congenital or acquired condition or in a more acute situation following a short illness or an accident. Technological developments and extensive research has led to ever-greater complexities in treatment options to manage life-critical conditions in children and the ability to extend and prolong life (Longden & Mayer, 2007). This in turn leads to increasingly more difficult and complex decisions, none more so than those involving the decision to forego treatment which was likely to result in the child's death. Ethical and clinical research has long explored and debated the issues around the level of parental involvement in these decisions and the impact it has on parents' emotional well-being in the years following the child's death (Brinchmann & Vik, 2002; Gillam, 2008; Caeymaex *et al.*, 2011). A study by Sullivan *et al.* (2015) involving twenty-five parents of children with long-term conditions found that all parents in the study wanted to be end-of-life decision makers for their children. Reasons included the parent's love and knowledge of their child, that parents have to live with the consequences of the decision and that they saw it as their moral responsibility as parents. The study found that those parents who did not perceive themselves as the ultimate decision maker experienced emotional difficulties in having been denied this role following the child's death. A prisoner, already imprisoned within the literal and figurative walls of the criminal justice system, will experience further isolation and detachment from the painful but necessary discussions and decisions involving possibly the most important person in their lives, and denying them the role which has been found to be vital to emotional recovery following the child's death.

Further studies involving such decisions in paediatric intensive care units emphasise the need for accurate, clear and understandable information and being physically present to support the child (Woodgate, 2006). There is a wealth of literature which highlights the positive benefits to grieving parents on the quality of care at the time of death which facilitates the wishes of parents to be involved in all aspects of their child's care, empowers parents to exercise choice and control and recognises the pivotal role that a parent plays in the child's life (Hinds *et al.*, 2009; Longden & Mayer, 2007). Structures, policies and procedures, inherent within the criminal justice system and aimed at protecting the public, require significant and demanding questions to be addressed to enable the incarcerated parent of a dying child the freedom to engage in meaningful end-of-life decision making.

When a child has died

Prisoners experiencing the death of a child during their imprisonment would suffer grief in its rawest form. The grieving process would be compounded by the multiple losses many of those incarcerated in the criminal justice system already endure, including loss of liberty, loss of family connections, loss of time, loss of control, loss of privacy and personal space and loss of making their own life decisions.

The environment they find themselves in would not be conducive to the need to grieve and it would be difficult to exhibit feelings which could be viewed by others as a weakness. When confronted with the reality of the death, these challenges, which must be managed concurrently, can complicate the grieving and the healing process.

As a bereavement counsellor, one of the authors has worked with groups of men who are journeying towards the loss of their children or who have lost a child and has often found them to express their feelings around their loss as an imprisonment. They recognise that they are in a world which does not understand what it really means to lose a child, and that there are limited places for them to express their feelings and explore their pain, both physically and emotionally, as they try to construct their own meaning of their grief. The group is a safe haven for them to talk, often with anger, tears and fears about how they now "do life". This expression is often used by parents as they move towards acceptance of their new norm. They repeatedly share their stories, recognising the need to do this in order to come to terms with the magnitude of their loss. There is also the added benefit of sharing together with men who are truly able to empathise.

Similarly, the women's group, benefitting from this mutually bereaved environment, tell the same story. They express that they are rarely alone, yet feel alone, in a world which does not understand their grief. In the early stages of grief, they feel imprisoned by feelings of powerlessness, hopelessness, anger, guilt and a meaningless existence. With the right support, however, they eventually accept that life will never be the same.

The grieving process is best described in Worden's (2009) tasks of grief, where he demonstrates the process people need to go through when grieving. He explores the four tasks of grief as the following.

To accept the reality of the loss

Denial is often a common occurrence even when death is expected. For example, many parents will experience waking up in the morning and expecting their children to be still sleeping, and then have to relive the reality of their deaths. Worden (2009) encourages the family to embrace the rituals of death, such as preparations for and attendance at a funeral, in order to accept the reality of death.

To work through the pain of grief

Avoidance is very common, particularly in men. They have been conditioned to avoid feelings and often immerse themselves in work, or practical matters surrounding the death, as opposed to facing the pain of grief. One bereaved father, who admitted to returning to work too early, subsequently experienced an emotional crisis which necessitated a prolonged absence to process his grief. He attended counselling to try to gain an understanding of his feelings, both physically and emotionally. During his recovery he examined the process of grief and concluded that he was avoiding the pain of grief and, in order to be able to move forwards with his life, he needed to accept the loss of his son and to embrace his pain.

To adjust to an environment in which the deceased is missing

Worden (2009) presents three areas of adjustment required for this task:

- the external adjustment, or what life will be without the deceased;
- the internal adjustment, or what one's life purposes is now, as the loss of their parenting role can result in feelings of helplessness and lack of purpose and meaning to life; and
- spiritual adjustment; having one's belief system questioned by itself can be difficult to process, but necessary to make sense of the loss.

To emotionally relocate the deceased and move on with life

This task means to have a healthy memory of the deceased and to find ways of going on with life. This task requires an acceptance and embracing of the new norm. Worden highlights that the tasks of grief are not a rigid process; in fact, people will move in and out of the tasks as they journey through life. This model is a useful indicator of where people are in their journey of loss, as a tool to explore with the client what grief looks like and to determine whether the client is experiencing complicated or unresolved grief. This would be a common experience for a person incarcerated in the criminal justice system. Prisoners are at the mercy of the system and their lives are determined by the decisions of others in a closely controlled environment. Daily life is governed by rules, and this, combined with lack of privacy and personal space, interferes with the strategies that the free person would use to combat stress, such as going for a walk, engaging in physical exercise or art therapies or writing in a journal. Grief and loss for prisoners is further complicated when others become the chief decision makers, adding to feelings of powerlessness and leading to unresolved grief.

Unresolved grief could result in a number of complicated grieving processes, amongst them disenfranchised grief (Gilbert, 2007). This is characterised by the inability to grieve because of external restrictions and ultimately results in grief which is not allowed to be publicly expressed. Harner *et al.* (2011), in a study exploring the experience of loss amongst incarcerated women, quoted women who expressed their grief in prison as "not my real life", "out of sight", "out of mind" and that "prison was no place to grieve" (p. 459).

Conclusion and recommendations for future practice

Denying the bereaved person the need to express his or her grief contributes to unresolved grief. The tasks of grief are difficult for most, but for those who have lost their freedom, grieving can be an added imprisonment. As a society, greater awareness of the need to embrace grief and loss with all its pain and uncomfortableness is required. A good place to start could be within the prison environment. The challenges for those who work across the criminal justice system when supporting offenders whose children are dying or have died are considerable. However, an examination of the evidence presented demonstrates that the likelihood of a parent to experience the serious illness or death of a child is greater in the prison population than it is in the general population and therefore, ultimately, cannot be ignored.

Recommendations for future practice

* the development of an infrastructure which identifies the children of prisoners in official statistics, taken at the time of remand or imprisonment;
* a system of joined-up, interagency groups working across health, social care and education to meet the holistic needs of prisoners and their families, especially at points of transition;
* the identification of prisoners who have lost a child, or have a seriously ill child, to enable a compassionate and practical approach to the need to express their grief;
* a child-centred approach to prison visiting which reflects the psychological needs of children and includes a policy on searching children which is proportionate to the risks posed; and
* bereavement training for prison staff relating to the death of a child.

References

Barnardos. (2014). *On the outside: Identifying and supporting children with a parent in prison*. Ilford, England: Barnardos.

Barnardos. (2015). *The evaluation of the community support for offenders' families service*. Ilford, England: Barnardos.

Boosfeld, B. & O'Toole, M. (2000). Technology dependent children: From hospital to home. *Paediatric Nursing* 12(6): 20–22.

Brinchmann, B. & Vik, T. (2002). Parents' involvement in life and death decisions in neonatal care: Norwegian attitudes. *Newborn Infant Nursing Reviews* 5: 77–81.

Caeymaex, L., Speranza, M., Vasiescu, C., et al. (2011). Living with a crucial decision: A qualitative study of parental narratives three years after the loss of their new born in the NICU. *PLoS One* 6: e28633.

Department for Education. (2016). *Children looked after in England, including adoption: Year ending 31 March 2013*. www.gov.uk/government/organisations/department-for-education/ (Accessed 30/08/2017).

Evans, J. (2015). *Locked out: Children's experiences of visiting a parent in prison*. Ilford, England: Barnardos.

Flouri, E., Narayanan, M. & Midouhas E (2015). The cross-legged relationship between father absence and child problem behaviour in the early years. *Child: Care, Health and Development* 41(6): 1090–1097.

Gilbert, K. R. (2007). Unit 9-ambiguous loss and disenfranchised grief: Grief in a family context. Cited in Harner H, Hentz P, Evangelista M (2011) Grief interrupted: The experience of loss among incarcerated women. *Qualitative Health Research* 21(4): 454–464.

Gill, O. & Jacobson Deegan, M. (2013). *Working with children with a parent in prison*. Ilford, England: Barnardos.

Gillam, L. (2008). End of life decision making in paediatrics. *Journal of Paediatric Child Health* 44: 399–403.

Glover, J. (2009). *Every night you cry*. Ilford, England: Barnardos.

Government UK. (2016). *Prison population statistics*. www.gov.uk/government/collections/prison-population-statistics (Accessed 05/12/2016).

Hardy, T. & Snowden, M. (2010). Familial impact of imprisonment and the specialist practitioner. *Community Practitioner* 83(10): 21–24.

Harner, H., Hentz, P. & Evangelista, M. (2011). Grief interrupted: The experience of loss among incarcerated women. *Qualitative Health Research* 21(4): 454–464.

Hatton, C. & Emerson, E. (2009). Poverty and the mental health of families with a child with intellectual disabilities. *Psychiatry* 8: 433–437.

Henshaw, P. (2014). Children make 1387 prison visits every day, but the impact is unknown, *British Journal of School Nursing* 9(8).

Hewitt-Taylor, J. (2005). Children with complex needs: Educating staff. *Primary Health Care* 15(3): 36–41.

Hinds, P., Oaks, L., Hicks, J., Powell, B., Srivastava, D. K., Spunt, S., Harper, J., Baker, J., West, N. & Furman, W. (2009). 'Trying to be a good parent' as defined by interviews with parents who made phase 1, terminal care, and resuscitation decisions for their children. *Journal of Clinical Oncology* 27(35): 5979–5985.

Joseph Rowntree Foundation. (2016). *UK poverty: Causes, costs and solutions*. England: JRF.

Kerker, B., Jinjin, Z., Nadeem, E., Stein, R., Hulbert, M., Heneghan, A., Landsverk, J. & Horwitz, S. (2015). Adverse childhood experiences and mental health, chronic medical conditions and development in young children. *Academic Paediatrics* 15(5): 510–517.

Longden, J. & Mayer, A. (2007). Family involvement in end-of-life care in a paediatric intensive care unit. *Nursing in Critical Care* 12(4): 181–187.

Morgan, J., Leeson, C., Dillon, R.C., Wirgman, A.L. & Needham, M. (2013). 'A hidden group of children'. Support in schools for children who experience parental imprisonment. *Children & Society* 28 (4): 269–279.

Neufeld, S. M. et al. (2001). Respite care users who have children with chronic conditions: Are they getting a break? *Journal of Paediatric Nursing* 16(4): 234–244.

Office for National Statistics. (2016). *Childhood mortality in England and Wales*. www.ons.gov.uk/peoplepopulationandcommunity/birthsdeathsandmarriages/deaths/bulletins/childhoodinfantandperinatalmortalityinenglandandwales/2014 (Accessed 30/12/2016).

Rodriguez, A. & Margolin, G. (2015). Parental incarceration, transactional migration and military deployment: Family process mechanisms of youth adjustment to temporary parent absence. *Clinical Child and Family Review* 18(1): 24–49.

Smith, R., Grimshaw, R., Romeo, R. & Knapp, M. (2007). *Poverty and disadvantage among prisoners' families*. York: Joseph Rowntree Foundation.

Sullivan, J., Gillam, L. & Monagle, P. (2015). Parents and end of life decision making for their child: Roles and responsibilities. *BMJ Supportive & Palliative Care* 5: 240–248.

Together for Short Lives. (2017). *Palliative care definitions*. www.togetherforshortlives.org.uk/search?q=palliative+care+definition (Accessed 30/08/2017).

Wolfe, I., Macfarlane, A., Donkin, A., Marmot, M. & Viner, R. (2014). *Why children die: Deaths in infants, children and young people in the UK Part A*. London: Royal College of Paediatrics and Child Health.

Woodgate, R. L. (2006). Living in a world without closure: Reality for parents who have experienced the death of a child. *Journal of Palliative Care* 22: 75–82.

Worden, W. (2009). *Grief counselling and grief therapy*. London: Routledge.

Conventions

The United Nations Convention on the Rights of the Child.

17 Beyond loss of liberty

How loss, bereavement and grief can affect young men's prison journeys

Nina Vaswani

Introduction

Recent UK statistics suggest that reoffending rates following release from custody remain stubbornly high, at 59.3 per cent of adults serving less than twelve months and 69.4 per cent of young people aged under 18 (Ministry of Justice, 2017). Successful rehabilitation and reintegration from prison are the foundation for reducing offending and providing the right environment for desistance. In order to best support these processes, it is essential that the needs of young people in custody are fully understood and met. Contemporary evidence-based practice in this field is frequently concentrated on identifying and managing risks through the Risk Factor Prevention Paradigm, which was developed from longitudinal studies of the antecedents of crime in young people (Kemshall, 2007). However, the reoffending rates indicate that there are limitations to the success of this approach, and it has been argued that the dominance of this model means that other pertinent factors that are deemed 'non-criminogenic', such as the trauma and grief caused by loss and bereavement, are often little understood and therefore overlooked by practitioners (Hester and Taylor, 2011).

In order to address this gap in knowledge and practice, this chapter will draw on the research literature to highlight the role that loss, bereavement and grief can play in shaping young men's journeys to prison, through prison and onwards into their reintegration back in to society.

A link between loss, bereavement, grief and offending behaviour?

Loss and bereavement are universal human experiences and are by no means confined to particular societal groups, but young people involved in offending do appear to be more vulnerable to these experiences than the general population. Draper and Hancock (2011) found that young people who had been parentally bereaved by the age of 16 were significantly more likely than those who had not been parentally bereaved to score above the cut-off for 'delinquent' behaviour in a teacher's assessment. Similarly, a study of persistent young offenders aged under 16 found that, although bereavement rates were similar to the general population, the occurrence of multiple, parental and traumatic bereavements (e.g. those precipitated by murder, suicide or overdose) was greater than anticipated (Vaswani, 2008). By the time the prison gates had been reached, bereavement rates had increased to more than 90 per cent of young offenders aged under 21, with at least three-quarters also having suffered a traumatic bereavement and two-thirds finding themselves bereaved on four or more separate occasions (Vaswani, 2014).

Although the death of a significant person is the image that most often springs to mind when considering the concept of loss and grief, these emotions can also be triggered by a much broader range of losses, many of which may appear on the surface to be small, transient or even inconsequential. Such losses can be caused by divorce and separation (Mooney *et al.*, 2009), parental imprisonment (Bockneck *et al.*, 2009), parental addiction or physical and mental ill health (Darbyshire *et al.*, 2001; Graham, 2012), moving house or school (Graham, 2012) and entering residential care or custody (Brodzinsky, 2009). Young people involved with the criminal justice system often have troubled and chaotic backgrounds characterised by these types of losses, with up to half of young people in young offender institutions previously or currently looked after (Blades *et al.*, 2011).

Whilst not necessarily as final as death, these losses can be difficult to deal with precisely because they are less understood or less validated by society, with little in the way of rituals to mark the loss and a lack of professional support (Boss, 2006). In addition, the uncertainty and ambiguity caused by these types of losses can mean that they are very difficult to resolve, with the resulting grief and trauma persisting indefinitely to the point that it becomes chronic (Boss, 2006). Last, multiple losses, and in particular losses that are perceived as a voluntary rejection such as abandonment, can result in problematic attachment relationships, meaning that young people withdraw from or reject the relationships and connections that can provide them with much-needed social support (Samuels and Pryce, 2008; Shaffer *et al.*, 2006).

The relationship between childhood experiences of loss and bereavement and later offending behaviour is complex and not easily unpicked from the current knowledge base. Multiple bereavements (four or more) are associated with a significantly increased risk of depression (Harrison and Harrington, 2001), and traumatic bereavements can result in a more complicated grieving response (Dowdney, 2000). Unresolved grief and trauma can lead to challenging and risk-taking behaviours in adolescence and adulthood, such as substance misuse (Vaswani, 2014), risky sexual behaviour, suicide (Felitti *et al.*, 1998) and a disregard for danger (Wright and Liddle, 2014). Bereaved young men in prison often link their bereavements with precipitating a downward spiral of destructive and offending behaviour, and at times directly attribute these experiences to their entry into prison (Vaswani, 2014). With this in mind, it is not difficult to see why, in their study of bereavement amongst young male offenders, Finlay and Jones (2000: 569) conclude that "severe emotional stressors, particularly traumatic bereavements, in childhood or adolescence are linked to offending and maladaptive behaviour".

It is not necessarily that straightforward, however; others suggest that loss is not a criminogenic factor in itself, but that mediating factors such as reduced parental monitoring (Isherwood *et al.*, 2007) or exclusion (Berridge *et al.*, 2001) are implicated. Last, there may be no causal association at all, and the relationship could simply reflect the parallels between the risk factors for offending behaviour and for premature death such as family conflict, poor housing, addiction and community violence (Childhood Bereavement Network, 2008). Whatever the mechanisms involved, the over-representation of substantial and challenging loss and bereavement experiences amongst young people involved in the criminal justice system is undeniable, to the extent that Leach *et al.* (2008) argue that the presence of traumatic grief should be considered in all prisoners.

The institutional context of dealing with loss and grief

The institutional context also needs to be considered in order to develop a comprehensive understanding of how young people in custody are affected by loss and grief. Entry into custody marks yet another loss in the lives of already-vulnerable young people, not only the obvious loss of liberty, but also separation from friends, family, social support and normative life experiences. The loss of these relationships is perceived to be one of the most painful aspects of custody (Murray, 2005). A study drawn from the narratives of twenty-three males aged 16–20 in a young offenders institution found that the shame of entering custody was often the final straw for already-strained and fragile relationships, with many of the young men feeling rejected by their parents or partners, or in turn rejecting their loved ones as a defensive mechanism (Vaswani, 2015). These disordered and problematic attachment relationships are formed over a lifetime of adversity but are exacerbated by the separation of custody.

There are also losses that are related to the ramifications of having a criminal and custodial record. Such losses include the very real loss of education and employment opportunities, and by extension, the loss of future hopes and ambitions that are experienced by young men as a result of a prison sentence (Vaswani, 2015). The pain caused by this loss of opportunities is ultimately about the loss of a future 'possible self' (Markus and Nurius, 1986). This possible self represents the 'ideal' person that the individual had imagined that he or she could become, shaped by the professional and social roles that were assumed possible to attain – father, husband, teacher, a mechanic, a success – but also shaped by the 'feared' self who is the person that the individual strives not to be: a drug user, a bad father, a failure. Finding these hopes dashed by the twists and turns of the life path can often be "experienced as a kind of bereavement for oneself; the loss involving lost worlds, lost futures and lost identities" (Jewkes, 2005: 370).

Another significant loss that can be linked directly to the prison environment is that of loss of 'status', in this context referring to the loss of position, power or respect in the social environment. With young people already afforded a lower status in society by virtue of their age, young prisoners can be further marginalised by the shame and stigma caused by their offences (Vaswani, 2015). Furthermore, by necessity, the prison regime creates power imbalances and removes individual agency to make simple everyday decisions about when to get up, or what to eat, or how to spend each day (Sykes, 1958; Vaswani, 2015).

These sometimes intangible losses often go unrecognised or may be viewed as the *just deserts* of a system ostensibly designed to punish as well as to rehabilitate. Not recognising, acknowledging or accepting these losses can disenfranchise young people's grief, meaning that grief can remain unresolved (Doka, 1999). Even dealing with unambiguous losses such as bereavement can be complicated by the custodial environment. Social roles and gender norms mean that young men in general are often reluctant to seek support, talk about their emotions or display signs of weakness, but in the hyper-masculine environment of a male prison these pressures take on a different magnitude. Bereaved young men in prison tend to put on a front in order to maintain their status and ensure that they do not appear vulnerable amongst their peers (Vaswani, 2014). Separation from usual sources of social support, such as family, further reduces opportunities to seek help (Leach *et al.*, 2008; Vaswani, 2014). Security restrictions on participation in important rituals such as funerals, graveside attendance and saying goodbye to the terminally ill, whilst understandable, also deny young men a socially acceptable occasion to express their grief (Vaswani, 2014).

The prison regime also interferes with the ability to grieve by reducing the autonomy to choose how to manage grief, which has significant consequences for successfully navigating the mourning process. Stroebe and Schut's (1999) 'Dual Processing Model' depicts two different categories of activities that characterise an individual's response to bereavement: loss-oriented activities such as reminiscing, yearning and crying that involve actively focusing on or processing aspects of the loss, and restoration-oriented activities that involve deliberately distracting oneself from aspects of the loss in order to allow time off from the pain of grief as well as restoring a sense of well-being and facilitating adjustment to new roles and circumstances. In the early stages of grief, loss orientation naturally predominates, but Stroebe and Schut's model emphasises the dynamic oscillation between both sets of strategies that is necessary for successful coping over time. Spending too much time in one activity or the other is perceived to be detrimental to both physical and mental health. Yet the confines of the prison environment can offer too little space to privately reflect on emotions and experiences (Irwin and Owen, 2005), or conversely too much time and space for unstructured reflection, with young people unable to distract themselves from their grief (Vaswani, 2014). When understood in the context of such models of processing loss and grief, it is easy to see how the ability to deal with grief in prison is severely impaired.

Thus, loss and bereavement affect young people in custody in a multitude of ways, creating layer upon layer of both small and large traumas that must be endured, often without societal or professional support. If these losses go unacknowledged or unaddressed they can manifest as acting out or offending behaviours (Leach *et al.*, 2008). These vulnerable individuals who have already experienced a lifetime of loss and disruption will have reduced reservoirs of resilience to deal with future losses or traumatic events (Ribbens McCarthy, 2006); the additional losses created by the justice system's response to this behaviour, such as the use of secure care or custody, can therefore be especially painful, if not, for some, retraumatising. To then have this loss and grief compounded by a regime that does not allow for individual or optimal ways to process loss and grief leaves grief unresolved. The initial impact of such a perfect storm of trauma is felt immediately in the prison by causing problems with engagement and behavioural and regime management, but in the longer term can cause problems with rehabilitation and reintegration into the community. The following section considers how loss and grief can impede these crucial processes.

Loss-related barriers to successful reintegration and desistance

Unresolved trauma and loss can affect prospects for rehabilitation most obviously and directly by leading to psychiatric, emotional and behavioural disturbance (Gorski, 2006; Leach *et al.*, 2008). Gorski's concept of 'Post Incarceration Syndrome' suggests that, in an already-traumatised population, the prison environment can lead to prisoners exiting in a worse state than that in which they entered custody. However, the impact of loss and grief can also be much more subtle. Successful engagement with interventions, reintegration and desistance from crime requires a number of key cognitions, processes and behaviours to coexist within an individual and his or her social network. First, there must be motivation to change, and the recognition that some form of external support may be required to effect that personal change. The supports and resources (internal, informal or professional) that are necessary to facilitate personal change must also be accessible to the individual (Kessler *et al.*, 1981). The individual must also believe that change is possible, be able to imagine a positive future with tangible goals and to have a clear road map to achieving those goals (Paternoster and Bushway, 2009) However, the legacy of a life characterised by multiple, traumatic and unresolved losses, as described earlier in this chapter, is that these optimum conditions for long-lasting personal change are less likely to occur due to the distinct, but interrelated, issues of problematic attachments and loss of agency, skills and self-concept.

Attachments and relationships

As described earlier, unresolved loss and grief are likely to be higher amongst the prison population due to a succession of adverse and traumatic life experiences, exacerbated by the ordeal of dealing with loss and grief whilst in care or custody. Bowlby (1980), in his work on attachment and loss, noted that unresolved loss in childhood frequently resulted in adverse psychological outcomes and attachment disturbances, most commonly overanxious attachment (e.g. clinginess and the tendency to form inappropriate bonds) or a complete deactivation of attachment behaviour (e.g. avoidant behaviour and an inability to form bonds with an appropriate caregiver or other adult). Although variations in the classification of attachments styles have been developed since Bowlby's original work, this broad distinction, and the avoidant attachment classification in particular, remains useful when considering the role of loss and grief in supporting or hindering the reintegration and desistance process.

Studies suggest that young people have a reduced tendency to seek help for social, emotional and other problems (Ribbens McCarthy, 2006), and that this is observed even more frequently amongst young men (Möller-Leimkühler, 2002). However, problematic attachment behaviours only serve to reduce help-seeking further, via two main mechanisms. First, individuals with avoidant attachment styles may have more negative views of others, perceiving them to be untrust-worthy rather than as a source of help, with this viewpoint extending to professional as well as personal relationships and reducing both help-seeking intentions and help-seeking behaviours (Shaffer *et al.*, 2006). Samuels and Pryce (2008) coined the term 'survivalist self-reliance' when describing this disconnection from relationships and active rejection of help amongst young people transitioning out of foster care. Second, social support networks facilitate help-seeking behaviours by providing sources of support, encouragement, advice, role-modelling and help (Rickwood *et al.*, 2005). Yet problematic attachments create deficits in social competencies, which in turn reduces the likelihood of help-seeking behaviour as individuals do not develop the kinds of social support networks within which sufficient help is available, or find their social relationships sources of stress rather than support (Mallinckrodt & Wei, 2005).

This latter point also has particular implications for the successful navigation of the desistance process, which crucially hinges on social relationships and the concept of social capital. Laub and Sampson (2001) argue that onset, persistence and desistance from crime occur with shifts in the predominant source of social bonds and the social control that such bonds exert over the individual. Over the life course, this tends to shift from family to peers (often associated with the onset of offending, and, in terms of social development, with the onset of adolescence) and later to spouses, partners or employment (with a corresponding move towards desistance, and, in terms of social development, with the onset of adulthood). Thus they conclude that "strong social bonds could explain desistance from criminal behaviour in adulthood, despite a background of delinquent behaviour" (2001: 19). However, losses and problematic attachments during childhood mean that young people often lack the *physical* presence of social bonds (e.g. due to the death of a parent) or do not have the *emotional* investments in their social relationships due to a lack of a secure, stable family base whilst growing up (Samuels & Pryce, 2008). In adulthood these attachment styles can hinder the development of the social relationships necessary to exert positive social control and facilitate desistance, such as prosocial intimate relationships.

Agency and skills

It was outlined earlier in this chapter how the use of custody can result in the loss of status, most notably loss of power and autonomy to make even everyday decisions. This loss of autonomy, first outlined by Sykes in his influential depiction of the five pains of imprisonment, can reduce individuals to a state of 'childlike helplessness' that has a negative impact on functioning upon release (Sykes, 1958; Jewkes, 2005) and interferes with the process of maturation (Maruna & Toch, 2005). Successfully, and rapidly, adapting to the restrictions and routines of prison life is important for navigating and surviving the custodial journey (Souza & Dhami, 2010; Vaswani, 2015). Yet the process of adaptation to the regime can result in what Clemmer, in his 1940 book *The Prison Community*, termed 'prisonisation' which erodes social roles. Over time "the loss of knowledge, skills and habits occurs. This leads to antipathy and loss of interest in social self-realisation. These changes create an obstacle for a later return to society" (Žukov *et al.*, 2009: 203).

It could be argued that these obstacles are even more insurmountable when considering the use of custody with young people. Whereas adults and young people alike are deskilled whilst in prison, young people are less likely to have had the opportunity to establish competence in these important life- or work-related skills in the first place, and therefore have little in the way of past knowledge, skills or confidence to draw on upon their return to the community. Employment can, for example, encourage increased self-esteem and engender an alternative and constructive self-concept, as well as positively influencing social relationships, all of which are associated with desistance from crime (Owens, 2009); being deskilled clearly poses a practical barrier to this process. Yet the *perceptual* barrier presented by a sense of powerlessness and loss of agency can present an equally formidable barrier for desistance, with a sense of motivation, of hope and of human agency being pivotal in this process (Maruna, 2001). Without a sense of efficacy and competence, goals and ambitions may appear to be unattainable and be written off. Indeed, continued involvement in crime can provide a much-needed sense of agency, autonomy and self-respect that may not be forthcoming from mainstream society (Maruna and Toch, 2005).

Self-concept

There are two key issues identified with a sense of self that might be implicated in unsuccessful reintegration and desistance. First, the loss of stability in the backgrounds of many young people in custody, with parents, siblings and friends caught in the revolving door of prison, can leave them with a sense that their own prison sentence was predetermined (Vaswani, 2015). This increases the likelihood of a self-fulfilling prophecy in which the negative view of self can lead to detachment and disengagement from prosocial peers and activities. This negativity is then reflected back in the disapproving response of other important figures, such as family or teachers, and can lead to a spiral of increasingly poor behaviour. Entering custody as a young person can cement these beliefs, as adolescence is a critical time in the development of a sense of identity, and prison is an environment that already provokes deep questions about self-identity (Maruna *et al.*, 2006). Given that adopting a prosocial identity is crucial in the process of desistance (Maruna, 2001), that such a self-concept becomes ingrained in many young people in custody is likely to impede sustained reintegration and desistance, as a positive future becomes difficult to align with the individual's self-concept.

Even for those who had some hope and ambition for the future, the practical barriers posed by a criminal history and prison record mean that employment opportunities and life chances are reduced (Maruna, 2011). Less tangible barriers also exist. The loss of the future possible self not only affects self-esteem by removing the imagery and potential of a positive future self but also removes a direct driver of behaviour (Paternoster and Bushway, 2009). The discrepancy between the current conceptualisation of self and a future possible self can act as a motivator for desistance and can hint at strategies and plans for attaining this goal, instilling a belief that change is possible (Paternoster and Bushway, 2009). Without a future possible self to strive for, and without hope, long-lasting personal change becomes a more challenging goal.

Conclusions

This chapter has drawn together the research literature to demonstrate the nature of the losses that have been experienced by young people in custody, losses that extend well beyond the immediate loss of liberty. From conspicuous bereavements, to less tangible losses, and to those losses caused by the system itself, these are not isolated cases but are reflective of a widespread problem amongst young people in all forms of institutions including residential care and across all reaches of the justice system. At a minimum, practitioners need to be alert to these losses that can precipitate or sustain involvement in offending behaviour, even if they are not defined as a criminogenic risk per se, and should also consider the presence of issues related to unresolved loss and grief for all people in care or custody (Leach *et al.*, 2008). Yet it should not be forgotten that loss and grief are universal human experiences and are not limited to one specific section of society. Many of these losses and traumas have occurred, and have been left to go unresolved, long before the prison gates are reached. This sad fact reiterates the importance of preventative action, especially through the provision of universal loss, grief and death education at the earliest possible stage (Ribbens McCarthy, 2006).

It is clear that loss and grief can affect every stage of a young person's journey to, through and from prison. Addressing such losses requires a multi-pronged approach from prevention, organisational and societal culture change, to specific therapeutic interventions. The breadth of such an approach may not only help to prevent some offending behaviour in the first place, and help to reduce behavioural management and non-engagement issues whilst in custody, but also facilitate the processes of reintegration and desistance back into the community. The justice sector cannot afford to continue to ignore these childhood losses.

References

Berridge, D., Brodie, I., Pitts, J., Porteous, D., & Tarling, R. (2001). *The independent effects of permanent exclusion from school on the offending careers of young people.* London: Home Office.

Blades, R., Hart, D., Lea, J., & Willmott, N. (2011). *Care: A stepping stone to custody?* London: Prison Reform Trust.

Bockneck, E. L., Sanderson, J., & Britner, P. A. (2009). Ambiguous loss and posttraumatic stress in school-age children of prisoners. *Journal of Child and Family Studies.* 18: 323–333.

Boss, P. (2006). *Loss, trauma, and resilience: Therapeutic work with ambiguous loss*. New York: W.W. Norton & Co.

Bowlby, J. (1980). *Attachment and loss (Vol. III): Loss, sadness and depression*. London: The Hogarth Press Ltd.

Brodzinsky, D. (2009). The experience of sibling loss in the adjustment of foster and adopted children. IN: D. N. Silverstein & S. L. Smith (Eds.). *Siblings in adoption and foster care: traumatic separations and honored connections* (pp. 45–56). Westport: Praeger.

Childhood Bereavement Network. (2008). *Bereavement in the secure setting*. London: National Children's Bureau.

Clemmer, D. (1940). *The prison community*. Boston: The Christopher Publishing Co.

Darbyshire, P., Oster, C., & Carrig, H. (2001). The experience of pervasive loss; children and young people living in a family where parental gambling is a problem. *Journal of Gambling Studies*. 17: 23–45.

Doka, K. J. (1999). Disenfranchised grief. *Bereavement Care*. 18: 37–39.

Dowdney, L. (2000). Annotation: Childhood bereavement following parental death. *Journal of Child Psychology and Psychiatry*. 41: 819–830.

Draper, A., & Hancock, M. (2011). Childhood parental bereavement: The risk of vulnerability to delinquency and factors that compromise resilience. *Mortality*. 16: 285–306.

Felitti, V. J., Anda, R. F., Nordenberg, D., Williamson, D. F., Spitz, A. M., Edwards, V., & Marks, J. S. (1998). Relationship of childhood abuse and household dysfunction to many of the leading causes of death in adults. *American Journal of Preventive Medicine*. 14: 245–258.

Finlay, I. G., & Jones, N. K. (2000). Unresolved grief in young offenders in prison. *British Journal of General Practice*. 50: 569–570.

Gorski, T. (2006). *Post incarceration syndrome and relapse*. Retrieved from www.tgorski. com/criminal_justice/cjs_pics_&_relapse.htm

Graham, A. (2012). Life is like the seasons. *Childhood Education*. 80: 317–321.

Harrison, L., & Harrington, R. (2001). Adolescents' bereavement experiences: Prevalence, association with depressive symptoms, and use of services. *Journal of Adolescence*. 24: 159–169.

Hester, R., & Taylor, W. (2011). Responding to bereavement, grief and loss: Charting the troubled relationship between research and practice in youth offending services. *Mortality*. 16: 191–203.

Irwin, J., & Owen, B. (2005). Harm and the contemporary prison. IN: A. Liebling & S. Maruna (Eds.). *The effects of imprisonment*. Cullompton: Willan.

Isherwood, T., Burns, M., Naylor, M., & Read, S. (2007). 'Getting into trouble': A qualitative analysis of the onset of offending in the accounts of men with learning disabilities. *Journal of Forensic Psychiatry & Psychology*. 18: 221–234.

Jewkes, Y. (2005). Loss, liminality and the life sentence: Managing identity through a disrupted lifecourse. IN: A. Liebling & S. Maruna (Eds.). *The effects of imprisonment*. Cullompton: Willan.

Kemshall, H. (2007). Risk assessment and risk management: The right approach? IN: M. Blyth, E. Solomon, & K. Baker (Eds.). *Young people and 'risk' (Researching Criminal Justice Series)*. Bristol, UK: Policy Press.

Kessler, R. C., Brown, R. L., & Broman, C. L. (1981). Sex differences in psychiatric help-seeking: Evidence from four large-scale surveys. *Journal of Health and Social Behavior*. 22: 49–64.

Laub, J. H., & Sampson, R. J. (2001). Understanding desistance from crime. IN: M. Tonry (Ed.). *Crime and justice: A review of research, Volume 28*. Chicago: University of Chicago Press Journals.

Leach, R. M., Burgess, T., & Holmwood, C. (2008). Could recidivism in prisoners be linked to traumatic grief? A review of the evidence. *International Journal of Prisoner Health.* 4: 104–119.

Mallinckrodt, B., & Wei, M. (2005). Attachment, social competencies, social support, and psychological distress. *Journal of Counselling Psychology.* 52: 358–367.

Markus, H., & Nurius, P. (1986). Possible selves. *American Psychologist.* 41: 954–969.

Maruna, S. (2001). *Making good: How ex-convicts reform and rebuild their lives.* Washington, DC: American Psychological Association Books.

Maruna, S. (2011). Judicial rehabilitation and the 'clean bill of health' in criminal justice. *European Journal of Probation.* 3: 97–117.

Maruna, S., & Toch, H. (2005). The impact of imprisonment on the desistance process. IN: J. Travis & C. Visher (Eds.). *Prisoner reentry and crime in America.* New York: Cambridge University Press.

Maruna, S., Wilson, L., & Curran, K. (2006). Why god is often found behind bars: Prison conversions and the crisis of self-narrative. *Research in Human Development.* 3: 161–184.

Ministry of Justice. (2017). *Proven re-offending statistics: Quarterly bulletin July 2014 to June 2015.* London: Ministry of Justice. Retrieved from www.gov.uk/government/statistics/proven-reoffending-statistics-july-2014-to-june-2015

Möller-Leimkühler, A. M. (2002). Barriers to help-seeking by men: A review of sociocultural and clinical literature with particular reference to depression. *Journal of Affective Disorders.* 71: 1–9.

Mooney, A., Oliver, C., & Smith, M. (2009). *Impact of family breakdown on children's well-being.* London: University of London.

Murray, J. (2005). The effects of imprisonment on families and children of prisoners. IN: A. Liebling & S. Maruna (Eds.). *The effects of imprisonment.* Cullompton: Willan Publishing.

Owens, B. (2009). Training and employment in an economic downturn: Lessons from desistance studies. *Irish Probation Journal.* 6: 49–65.

Paternoster, R., & Bushway, S. (2009). Desistance and the feared self: Toward an identity theory of criminal desistance. *Journal of Criminal Law and Criminology.* 99: 1103–1156.

Ribbens McCarthy, J. (2006). *Young people's experiences of loss and bereavement.* Berkshire: Open University Press.

Rickwood, D., Deane, F. P., Wilson, C. J., & Ciarocchi, J. (2005). Young people's help-seeking for mental health problems. *Australian E-Journal for the Advancement of Mental Health.* 4: 1–34.

Samuels, G. M., & Pryce, J. M. (2008). 'What doesn't kill you makes you stronger': Survivalist self-reliance as resilience and risk among young adults aging out of foster care. *Children and Youth Services Review.* 30: 1198–1210.

Shaffer, P. A., Vogel, D. L., & Wei, M. (2006). The mediating roles of anticipated risks, anticipated benefits, and attitudes on the decision to seek professional help: An attachment perspective. *Journal of Counselling Psychology.* 53: 442–452.

Souza, K. A., & Dhami, M. K. (2010). First-time and recurrent inmates' experiences of imprisonment. *Criminal Justice and Behavior.* 37: 1330–1342.

Stroebe, M., & Schut, H. (1999). The dual process model of coping with bereavement: Rationale and description. *Death Studies.* 23: 197–224.

Sykes, G. M. (1958). *The society of captives: A study of a maximum security prison* (Vol. 227). Princenton: Princeton University Press.

Vaswani, N. (2008). *Persistent offender profile: Focus on bereavement.* Edinburgh: Criminal Justice Social Work Development Centre.

Vaswani, N. (2014). The ripples of death: Exploring the bereavement experiences and mental health of young men in custody. *The Howard Journal of Criminal Justice*. 53: 341–359.

Vaswani, N. (2015). A catalogue of losses: Implications for the care and reintegration of young men in custody. *The Prison Service Journal*. 220: 26–35.

Wright, S., & Liddle, M. (2014). *Young offenders and trauma: Experience and impact*. London: Beyond Youth Custody.

Žukov, I., Fischer, S., Ptáčak, R., & Raboch, J. (2009). Imprisonment and its influence on psychobiological needs. *Prague Medical Report*. 110: 201–213.

18 Grief, chaplaincy and the non-religious prisoner

Katie Hunt and Sue Read

Introduction

This chapter calls for a clearer distinction between religious and pastoral support. Prisoners experience bereavement at a very high rate and there are strong links between unresolved grief and offending, but what little bereavement support is provided tends to be available largely through prison chaplaincies. The experience of some criminal justice professionals is that many inmates feel uncomfortable accessing religious services and do not receive the help they need. It will be argued that multi-faith spaces, which seek to cater to inmates of all faiths and none, may be unable to support all offenders equally, and that the importance of effective pastoral care in the criminal justice system puts pressure on the Prison Service to do more to support those whom the chaplaincy cannot reach. A secular service independent of chaplaincies and their staff would be accessible to all, so that no prisoner feels alienated from vital support.

Bereavement and loss in prison

The contemporary English prison is an extraordinarily difficult environment in which to live and work, and the plethora of practical, emotional and social challenges facing prisoners is well documented. Overcrowding, underfunding and staff shortages leave institutions ill equipped to meet the complex mental and physical needs of the people they confine. Towards the end of 2016, worrying increases in deaths, violence, self-harm, drug use and a series of riots led academics and commentators to refer to a 'prison crisis' in the United Kingdom.[1] Life in these unsustainable conditions punishes offenders well beyond the loss of liberty that constitutes a lawful sentence, limiting them in every way, from higher aspirations of personal growth and skill development, to the most basic requirements of hygiene, safety and nourishment. The effects of incarceration endure long after release, for those who live to see it, but with an ageing prison population, and suicides at an all-time high, record numbers of inmates are now dying during their sentences.

In addition to the what Sykes (1958) calls 'the pains of imprisonment' (i.e. the hardships particular to the prison environment and the experience of incarceration), there is evidence that offenders are highly likely to have experienced traumatic life events before arriving in prison. Histories of addiction, child abuse, serious illness or injury, domestic violence and poverty are far more common amongst people with convictions than in wider society (Maschi *et al.*, 2011).

The figures vary, but studies in this area have consistently shown that offenders suffer bereavements at a much higher rate than the general population (Hester & Taylor, 2011). A study of inmates at Holloway Prison in the United Kingdom found that 82 per cent of the participating prisoners had experienced the death of someone close within the previous five years (cited in Northern Ireland Prison Service, 2005), whilst around 90 per cent of 16- to 20-year-olds at the young offender institution in Vaswani's research had suffered the death of someone close to them at least once (2014). The bereaved are vastly over-represented in the criminal justice system, and yet the subject of loss in these settings is often ignored. Incarceration hinders the 'tasks of mourning' at every stage, presenting unique challenges that complicate and amplify this pain (Worden, 2009). For example, offenders' confinement often means that they are unable to visit a dying relative or participate in funeral services, which makes it harder to accept the reality of the death. Cut off from their social networks, offenders can do little to support or be supported by their loved ones and will often be left to grieve alone. Feelings of despair, anger, abandonment and powerlessness are commonplace during mourning, but must be suppressed in prison, where emotional expression or displays of vulnerability are interpreted as signs of weakness. Finally, the incarcerated offender has no opportunity to adapt to a world in which the deceased is missing and adjust to life without him or her. In this way, the opportunity to move on is suspended until the end of the sentence.

There are strong links between bereavement and offending. Stevenson and McCutchen (2006) draw a parallel between emotional responses to grief and to incarceration, highlighting the similarities between the feelings experienced by mourners and inmates. We submit that the grieving prisoner is in this sense doubly bereaved, first by the imprisonment and then by the loss of a loved one. As marginalised and vulnerable people who are often excluded from grief rituals and unable to mourn openly, prisoners are disenfranchised grievers (Doka, 1989). Disenfranchised grief impedes an ex-offender's reintegration into the community (Vaswani, 2014) and can have serious mental and physical health consequences, often leading to destructive behaviour and recidivism on release (Hester & Taylor, 2011; Wilson, 2010). This creates a pressing need for comprehensive pastoral care.

Prison chaplaincy and pastoral care

Some help is available. A multi-faith chaplaincy is established in every prison in England and Wales, with teams of staff dedicated to providing religious and spiritual guidance to offenders and colleagues alike. Some institutions also work with organisations like Cruse Bereavement Care, which has a presence in approximately thirty establishments in England, Wales and Northern Ireland (Wilson, 2010). Many prisons employ full-time imams or representatives of minority faiths, whilst others offer counselling, whether by trained counsellors and volunteer listeners from the local community, or through access to external support services. In most prisons, however, there is no formal bereavement counselling available. What little support is provided for those dealing with grief and loss tends to be available only through the chaplaincy.

Anglican chaplaincy has been a part of the prison system since its inception. Church of England priests played a large part in attempts to reform the system in the eighteenth century (Beckford, 2013). The chaplaincy was at the heart of Victorian prison life, and Priestly writes that the daily summons to communion was 'experienced by prisoners as unmistakably disciplinary . . . part of one's punishment' (1985: 91). In 1773, recognising the centrality of the chaplain's role in the judicial process, Parliament passed the Gaol Chaplains Act authorising the appointment of paid prison chaplains. Those chosen were always Anglican. The Prison Act of 1865 stipulated that every prison '*must appoint a chaplain, being a clergyman of the established church*', and this requirement was renewed at section 7 of the Prisons Act of 1952.

More recently, increasing religious diversity has been an important catalyst for change, and the pressures faced by institutional religion have had an impact in prisons (Gilliat-Ray, 2005). In the early twentieth century, the ethos of the prison chapel moved away from discipline and spiritual redemption and towards education and rehabilitation. Worship was no longer compulsory, and prison chapels altered in size and function, becoming smaller, multipurpose spaces used for private reflection, meetings and even entertainment. Section 10 of the Prison Act of 1952 permitted, for the first time, the appointment of non-Christian chaplains, at the secretary of state's discretion. Today, imams, rabbis and ministers of other faiths have an active presence in many institutions, although they are always appointed in addition to – never instead of – the Anglican chaplain.

Religion and non-religion in prison

It is difficult to overstate the contribution that the chaplaincy can make to prisoner welfare and to the atmosphere of the establishment itself, under the right circumstance. The chaplaincy is the 'community centre' of the institution, and welcomes visitors of any belief system for worship, conversation or quiet reflection. Many people turn to faith for a sense of meaning and moral strength in times of crisis, and faith communities are a valuable source of friendship, company and a feeling of belonging. In prison, religion serves as an important buffer against the fear of death, fostering optimism, humanity and a sense of security at a time when those feelings are scarce (Aday & Wahidin, 2016). It is clearly a crucial coping mechanism for many people, but one that is, by definition, unavailable to atheist or non-faith prisoners. These men and women face the same challenges as believers and must also come to terms with their 'double bereavement' of mourning whilst imprisoned, but they are further disadvantaged in that theirs is a grief without God. The non-religious griever confronts his losses unsupported by a faith from which to derive comfort, a religious community in whom to find kinship or a minister to provide guidance and compassion. Religious prisoners can find, in the chaplain, a like-minded person in whom they can confide; for those of no faith, this valuable figure is absent.

How realistic is the aim, set out in Ministry of Justice guidelines, for prison chaplaincies to be equally supportive to people of 'all faiths and none' (2011: 25)? As Gilliat-Ray has observed, the phrase is 'employed to convey positive messages about inclusivity, but often also masking the virtual impossibility of providing a sacred space for use by all faith groups that is free from on-going battles and politics' (2005: 288). Whilst it is true that the modern prison chaplaincy opens its doors to all inmates regardless of belief, its capacity to provide true equality of opportunity, whereby all religious groups (including the non-religious) feel equally welcome in the space and comfortable accessing its services, is necessarily limited.

In the summer of 2015, the second of the authors conducted interviews and focus groups with prison counsellors and healthcare professionals.[2] Their experience was that many non-religious offenders were not accessing bereavement support because it was provided through the chaplaincy. Whilst some non-religious prisoners do use the chaplaincy services and have positive experiences with them, a significant number felt uncomfortable having to engage with religious people and places in order to receive counselling, and this prevented them from getting help:

> Participant 1, bereavement counsellor: '*Some people can be put off by a member of the chaplaincy because they don't have any religious beliefs, you know, they might not even go there and know that this* [bereavement counselling] *exists.*'
>
> Participant 6, bereavement counsellor: '*There's also an issue because the chaplaincy is where we get most of our referrals. There is an aversion to the chaplaincy for some prisoners because, you know, it's religious . . . We're completely diverse, but they don't see that because to access our service they have to go in the chapel.*'
>
> Participant 16, prison nurse: '*If somebody wasn't religious, they just completely did not want to engage with that kind of support. So, if they said, "I'm not religious, I'm not really interested", then they wouldn't engage or even access the support group.*'

Frances Crook, the chief executive of the Howard League for Penal Reform, has recognised this problem herself and articulated it publicly. Speaking on the BBC's Radio 4, she said,

> Traditionally we've always had Church of England priests in the prisons providing some kind of support service. My concern is that this is only for a minority of prisoners, of whatever faith they are, because actually more than half of prisoners have answered a survey saying they don't have a religion. All prisoners are very vulnerable, all prisoners are often frightened and in need of support and help but the people who don't have a faith can't get that support because there is no comprehensive service offering moral support to them.
>
> (Crook, 2010)

The prison population has long been recognised as a disenfranchised group, and these quotes suggest that prisoners of no faith are further excluded in terms of using and benefiting from pastoral care in the many institutions that offer no alternative to chaplaincy. This means that large numbers of inmates are unlikely to receive the help they need at the time when they most need it.

Although chaplaincies welcome all members of the prison community, and so provide *prima facie* equality, their structures have always been Anglican. Gilliat-Ray reminds us that these spaces are 'emerging out of a religious history predominately shaped by Protestant Christianity, and with this history comes [*sic*] particular ideas and assumptions about what constitutes religion and religious practice' (2005: 304). The fact that pastoral care services are offered through a religious institution makes them more accessible to some than to others. The pastoral care itself may be secular, but the people and places providing it are not. This has a disparate impact on prisoners of no faith who may have fewer support mechanisms available to them in practice and are the least likely to receive the help that they need. Crompton and Hewsom summarise: 'Although it aims at equality of opportunity, users can never truly be served equally. In one sense everyone is disadvantaged, but some more than others' (2016: 8).

Need for change

It is evident that there is a need for enhanced support structures in this area. Recent literature has exposed a disturbing lack of effective bereavement interventions (Hester & Taylor, 2011), as well as a shortage of time, knowledge and resources amongst bereavement caregivers and correctional staff to meet the needs of grieving offenders, who are released back into their communities with very little support. We argue that the position of the chaplaincy, an inherently religious organisation, as the primary source of, or gateway to, counselling and pastoral support services intended for all inmates is unjustified and unhelpful, considering the increasingly secular prison population. Today's prisons are occupied by a great many people who do not have a faith or do not regularly attend religious services (Todd & Tipton, 2011). Offender population statistics from 30 September 2017 show that less than half of all prisoners are Christian, and only one in six identify as Anglican (Ministry of Justice, 2017). Far from representing a majority of the inmate population, Anglicanism is not even the dominant Christian denomination; a higher number of prisoners identify as Roman Catholic. After Christians (taken as a whole), the next largest category is the non-religious, who make up almost a third (31 per cent) of the prison population, yet do not have the option to seek pastoral or spiritual support from a person with the same world view.

Although the prison population is not representative of the general population, certain groups being dramatically over- or under-represented, the decline in religiosity in prison mirrors the steady secularisation of the society as a whole, through sequential waves of immigration as well as a wide-scale rejection of formal religious observance. NatCen's British Social Attitudes survey (2016) found that a majority of Britons (53 per cent) are non-religious, with faith membership at an all-time low. Woodhead (2016) noted that, the younger you are, the more likely you are to be non-religious, whereas, the older you are, the more likely you are to be a Christian; in that sense, Christianity is literally dying out, whilst non-religion is expanding. Counting the numbers of non-religious people is problematic, however, and the systems used are bound to lead to underestimates. The 'census effect' – whereby many non-believers who were raised according to a certain faith or whose parents are religious are inclined to indicate a religious affiliation on official documents – suggests a further, hidden secularisation.

Spiritual needs

Although the importance of religious support should not be underestimated, chaplaincies should not be permitted to dominate pastoral care. We recommend a policy shift towards a clearer separation of services and the availability of secular support in every prison, thereby removing the religious disincentive so that every person serving a custodial sentence feels able to access the help that is right for him or her. Non-religious people have spiritual needs (i.e. needs relating to inner well-being, morality and the human psyche) like everybody else. Chaplaincies are inappropriate for a large proportion of our diverse population, who rightly expect state institutions to be secular and equally welcoming to all at the point of use.

Of course, the boundaries between spiritual and secular support are far from clear. In Todd and Tipton's research (2011), most prison chaplains, and some officers and governors, saw an attempt to divorce faith from pastoral care as deeply problematic, arguing that personal faith and a sense of a 'calling' motivated, informed and sustained their pastoral work. Emotional support is a large part of the work of chaplains, and it is certainly not envisioned that ministers should limit their guidance exclusively to religious matters. Rather, it is recommended that services be restructured so that chaplaincies are never the sole – or even primary – source of guidance for the largely non-Christian prison population, and that high-quality secular care is always available.

We would argue that this proposal does not undermine but rather advances the aims of prison chaplaincy. The entrenchment of religious people and provisions in the prison system derives from the idea that nobody is beyond reform, and that all individuals, regardless of belief, deserve support in overcoming their emotional conflicts and leading healthy lives. If this is so, and few could argue otherwise, then a different approach is required to help those in need that the chaplaincy cannot reach.

Different alternatives

In some cases, change has come naturally. Because of the large number of offenders who are not religious but who, in many prisons, have no other source of pastoral support, it is not surprising that researchers have identified a change in the ways that chaplaincies and other sacred spaces are used and viewed in public institutions. Gilliat-Ray explains:

> From a time when Chapel attendance was part of the disciplinary mechanism of the institution, the religious spaces in today's prisons have a multiplicity

of meanings for inmates. For example, they are places where inmates might find the privacy for tears, or counselling with the chaplain . . . or to simply to [*sic*] 'escape' from their cell.

(2005: 290)

For many prison chaplains, their role has also evolved to suit the requirements of their multicultural and confined congregation. In a closed setting, where people of many different world views are suffering, it no longer makes sense to offer religious pastoral care in the absence of a secular alternative. Instead, the religious element of the work is in many cases greatly diminished, and the emphasis shifts to friendship and mentoring, rooted in empathy and common humanity rather than shared faith. In this way, the function of the prison chaplain is very different to that of the university or hospital chaplain, whose work is closer to ministry, because of the wider range of religious and pastoral facilities available to those they serve.

Another response has been to add non-religious staff members to chaplaincies. Traditionally only members of the Christian clergy, chaplains today are increasingly likely to be lay people providing universal support. We submit that the inverse solution is the more logical; instead of bringing secular staff *into* the chaplaincy, prisons should seek to take secular services *out* of it. There would be no need for non-religious chaplains – something of an oxymoron – if non-believers were not compelled to consult with faith representatives in order to receive support with bereavement and loss.

Whatever non-denominational supplements to chaplaincy may be in place, such as the services of Cruse Bereavement Care or Samaritans-trained listeners, the only pastoral care that is currently targeted to the non-religious (as a counterpart to chaplaincy, which is inherently religious) is the work of the Non-Religious Pastoral Support Network (NRPSN), a group of trained and accredited volunteers operating in prisons, hospitals and hospices (http: //nrpsn.org.uk/). Members come into the prison to provide the sort of support to the non-religious that might be provided to religious people by chaplains. The help that they give can include breaking the news of a death, facilitating group work or offering a sympathetic ear to a person in need. The network began with a pilot group at Her Majesty's Prison Winchester in the United Kingdom, working with prisoners who identified as having 'nil' religion on admission, by holding discussion groups and providing bereavement support. The project was well received by both offenders and prison management; it is now a permanent aspect of pastoral care at Winchester, and is expanding into institutions across the country.

The input of the NRPSN has been welcome and effective, but the impact that members are able to make is limited. Their help is provided informally, without payment and at the initiative of the members themselves rather than the prisons they serve, whereas chaplains are salaried full-time staff members with a legislative mandate. This vast difference in standing speaks volumes about the Prison Service's approach to religious equality. Many non-religious carers volunteer alongside busy work lives and other commitments and are not able or, in some cases, permitted to come in for more than a few hours a week. Volunteers are not usually informed of the non-religious people in their prison and their presence is rarely advertised. Thus, the barriers to service provision operate in both directions; non-faith prisoners struggle to access secular pastoral care, and secular pastoral carers struggle to access non-faith prisoners. Their help is clearly not enough to support the third of the prison population who identify as non-religious, but this demographic is not accommodated, funded or even recognised in the same way as other groups. The result for many prisoners is that the contribution of groups like the NRPSN – if they are present at all – is the only available support that is appropriate to their beliefs.

Concluding thoughts

The multi-faith chaplaincy is alienating to atheist and non-faith offenders, who are entitled to support that is relevant to their beliefs. This chapter calls for bereavement counselling and other neutral services to be provided independently of chaplaincy, and for non-religious pastoral carers to be appointed in every prison in order to offer to non-faith prisoners the same opportunity as their religious counterparts – the choice to seek pastoral or spiritual support from a person with the same world view. The Prison Service has a duty to address secular prisoners' unmet needs and inequality of opportunity. A safe space in which inmates can share their experiences would be accessible to all, so that no offender feels discouraged from accessing vital services.

Certainly, we do not seek to diminish or ignore the excellent work done by chaplaincy teams. The argument is simply that the interventions of chaplaincy team members are not suitable for everybody. Providing an alternative source of pastoral support separate from the chaplaincy and its staff redresses this imbalance. If, as Thomas and Zaitzow argue, the person best suited to support an offender is 'the minister or pastor of that particular faith' (2006: 251), it surely follows that the best person to assist an atheist, secularist or humanist prisoner cannot be a religious minister.

Developing and implementing neutral pastoral care programmes within a secure environment carries financial implications and does not happen overnight. Implementing these services demands time, resources and staff energy, all of which are already overstretched, in many cases to breaking point, in UK prisons. We nevertheless anticipate that such a policy would swiftly pay dividends, cutting costs dramatically in the long term. It is anticipated that many of the issues that put pressure on staff and budgets in a prison environment – inmate unrest, threats to staff safety, physical and mental health problems and so forth – would be improved significantly if every offender in the penal estate had meaningful access to pastoral support, whether voluntary or professional, from a compassionate and like-minded individual. Where financial resources do not allow for salaried staff, prison management teams should be encouraged to cooperate with organisations like the NRPSN and commit to raising awareness of the need for, and sources of, secular support for offenders.

Given the difference that help of this kind can make, particularly in reducing destructive behaviour and recidivism, the Prison Service cannot afford to exclude such a large and fast-growing section of its vulnerable population and has a duty to provide services that all inmates feel able to access. Effective support for those facing bereavement behind bars is not only an issue for those in criminal justice professions; it is a public policy matter of concern to us all. Counselling and pastoral care that facilitates an offender's bereavement and addresses his or her mental health needs prior to release is likely to have a beneficial impact that extends beyond the individuals themselves to the prison culture, the offender's family and society as a whole.

Notes

1 See, for example, Johnston, E. (2017). The prison system is in crisis: Let's not look to Hollywood for the answer. *Criminal Law and Justice Weekly*, 181; Crook, F. (2016). The answer to the prison crisis is simple: Less is better. *Howard League for Penal Reform*, 20 December, blog post available at http://howardleague.org/blog/the-answer-to-the-prison-crisis-is-simple-less-is-better/; and Warrell, H. (2017). UK prisons in crisis as suicides and assaults hit record levels. *Financial Times*, 26 January.
2 About this qualitative project, see chapter 1, endnote 1.

References

Aday, R. & Wahidin, A. (2016). Older prisoners' experiences of death, dying and grief behind bars. *The Howard Journal of Crime and Justice*. 55: 312–327.

Beckford, J.A. (2013). Religious diversity in prisons: Chaplaincy and contention. *Studies in Religion*. 42: 190–205.

Crompton, A. & Hewson, C. (2016). Designing equality: Multi-faith space as social intervention. IN: D. Llewellyn, and S. Sharma (Eds.). *Religion, Equalities and Inequalities*. Abingdon: Routledge.

Crook, F. (2010, September 27). Religion in prison. Beyond Belief. BBC Radio 4.

Doka, K. (1989). *Disenfranchised Grief: Recognizing the Hidden Sorrow*. New York, NY: Lexington Books.

Gilliat-Ray, S. (2005). From 'chapel' to 'prayer room': The production, use, and politics of sacred space in public institutions. *Culture and Religion*. 6: 287–308.

Hester, R. & Taylor, W. (2011). Responding to bereavement, grief and loss: Charting the troubled relationship between research and practice in youth offending services. *Mortality*. 16: 191–203.

Maschi, T., Gibson, S., Zgoba, K.M. & Morgen, K. (2011). Trauma and life event stressors among young and older adult prisoners. *Journal of Correctional Health Care*. 17: 160–172.

Ministry of Justice (2011). *Faith and Pastoral Care for Prisoners*. Prison Service Instruction (PSI) 51/2011. Updated 18 November 2013. London: Ministry of Justice.

Ministry of Justice (2017). *Prison Population: 30 September 2017', Offender Management Statistics Quarterly: April to June 2017*. London: Ministry of Justice.

NatCen (2016). *NatCen's British Social Attitudes Survey: Change in religious affiliation among adults in Great Britain*. Available at: www.natcen.ac.uk/media/1236081/religious-affiliation-over-time-british-social-attitudes.pdf

Northern Ireland Prison Service (2005). *Hydebank Wood Prison: The Re-Integration Needs of Women Prisoners in Northern Ireland*. Belfast: Northern Ireland Prison Service.

Priestly, P. (1985). *Victorian Prison Lives*. London: Methuen and Co.

Stevenson, R.G. & McCutchen, R. (2006). When meaning has lost its way: Life and loss 'behind bars'. *Illness, Crisis and Loss*. 14: 113–119.

Sykes, G. (1958). *The Society of Captives*. Princeton, NJ: Princeton University Press.

Thomas, J. & Zaitzow, B.H. (2006). Conning or conversion? The role of religion in prison coping. *The Prison Journal*. 86: 242–259.

Todd, A. & Tipton, L. (2011). *The Role and Contribution of a Multi-Faith Prison Chaplaincy to the Contemporary Prison Service*. Cardiff: Cardiff Centre for Chaplaincy Studies.

Vaswani, N. (2014). The ripples of death: Exploring the bereavement experiences and mental health of young men in custody. *The Howard Journal of Criminal Justice*. 53: 325–447.

Wilson, M. (2010). 'This is not just about death: It's about how we deal with the rest of our lives': Coping with bereavement in prison. *Prison Service Journal*. 190: 10–16.

Woodhead, L. (2016). The rise of 'no religion' in Britain: The emergence of a new cultural majority. *Journal of the British Academy*. 4: 245–261.

Worden, J.W. (2009). *Grief Counseling and Grief Therapy: A Handbook for the Mental Health Practitioner*. London: Routledge.

Index

Note: Page numbers in *italics* indicate figures and page numbers in **bold** indicate tables.